the truth about

Angels

TERRY LAW

CHARISMA
HOUSE

Most CHARISMA HOUSE BOOK GROUP products are available at special quantity discounts for bulk purchase for sales promotions, premiums, fund-raising, and educational needs. For details, write Charisma House Book Group, 600 Rinehart Road, Lake Mary, Florida 32746, or telephone (407) 333-0600.

THE TRUTH ABOUT ANGELS by Terry Law
Published by Charisma House
Charisma Media/Charisma House Book Group
600 Rinehart Road
Lake Mary, Florida 32746
www.charismahouse.com

Unless otherwise noted, all Scripture quotations are from the King James Version of the Bible.

Scripture quotations marked AMP are from the Amplified Bible. Old Testament copyright © 1965, 1987 by the Zondervan Corporation. The Amplified New Testament copyright © 1954, 1958, 1987 by the Lockman Foundation. Used by permission.

Scripture quotations marked NIV are from the Holy Bible, New International Version. Copyright © 1973, 1978, 1984, International Bible Society. Used by permission.

Scripture quotations marked NKJV are from the New King James Version of the Bible. Copyright © 1979, 1980, 1982 by Thomas Nelson, Inc., publishers. Used by permission.

Scripture quotations marked TLB are from The Living Bible. Copyright © 1971. Used by permission of Tyndale House Publishers, Inc., Wheaton, IL 60189. All rights reserved.

Cover design by Karen Grindley
Design Director: Bill Johnson

Library of Congress Cataloging-in-Publication Data:
Law, Terry.
    The truth about angels / Terry Law. -- 1st ed.
       p. cm.
    Includes bibliographical references.
    ISBN 1-59185-959-X (pbk.)
    1. Angels--Christianity.   I. Title.
    BT966.3.L39 2006
    235'.3--dc22   2006014560

ISBN-13: 978-1-59185-959-8
E-book ISBN: 978-1-59979-931-5
Available at Amazon and Barnes & Noble

11 12 13 14 15 — 10 9 8 7 6 5
Printed in the United States of America

I would like to dedicate this book to the many heroes of the faith in hostile lands who have risked their lives and families as we spread the gospel together over the last thirty-five years.

Speaking of the faith believers of the ages, the Hebrews writer says:

[Many] through faith subdued kingdoms, wrought righteousness, obtained promises...escaped the edge of the sword, out of weakness were made strong....Others had trial of cruel mockings and scourgings, yea, moreover of bonds and imprisonment...wandered in deserts, and in mountains, and in dens and caves of the earth...of whom the world was not worthy. —Hebrews 11:33–38

Some of these heroes who worked with our ministry were still in prison at the time of this writing. Remember them.

How busy they have kept God's angels!

Acknowledgments

My deepest appreciation to:

My family, who gave up my presence while I wrote this book.

Connie Ferrier, my writing and research assistant. Without her, there would be no book. Thanks for hanging in there, Connie, and seeing it through to the end. What a tremendous amount of work you have done! And thanks to your husband, Jim, for making sure all the details were handled smoothly.

Deborah Poulalion, the patient and sensitive editor who edited the original version of this book. Lillian McAnally, for making this tenth anniversary edition possible.

My ministry staff—Ben, Vivian, Koes, Dara, John, and Marilyn, who help make the ministry possible; Joel, who does the work of the Lord with me; David, Scot and Kathy, Jason, and to editors Roone Acree and Joshua Lease. Many thanks for understanding my long absences from the office. You made sure our ministry continued around the world.

The people who shared with me their stories of experiences with angels.

The Lord, who sent His angels to watch over and assist me since my childhood.

Contents

Preface

Years ago, a good friend approached me and told me that I should write a book about angels. "After all," he pointed out, "angels have had a major influence on your life and ministry."

I hesitated for several reasons, the chief one being that I had never seen an angel, though it was true that they had impacted my life several times. However, in the 1990s I had a growing desire to study and write on the subject. My research began.

In December 1993 the issue came to a head. I sensed an overwhelming impression that I was to move ahead with the project, and so I decided to do it early in December. Interestingly, two weeks later, both *Time* and *Newsweek* came out with major articles on angels.

What startled me was the plethora of angel sightings that did not correlate with biblical data. They obviously were New Age (metaphysical) in flavor. I began to realize that good people were being influenced by supernatural events that they assumed came from God. I believe these angel sightings found such fertile ground because our society, schooled in rationalism, is hungry for anything spiritual.

As I researched existing material on angels, I discovered there was almost no literature that promoted a strong biblical teaching on this important area. Since I have embarked on my adventure, my decision has been confirmed by subsequent events.

The following year, 1994, the American Booksellers Association declared that it was the year for angels. The subject of angels was the most popular category featured on the exhibit floor. Hoping to ride the wave of successful sales, a number of New York publishing houses released titles on angels—most from a New Age perspective. Thirty-two books on the subject were scheduled to release by February 1995. Since then, countless of articles and books have been written about angels. Very few books have been written from a biblical standpoint.

I wrote this book as an answer to the deluge of information and to provide a biblical basis for examining the angel phenomena.

First, I want to let you know what people are saying and experiencing concerning angels. I quote a broad spectrum of opinions

—evangelical, Charismatic, Roman Catholic, New Age, and secular ideas. However, simply because I quote a person *does not* necessarily mean I endorse that person or even agree with what he or she has said. Conversely, it certainly doesn't mean the person would agree with everything I believe or say either!

Second, I want to give you practical, biblical teaching about the role God has given angels in our lives. It is important to know that real angels (good angels) are seldom visible to us because of our human propensity to worship them. But I believe good angels and bad angels are active today, and it is imperative that every one of us recognizes the differences between them.

In a time when a spiritual vacuum seems to have created a rush of supernatural events, I am convinced that we need to know the truth about angels.

Introduction

One of the most beautiful sights in the world is a rainbow arching across the vast expanse of sky on the Canadian prairies where I grew up. There were times when I sat on my tractor after a day's work on the farm and gazed at the horizon, wondering if there was a place where the heavens actually touched the earth.

When things belonging to the supernatural realm intersect with the natural world, a meeting of heaven and the earth *does* occur. One unmistakable example is a visitation from an angel.

In the past, only "religious" people saw angels. But today the sightings and stories have spilled over into the secular world. In fact, most of the interest in angels during the 1990s was concentrated in the secular world until the church realized it needed to respond.

This supernatural interest raised numerous questions: Is there another dimension or realm with beings as real to that dimension as people are to this one? Is it possible for "aliens"—beings from another place—not only to operate in this place but also to be seen in it? And if there were beings from another realm, why did they seem to be seen more in the 1990s?

In this book I hope the reader will find answers to these questions and others that emerge from them. At a time when many people—believers in Jesus Christ and nonbelievers alike—are reporting encounters with angelic beings, we need to outline our facts and explore problems.

For example, why the strange bedfellows in this deluge of material about angels, such as the Bible being quoted next to New Age writings? There was a Broadway play that fuses biblical and Mormon angelology. The combination results in a "gay fantasia on a national theme," says the playwright.[1]

When I wrote this book, I wondered if the craze over angels was simply another passing fad promoted by merchandisers out to make a profit. Even Hollywood began producing films and television shows such as *Touched by an Angel, Highway to Heaven, Michael,* and *City of Angels* on the subject of angels. Were the stories of personal encounters with angels products of people's imaginative fancies and desires, outright fabrications, or actual events?

Perhaps a *Time* magazine article put the situation in a nutshell: "For all those who say they have had some direct experience of angels, no proof is necessary; for those predisposed to doubt angels' existence, no proof is possible. And for those in the mystified middle, there is often a growing desire to be persuaded."[2]

That growing desire to be persuaded can be dangerous.

Time reporter Nancy Gibbs noted that the fascination with angels was "more popular than theological, a grass-roots revolution of the spirit." She said, "All sorts of people are finding all sorts of reasons" to find out about angels for the first time.[3] Literary critic Harold Bloom of Yale University, who wrote a book on angels, the millennium, and memory, believed modern interest in angels is "about not wanting to die."[4]

One of the saddest—and most ironic—parts of the popular interest in angels is that many theologians who have read and taught the Bible for years apparently do not know what to think about this fascination. They also do not know what to do about it or how to correct it if it is wrong.

George Landes, professor of Old Testament at Union Theological Seminary, told *Time*:

> In the eyes of traditional Church leaders, the popular authors who render angels into household pets, who invite readers to get in touch with their inner angels, or summon their own "angel psychotherapists," or view themselves as angels in training are trafficking in "discount" spirituality. And the churches are at a loss for a response.[5]

I believe angels are real. In fact, I've been unmistakably aware of angelic intervention several times in my own life, and I'll tell those stories later in the book. However, I also believe the reason for a person's interest in angelic encounters is crucial. A desire for knowing angels that is greater than a desire for knowing the Creator will lead to trouble.

1

Personal Encounters
of an Angelic Kind

*There are more things in heaven and earth, Horatio, than
are dreamt of in your philosophy.*[1]
—William Shakespeare

A man and his wife were out for a walk one spring morning when they saw, about ten feet above them, a "floating group of glorious, beautiful creatures that glowed with spiritual beauty." This group of six young women, described as "the host of heaven," wore flowing white garments and talked together earnestly in a language the couple could not understand. They said the experience changed their thinking about angels.[2]

A woman woke one night to see an angel standing at the foot of her bed. This angel wore "ecru-colored robes" that covered her feet, and she had beautiful wings, "like the feathers or wings of a big bird." The angel simply stood there with no mysterious light and left no message.[3]

A young man from a wealthy family was trying to escape from joining a particular church that seemed full of superstition. As he attempted to leave the church building, a large black dog appeared and blocked his way. The dog seemed threatening and kept him from leaving. When the dog disappeared, rays of light radiated from the building. The young man followed the light and saw a vision. He not only joined the church but also became well known in it.[4]

George Washington, the first U.S. president, reportedly had a vision at Valley Forge in 1777. Washington is said to have seen a beautiful female appear before him as he worked at his desk one afternoon. She showed him visions of three wars to roll over this continent, two

3

of which many have considered to be the Revolutionary War and the Civil War, with the third a "red" menace still to come.[5]

Angel Fever

The stories I've repeated are just minuscule examples of the ongoing interest in angels.

When I originally wrote this book over a decade ago, the number and frequency of such reports had grown so much that the national news media devoted major news stories to the phenomenon. Both *Time* and *Newsweek* featured cover stories on angels (December 1993). Articles also appeared in other magazines and in major newspapers across the country, including the *Wall Street Journal.*

The Angel Collectors Club of America located in Golden, Colorado, holds a national convention every two years for those who collect angel art, books, and statuettes. Across the country, stores and boutiques opened that sell nothing but angel collectibles— calendars, perfume, napkin rings, place mats, stationery, *ad infinitum*. In many places people are sending angel collectibles in lieu of flowers to funerals.[6]

Seminars and workshops were being held across the country, with some of these designed to help you "get in touch" or communicate with your angel.[7] Computerized conferences on angels were available for those with computers.

The book that seemed to have kicked off the 1990s explosion of interest in angels was Sophy Burnham's book titled *A Book of Angels.*[8] By the end of 1993 it had sold more than a half-million copies, which, at that time, was phenomenal for the publishing industry. Her book is a mixed stew of folklore, personal experiences, and other stories she collected. In 1991 Burnham published a sequel, *Angel Letters*, containing letters from readers of the first book, which sold a quarter-million copies.

Many other books followed Burnham's, and the only major books that were published about angels from 1975 until 1990 were reissued: evangelist Billy Graham's best seller (now revised) *Angels, God's Secret Agents*, Moody Bible Institute professor C. Fred Dickason's *Angels: Elect and Evil*, both published in 1975, and world-renowned philosopher Mortimer Adler's *The Angels and Us*, published in 1982.

(There were a few other angel books published, but they reached only a small, specific audience in the Christian market.)

Graham said of his 1975 classic that when he started to preach a sermon on angels there were so few modern publications available, he decided to write a book about them. Similarly, Adler's book was the result of a lecture on the philosophical significance of angels presented at the Aspen Institute for Humanistic Studies. This lecture drew a larger audience than he had drawn for thirty years. He too decided to write a book on the subject.[9]

For those who notice trends, a portent of things to come might have been the popular television show of the eighties called *Highway to Heaven*, starring the late Michael Landon as an angel trying to "earn his wings." In the nineties, the television show *Touched by an Angel*, starring Della Reese and Roma Downey, showed how two angels portrayed as ordinary humans are sent from heaven to earth to help people with their problems and come to understand how much "God loves them."

Before that, Jimmy Stewart's classic Christmas film, *It's a Wonderful Life* (1946), was the only film about angels that caught the fancy of the general public, although other movies have been made with the same theme.

Was this angel phenomenon fad, fantasy, or reality? Are the heavenlies now meeting the earth in a greater way, allowing more supernatural beings to impinge into the material universe?

Fad, Fantasy, or Reality?

People who do not believe in the supernatural think this is a passing fad. Others believe masses of people are buying into a counterfeit because they have refused the reality of God.

One cultural critic said:

> Psychoanalysts are beginning to acknowledge that the major disease of our century is the loss of the soul. When we talk about angels, we see a culture trying to develop a sense of soul-making.[10]

Someone once said that a disbelief in God does not result in a belief in nothing; disbelief in God usually results in a belief in anything. Many people think a spiritual vacuum in America is the root cause of the interest in angels.

Time magazine found that 69 percent of those they polled believe in the existence of angels, and 46 percent believe they have a guardian angel.[11]

In the spring of 1993, an article on angels in *Christianity Today* pointed out that society seems "bent" on contact with the supernatural and is threatening to outdo the church in asking and talking about angels.[12] It was predicted that the "quest for spiritual meaning" would be among baby boomers' greatest concerns in the nineties.[13]

So the nineties' interest in angels was a combination of all three: fad, fantasy, and reality.

The faddish part will definitely fade over time. Before World War II, people collected mostly fine art, stamps, crystal, china, and antiques. As the decades progressed, the diversified collections of campaign buttons, license plates, and Elvis artifacts surfaced. In the eighties people collected figurines and items picturing cows, geese, ducks, pigs, and chickens. In the nineties, people were collecting angels.

Just as certainly as this is a fad fueled by merchandising, some of the stories and "personal encounters" are the result of people's imaginations.

One theologian at St. Charles Borromeo Seminary said he would be "very suspicious" of a spiritual or supernatural experience not based on a moral code or a religious framework. He added, "You know, we have asylums filled with people who have spoken to angels and Napoleon and others."[14]

But even if some of this explosion is fad and some is fantasy, what about the *reality*? What standard can you use to test it?

Some people say you can rely on religious books, other historical accounts, or personal experience. Believers in Jesus as Christ would say there's only *one* proof: the Bible. According to that standard, all of the encounters listed at the beginning of this chapter fail the ultimate authenticity test: None of them fit biblical facts about God's angels. The discrepancies include the following:

1. In Scripture, angels of God always appear masculine. Angels appearing as female show up in some historical accounts and in some personal experiences but *never* in the Bible.

2. An angel of God never appears as an animal or bird. (An angel appeared to a donkey once.)

3. According to the Bible, angels are a created class of beings and are never represented as spiritually progressed humans. In other words, humans do not evolve into angels.

Every supernatural experience is not necessarily from God. Every spirit that calls itself "the Lord" is not necessarily the Lord of lords and King of kings, Jesus Christ.

Many books portray angels as "good fairies," selflessly eager to help human beings. This is a one-sided view, and it is dangerous.

Are Angels Always Benign Spirits?

Human beings know instinctively there has to be *something* out there. But whole civilizations have scoffed at the idea of a Supreme Being who created and "owns" the universe and mankind. Yet they embrace lesser gods who lead them into bondage and degradation.

Is that what is happening in America?

For one thing, this is the first time in the history of the United States when a belief in God has been so depopularized that a belief in *anything* could happen. The lesser gods of humanism, materialism, and rebellion against authority (independence) no longer satisfy. The search is on for spiritual values—but without God.

Even secular writers have noticed the difference between the angels of the Bible and those being written and talked about now. The article in *Time* pointed out:

> Jehovah's angels are powerful creatures... [but] in their modern incarnation, these mighty messengers and fearless soldiers have been reduced to bite-size beings, easily digested. The terrifying cherubim [of the Bible] have become Kewpie-doll cherubs...
>
> The emphasis on angels as divine intermediaries, theologians worry, just creates a greater distance from an ever more abstract God. And to the extent that angels are always [presented as] benign spirits, it evades any reckoning with the struggle between good and evil.[15]

Presenting angels as always benign is the equivalent of putting bias into a laboratory experiment, leaving out some of the data to achieve a predetermined desired result. It begs some logical questions.

Where did angels come from? Did they evolve? What kind of amoeba could evolve into a heavenly creature? If it wasn't evolution, who created angels? Was their creator good or evil?

What about people's encounters with dark beings? Do we claim all these stories simply aren't true? Are only benign angels real?

One can understand secular writers not being educated in biblical facts about angels. But to find that many Christians do not know the answers to these questions is disturbing. In 1994, one of the largest mainline denominations in America at the time, one with a strong evangelical community, offered a variety of books from many publishers in its catalog. Two of these were angel books—one was for "advanced aspiring angels," and the other was a "guidebook to awaken the angel within each of us."[16]

Several novels published by Christian companies that year also showed the same lack of familiarity with biblical data about angels. In fact, some plots followed the theme of *Highway to Heaven* and had people turning into angels or angels earning their wings. Other novels had more complex themes.

In one, a young angel was made a normal boy, complete with the hurts and insecurities of any child. He was told by the archangel Michael that he would live as five different boys in different time periods. Furthermore, he was unaware that he was an angel and would live his five lives simultaneously.

That is more than Jesus did—live five different lives at once. Also angels in Scripture do not age or "earn their wings" but exist eternally as they were created.

A second Christian novel had a woman journalist actually being the third angel of "woe" of Revelation. (Compare Revelation 8:13 and 11:15).

Does literary license excuse taking liberty with biblical facts? Christians and non-Christians need to wake up and start thinking about what's being said.

Are we entertaining lies that are centuries old?

2

Nothing New Under the Sun

The thing that hath been, it is that which shall be; and that which is done is that which shall be done: and there is no new thing under the sun.
—Ecclesiastes 1:9

Progress, far from consisting in change, depends on reten tiveness.... Those who cannot remember the past are condemned to fulfill it.[1]
—George Santayana

Secular histories, religious histories, and archaeology show that nearly all of the world's cultures accepted the existence of supernatural beings. Many societies made no distinction between good and bad spirits. The ancient Egyptians believed supernatural beings controlled all affairs of life. This was also the case in Persia, Babylon, and India.

In spite of a culture focused on philosophy and humanistic ideas, even the ancient Greeks believed in spirits, with spirit worship playing a part in their daily lives. Socrates claimed to have a personal guardian spirit. He called it a *daimon*, and it warned him of trouble but never told him what to do.[2]

The Romans absorbed most other religions into their own. That is, they did this as long as the other religion was polytheistic. They simply added new gods to their pantheon.

Geddes MacGregor wrote in *Angels, Ministers of Grace*:

From Scandinavia to Iran, from Ireland to South America, popular folklore is full of allusions to such elemental spirits...who have been carried over from old Celtic, Scandinavian, Teutonic, or other old folklore.[3]

9

Even in the Far Eastern cultures of China, Japan, and Korea, angels and/or demons were an integral part of their religions, although many times these beings were called gods. In the Far East, spirits were thought to be dead humans, resulting in ancestor worship instead of direct worship of angels or demons.

The Bible first mentions heavenly beings in the third chapter of Genesis. God placed cherubim at the east end of the Garden of Eden to guard the tree of life after Adam and Eve sinned. Some theologians think cherubim are a separate class of beings from angels. Others think cherubim, seraphim, living creatures, and angels—all mentioned in Scripture—are simply various angelic orders.

A very curious story found in Genesis 6 is the oldest written mention of what the ancient Jews and even the Jews of Jesus' day thought were angels.

> And it came to pass, when men began to multiply on the face of the earth, and daughters were born unto them, that the sons of God saw the daughters of men that they were fair; and they took them wives of all which they chose....There were giants in the earth in those days; and also after that, when the sons of God came in unto the daughters of men, and they bare children to them, the same became mighty men which were of old, men of renown.
>
> —Genesis 6:1–2, 4

These "children" (called Nephilim, Rephaim, or Anakim) are mentioned a number of times throughout the Old Testament. Often they are simply called giants.

Goliath, the Philistine champion who was defeated by the shepherd youth David may have been a descendant of these unions. He was said to have been more than nine feet tall (1 Sam. 17:4), so certainly he and his brothers would have been considered giants in a society where the average man was just a little less than five and a half feet tall[4] (2 Sam. 21:19, 22).

There are two schools of thought about Genesis 6:1–4 among well-respected church leaders on both sides of the question. One is that angels cohabited with women and produced giants as offspring, which was the majority position of the church until the Age of Enlightenment. The other is that "sons of God" referred to the sons of Seth, the righteous line from Adam, and "daughters of men" referred to women from the wicked line of Cain.

It seems unlikely that it can be proved one way or the other, but ancient writings give most support to the idea that the sons of God were fallen angels. (See Appendix A for more details.) A story about angels who allegedly mated with women was included in the writings of Josephus, a well-known Jewish historian whose books date from about A.D. 90. The editor for a modern publication of Josephus's works noted that, "This notion, that the fallen angels were, in some sense, the fathers of the old giants, was the constant opinion of antiquity."[5]

The importance of this story is that it appears in one form or another in all ancient civilizations and cultures. It is impossible to study angels, religion, or even culture and everyday life in the pre-Christian era without finding stories about some form of supernatural beings mating with women.

A theologian named Alexander Hislop did a monumental job in the late 1800s of tracing connections between all of the early religions. He compared the belief and worship of supernatural beings across nation after nation and religion after religion. His report gives more evidence that indeed something happened somewhere in the ancient times involving the natural and supernatural realms. Whatever that was, it still influences many peoples today.[6]

Hislop's book also certainly shows that "there is nothing new under the sun"—in the occult realm, at any rate.

A Cycle Being Repeated

Periods of heightened interest in angels occurred in the past, but they did not lead to an increased interest in the God of the Bible. Angels were emphasized in the arts in the 1800s. A movement came afterward that was similar to Far Eastern practices in that it did not focus on angels but on what adherents called ghosts, the spirits of the dead.

This interest in hypnosis, psychic phenomena, and mental healing came to be called *spiritism* or *modern spiritualism*. Several hundred churches of that belief system still exist today, with about a hundred thousand members in the United States.

Intellectuals and people in the arts were the greatest promoters of spiritualism. They accepted the theory of evolution, they refused to believe in God, and they denied the existence of heaven or hell. However, they did not want to give up the belief that man lives forever. This combination of beliefs made them vulnerable to the idea that those who have died could be contacted through a living person. Séances (gatherings where a medium contacts dead friends or relatives) were not only popular but also fashionable in Great Britain and America until the days of World War II.

One cult that rose up had angels appearing under the name of "ascended masters." That name came from a belief that man continued to evolve through lifetime after lifetime on earth and then in the supernatural realm after he died.[7]

Many other movements and groups developed during this period, including the Christian Science Church, the Unity School of Christianity and New Thought.

New Thought was the first Gnostic American cult. Why is that significant? Because Gnosticism has been a perversion of truth since the earliest days of the church. A belief system is considered Gnostic when it is built on a system of "secret knowledge" or direct divine revelation, in addition to the Bible.[8] People in the New Thought movement thought they had special knowledge that would give them health and prosperity.

Gnosticism comes from the Greek word *gnosis*, meaning "knowledge" or "science."[9] This system of thought or belief is a complex religious movement that surfaced in the second century. By the end of that century, Gnosticism was no longer a school of thought in the church but had divided into separate sects.

Many historians think Gnostics in the church (A.D. 250–350) derived their ideas from pagan religions such as Hinduism and Greek philosophy. Also, it seems from comments in some of the New Testament pastoral letters that the "false teaching" denounced by the apostles was similar but less well developed than that openly taught in the second-century church. (For a more complete definition of Gnosticism, see endnote 8.)

In the twentieth century, Gnosticism appears to be raising its head again. This new version of old pagan systems is called New Age.

The New Age Movement

A large number of Gnostic texts (the Nag Hammadi collection) found in Upper Egypt in 1945 helped to fuel the New Age movement, which emerged from the ashes of New Thought. The New Age movement surfaced almost full-blown in the mid-1960s.

New Age is not an official religion. There is no central organization to join, no creed to confess, and no one particular Vatican or Mecca. Instead of denominations, it is a collection of independent groups that may or may not contain permanent members or even meet in one place.

Russell Chandler, author of *Understanding the New Age*, says it is a hybrid mix that includes modern philosophy and psychology, religion (mostly Eastern mysticism), medicine (with a holistic emphasis), humanism, Gnosticism, and self-potential and self-improvement schools, mixed with the counter-culture of the 1950s and 1960s.[10]

New Age also includes astrology, science fiction, and environmentalism. Real concern over the state of the planet has metamorphosed in some groups into the worship of the Greek goddess Gaia in the guise of the Earth Mother (Mother Nature). New Age also includes psychic phenomena, white witchcraft, and magic.

"New Age magic" is the result of a desire for "a certain and secret wisdom." That is essentially the same enticement Eve faced in the Garden of Eden—to eat of the tree of the knowledge of good and evil and become a god.[11] This desire affects everything else, even the yearning to change the politics of the world.

Chandler wrote about the political aspect of the movement:

> Thus, the New Age agenda calls for an emerging global civilization and one-world government, including "planetary taxation" and the United Nations as the sole governing agency. It would also create an eclectic "world religion" that closely resembles Eastern religious systems rather than Western monotheistic faiths.[12]

Many Christians are being drawn into the New Age movement. Also, many New Age teachings are showing up in the belief systems of some Christians and some churches—often without their realizing it.

At the other extreme, some well-meaning Christians have criticized doctrines that really are Bible truths but have been counterfeited by some New Age teachings. In 1985 the Southern Baptist Convention issued a very balanced statement to Christians about the New Age:

> Be particularly careful that you are not inclined toward a kind of uninformed hysteria characterized by oversimplification and indiscriminate fear that you are threatened by conspiracies of all sorts. While New Age thinking and New Age–oriented activities are serious and dangerous, do not allow their presence and influence to drive you to indiscriminate distrust of fellow Christians and blanket disenchantment with authentic Christian institutions.[13]

For example, when New Agers made the rainbow an accepted symbol of the movement, many Christians began to treat it as an occult sign. However, the rainbow is God's sign given especially to man, signifying His love and mercy (Gen. 9:12–17).

It is important to keep in mind that the connection between Gnosticism and New Age is very real and dangerous. Peter Jones, professor of New Testament at Westminster Theological Seminary, says New Age and Gnosticism "resemble one another like two Siamese cats, sometimes in the smallest detail."[14]

If the New Age movement is Gnostic, then that means it is premised on "special knowledge." So where does that special knowledge come from? Right now the source of choice is angels who claim to come from God.

The main theme in modern books about angels is that each person has his or her own personal angel who will help with direction, understanding, and knowledge. These "helpers" are female as well as male, short, tall, fat, thin, and of all races. Most are described as "wonderful beings" who only intend good for mankind. Some are lights, some are birds, some have wings, and some do not.

The only standard of measurement is that the person reporting the incident believes an angel was involved or says the being claimed to be an angel. Good, bad, or indifferent, any kind of apparition, ghost, or manifestation is considered angelic.

Parallels: The Way It Was and Is

Hollywood's elite group is searching for a "higher power" and is finding it in the mystic stream of Judaism called Kabbalah (Cabbalah), which dates back to Babylonian captivity in the sixth century B.C.[15] In Kabbalism, these twenty-two "divine agents" are the sounds (or tones) produced by God that became ministering angels who govern for Him.[16]

The modern Jewish attitude toward angels tends to regard them as symbolic, poetic, or representing earlier cultures' ideas of the unknown. The *Encyclopedia Judaica* says Jews feel a belief in angels cannot be reconciled with modern rationalism. Only among the small fundamentalist sections, such as the Hasidim and some oriental Jewish communities, is the belief in literal angels still upheld.[17]

Historically, angels were thought of as gods and goddesses that one could get in touch with through trances by priestesses and oracles. Next, angels became known as spirit guides who could be contacted through mediums. A couple of decades ago, *medium* became an old-fashioned word. Today, those who contact spirits are called *channelers.*

In this present surge of angelology, spirit guides, channelers, and ascended masters have once again become known as angels, and anyone can talk to or become one. We have come full circle, returning to two thousand years ago when the apostle Paul warned Christians not to worship angels or entertain false teaching from them (Col. 2:18; Gal. 1:8).

As one scholar commented: "The way it was is the way it is"—a good enough bottom line for the theme of this chapter: parallels in history.[18]

On the other hand, we cannot stop believing in God's angels simply because some people misinterpret, misunderstand, or falsify their appearances, behavior, and purpose.

Nor do we want to be like the Sadducees, who, as Mortimer Adler pointed out, did not believe in angels or in anything supernatural despite all the references to angels in the Old Testament.[19]

Now that we've seen what people have thought of angels from outside of the church, let's look at what the church has said.

3

Angels and the Church

*The sound of heavenly voices, sweetly and softly joined in
harmony, without an apparent melody, was overpowering.
The effect on the hearer was to render him as incapable of
movement as though nailed to the spot.*[1]

—Hope Price

Angels have been reported as participants in the activities of
the Christian church since the first century. (See the Book
of Acts.)

The warnings of the apostles against angel worship (Col. 2:18–
19) and false angels (Gal. 1:8) kept Christian focus on angels at a
minimum for three centuries. But in A.D. 325, the Christian Council
of Nicea included a belief in angels as part of orthodox church
dogma, which may have sparked some worship of angels in the
church. This caused another council less than twenty years later
(A.D. 343) to prohibit angel worship, calling it idolatry.[2]

From about A.D. 500 until the time of the bubonic plague in A.D.
1347, however, angels were so much a part of the Roman Catholic
Church doctrines, worship services, and thinking that an entire
angelology developed as church dogma. This time has become
known as the Golden Age of Angels.

During the Middle Ages, theologians constructed an intricate
picture of the heavenly host based on a book that was hundreds of
years old called *The Celestial Hierarchy*. It outlined nine "choirs" of
angels arranged in three triads as follows:

- The highest triad—seraphim, cherubim, thrones

- The middle triad—dominions, virtues, powers

- The lowest triad—principalities, archangels, angels

Supposedly, in this angelic bureaucracy, the higher ranks worshiped God, the middle ranks kept the universe running, and the lower ranks carried out specific tasks.[3] (I'll describe what I believe Scripture says about the ranks of angels in chapter twelve.)

The author of *The Celestial Hierarchy* wrote under the pseudonym of Dionysius the Areopagite, the name of a man converted by Paul at Athens (Acts 17:34).[4] Years later it was discovered that the manuscript was dated much too late for its author to have been Paul's convert. Today he is called "pseudo-Dionysius."[5]

However, pseudo-Dionysius's hierarchical arrangement of heavenly beings was accepted by the Roman Catholic Church as authentic. It was retained as the basis of the Catholic angelology system until modern times.

Not only were orders of angels introduced by pseudo-Dionysius but also personal names of angels. Angels underwent what some have called a "population explosion" in those years, so much so that in A.D. 747 the Seventh Ecumenical Synod established a limited dogma on angels. This banned the use of names or calling on angels for help, except for Michael, Gabriel, and Raphael (the latter is not mentioned in the Protestant Bible but is in the Roman Catholic Douay Bible).

Whether or not their names were sanctioned by the church, angels were the subject of many books and articles by theologians during the Golden Age of Angels. These men thought that angels existed to fill the gap between God and man. Until science began to explore the universe, the church thought angels were the power behind the moving of the planets and everything in nature. But contrary to common belief, theologians never tried to estimate how many angels could stand on the head of a pin. Adler wrote that this was a sarcasm developed in later ages by writers scoffing at the medieval preoccupation with angels.[6] After all, the Middle Ages was the period during which most of the art depicting angels—still used today as models—originated. The *New Catholic Encyclopedia* says that actually the figural type of the Christian angel was derived from the winged Greek goddess of victory, Nike.[7]

This artistic source and the fact that many medieval angels were depicted as feminine or effeminate is perhaps why many people "see," paint, or think of angels as being feminine. However, the Bible always portrays angels as masculine.

Fat little cherubs such as Cupid are not found in biblical reference either. *Time* magazine commented:

> Only in the New Age would it be possible to invent an angel so mellow that it can be ignored. According to the rest of history, anyone who invites an encounter with an angel should be prepared to be changed by it.[8]

In fact, the *cherubim* of the Bible don't look anything like a *cherub!* This is how the apostle John described one of the angels he saw:

> And I saw another mighty angel come down from heaven, clothed with a cloud: and a rainbow was upon his head, and his face was as it were the sun, and his feet as pillars of fire.   —Revelation 10:1

With the advent of the Reformation (1500s), the focus on angels subsided. Early Protestants thought Renaissance paintings were decadent and argued that angels or saints were not needed as mediators between God and man.

Martin Luther, who was the catalyst for the Reformation, did refer in a sermon to "his guides, the holy angels," but he had an entirely different attitude about them than the church world from which he came.[9] To Luther, angels were created by God to serve His people, so they did not require special veneration.

The Western church became interested in angels again during the 1700s and 1800s, probably because of the arts and their influence on religious thinking. Poets and artists were inspired by John Milton's *Paradise Lost,* Dante's *Inferno,* and other works that spoke of the angelic realm.

One of these artists was William Blake, whose writings and art often featured angels, many of them appearing feminine.[10] The Victorian artists continued this tradition.

Essentially, this time of interest in angels extended into what is known as the Romantic period, which Christian scholar Edward T. Welch calls:

> …an ideological revolution that resulted in a remaking of God and the human soul. It emerged at a time when the influence of

Christianity seemed to be waning and people were changing their view of themselves and their world....The Romantic movement also grappled with the relationships among God, man, and creation. The conclusion, however, was decidedly anti-Christian and pantheistic.[11]

One of the most influential teachers on angels at the time was Emanuel Swedenborg (1688–1772), a Swedish mystic and clairvoyant who was also the son of a Protestant bishop. Until his mid-fifties, Swedenborg's interests were mostly in technical and mechanical inventions. One author says he actually succeeded in getting an aircraft to fly for a few moments.[12]

Swedenborg's thirst for knowledge led him to investigate dreams, and from that he began to have visions. He felt his new mission was to discover the "hidden meaning" of the Bible and to describe the world of the spirit. Some of his descriptions came in the form of automatic writing.

He said angels live like men with clothes, houses, and other things. He was one of the first to teach that angels (and demons) are really people who have progressed or regressed.

Swedenborg drew so many followers that he left Christianity and formed a new sect, the Church of the New Jerusalem. Swedenborgianism still has about one hundred thousand members worldwide.[13] His followers are considered spiritualists, not orthodox Protestants.

The focus on angels seems to have been largely with individuals or revival movements. The traditional Protestant church played no large part in this wave of angelology, though many believed in biblical angels who would protect and assist in times of trouble as an answer to prayer.

Throwing Out the Baby With the Bath Water

With the advent of the twentieth century, and especially during World War I, the Great Depression and then World War II, the idea of angels was deemed esoteric or out-and-out strange, even in much of Christendom.

Much of the skepticism about the supernatural may have had its roots in the epidemic of influenza in 1918 and 1919 called "the forgotten pandemic."[14] It seemed to have the same effect as the Black Death of the fourteenth century in that people became depressed and disillusioned with the supernatural. The result was a move away from a preoccupation with the supernatural. However, instead of arriving at a position of balance, the pendulum swung to the other extreme—rationalism.

Yet if people in the church denied the existence of angels, it struck at the very deity of Jesus. In other words, if Jesus taught that angels existed and they didn't, then He couldn't be God.[15]

Seeing this historical pattern of swinging from extreme gullibility to extreme cynicism, from romanticism to rationalism, makes a strong argument for finding balance in the extremes of angelology today.

The Supernatural Visits Churches

Even though society took a turn to extreme rationalism in the twentieth century and the church seemed in danger of going with it, there were still reports of angelic activity among Christians.

Around the turn of the century, evangelist Maria Woodworth-Etter became very well known for the supernatural manifestations in her meetings. A number of angel sightings and visions of angels were reported in the services. Also, a large portion of the congregation from time to time were said to have heard angelic choirs.[16]

Angels also were reported in the services of Aimee Semple McPherson, who founded the International Church of the Foursquare Gospel in the early part of this century.

Roy Hicks Sr., retired general supervisor of the International Church of the Foursquare Gospel, wrote in *Guardian Angels* about one of the incidents that took place in the early days of McPherson's ministry. She was holding outdoor meetings and unknowingly pitched her tent on a lot where the locals played baseball.

> As the service began, she saw the angry young men coming from the bushes around the tent. They were carrying gasoline cans, and she knew they intended to burn the tent.
>
> She related, "I said to the Lord, 'What shall I do?'"

The Lord told her to lift her hands and begin to worship Him. As she obeyed, her eyes were opened in the Spirit, and she saw the tent completely surrounded by a host of angels with their wings extended and touching, wing tip to wing tip. As she opened her eyes, she saw the men, all with looks of astonishment on their faces. They had dropped the cans and stood there with mouths agape. Later on, many of them began to attend the services, and many were saved.

When Angelus Temple...was erected, she had the painters stencil angels, wing tip to wing tip, around the perimeter of the auditorium just under the huge dome to commemorate the event.[17]

One of the most well-known accounts of an angel working in the church in twentieth-century Protestantism took place during the ministry of William Branham, who was called "the healer-prophet."[18] His crusades spanned the years from World War I to the 1960s.

Branham said an angel stood behind his right shoulder and gave him exact details and events about people's lives that Branham then spoke forth and used for ministry. Even church leaders who were not impressed with Branham's ministry had to admit that the accuracy of what he told people was phenomenal.

Branham also said the angel performed all the healings in his ministry. He cited John 5:4, which says those who dipped in the Pool of Bethesda immediately after an angel stirred the water were healed (KJV).

Skeptics in the Church Today

While the secular world is grasping for the supernatural today, it seems that some people in the church have polarized in the opposite direction toward skepticism.

J. Rodman Williams, professor of theology at Regent University (formerly CBN University), says that in many Christian circles today angels are viewed as symbolic or "as mythopoetic pictures of various dimensions of human existence."

In 1988 Professor Williams cited a "growing skepticism" among Christians concerning the existence of angels, not because of an "antisupernatural" belief but from a question of relevance.[19] He raised some key questions:

- Does Christian faith need angels?

- Is it not enough to believe in God without adding to the superstructure by bringing in angels?

- Are we ill-advised in Christian doctrine to venture again into this area considering how angelology went beyond the scriptural record during the Middle Ages?

As the author of *Systematic Theology From a Charismatic Perspective*, Williams comes from a movement with an emphasis on the supernatural gifts of the Holy Spirit. Yet he believes the church has been so "burned" with false manifestations and theology that it might be better to leave angelology alone.

On the other hand, he added, "If angelic visits are still possible, there is all the more need for such study to be done." He cited a 1980s book *Angels on Assignment* in which a local pastor, Roland Buck of Boise, Idaho, describes his visits by angels.[20] (The late Rev. Buck was a personal friend of mine. I'll tell more about his story later.)

It seems that Williams has the best answer: If angels or beings calling themselves angels are making appearances, and if the general public is about to plunge off the deep end into "angelolatry," then it behooves the church to find the truth in the middle of extremes and have some answers for Christians and for non-Christians.

Branham, McPherson, and others provide examples of angelic activity in the church during the time of rationalism in the mid-twentieth century. As we shall see, angels were active among believers and nonbelievers in one of the most stressful of all human situations—war.

4

Angelic Warriors in the Twentieth Century

For he shall give his angels charge over thee, to keep thee in all thy ways.

—Psalm 91:11

[God] has all eternity in which to listen to the split second of prayer put up by a pilot as his plane crashes in flames.[1]

—C. S. Lewis

Many stories from times of war include incidents in which seemingly miraculous things happened—things with no natural explanation—that are attributed to angels. Some of these stories involve nations, and some involve individuals. Some have more than one witness who saw the same thing or similar things.

Why do angels appear at some times and not at others?

Does God "take sides" with one nation over another?

It seems, as John Wesley once said, "God does nothing unless somebody prays." As we will see when we look at stories of angels in the Bible, it appears that the earnest prayers of people who cry out to God often bring deliverance. At times, that deliverance is in the form of angelic ministry.

The other major factor that appears in biblical patterns of angelic assistance is that God has an overall plan for this planet and for His children. If human events directly affect His plan, you may be sure that angels will be involved.

And, no, God does not "take sides." What happens in battles and wars is that sometimes one side is on God's side. God's angels do not fight on the side of those who do not believe in Him. In fact, angels will eventually be involved in judgment handed down against those who have been against God. (Look at the role of angels in the Book of Revelation.)

Several of the most well-known incidents of angels related in this chapter involve Great Britain and the Allies on one side and the Axis powers on the other. Angels appear to have intervened on behalf of the Allies more than once. These stories have appeared in print many times before, but they are so important and have so many witnesses that they bear repeating.

Does the fact that angels intervened on behalf of the Allies mean that God opposed every citizen of the Axis nations?

Of course not. However, the people in Axis countries were under governmental authorities who were opposed by God. Particularly in Germany, the ruling Nazi party obviously opposed God's moral laws and God's people. We hear and read frequently about Hitler's intention to wipe out the Jewish race.

God does not "take sides" but rather helps those on His side, and He does pull down evil kingdoms, as we see in the Old Testament.

Angels in World War I

A story from World War I involving angels known as "The Angels of Mons" was told throughout England within a month after the battle.

Near Mons, France, in August 1914, heavily outnumbered British troops had fought with no respite for days. They had lost many men and guns, and defeat looked inevitable.

Captain Cecil W. Hayward was there and tells how suddenly, in the midst of a gun battle, firing on both sides stopped. To their astonishment, the British troops saw "four or five wonderful beings, much bigger than men," between themselves and the Germans. These "men" were bare-headed, wore white robes, and seemed to float rather than stand. Their backs were to the British, and their arms and hands were outstretched toward the Germans. At that moment, the horses ridden by German cavalrymen became terrified and stampeded off in every direction.[2]

Of all the angel war stories, the incident at Mons probably has the largest number of witnesses reporting similar sightings.

Hayward also told of another battle sometime later in World War I when matters again seemed hopeless for British soldiers who were surrounded by German troops. Suddenly the heavy enemy fire stopped completely, and everything grew strangely quiet. Then "the sky opened with a bright shining light, and figures of luminous beings appeared" floating between the British and German lines.

German troops retreated in disorder, allowing the Allied forces to reform and fall back on a line of defense farther to the west. German prisoners were taken that day, and when they were asked why they surrendered when they had the British troops surrounded, they looked amazed, saying, "But there were hosts and hosts of you."[3]

Captain Hayward also wrote of the incident of the "white battalion" at Bethune three and a half years later. He was one of the intelligence officers who interrogated German prisoners from that battle.

In April 1918, near the close of World War I, a mysterious white battalion was seen by hundreds of German soldiers near Bethune, France. One German officer told of his troops marching along in excellent spirits because they thought the British were defeated. Suddenly a lieutenant grabbed him by the arm, saying:

> Look, Herr Captain, there is a large body of mounted men approaching Bethune from the other side. See, the smoke of the burning houses is blowing away and I can discern their uniforms. Why, they are all dressed in white and are mounted on white horses. Who can they be?[4]

At first the captain thought the troops might be British Colonial mounted troops, but they knew of none who wore white uniforms and rode white chargers. The Germans stopped to watch the cavalrymen advancing through the smoke, their figures clearly outlined in the sun. Mortar shells shook the ground, and intensive machine gun fire raked the men, but the cavalry unit dressed in white rode on at a slow trot. Not one man or horse was hit.

Riding in front of them was "a fine figure of a man" who had a sword by his side like those used by the Crusaders, but his hands quietly held the reins of his horse. Suddenly terror seized the German troops, and they fled.

The British troops did not see the cavalrymen dressed in white. Only the Germans did. The Prussian captain said he knew at that moment Germany had lost the war due to these mysterious troops on the side of the British.

This incident reminds us of Old Testament battles when God confounded Israel's enemies with fear and terror, causing a complete rout. Also, in Exodus 23:27 God had promised the Israelites He would send His fear before them and make their enemies "turn their backs" to them.

Hope Price, who recorded the World War I stories in a book, noted that the British government officially sponsored national days of prayer during the conflict. She believes the government's commitment to prayer played a role in the angelic intervention on behalf of British soldiers.[5]

In other words, the official government of a nation can represent that nation. Actions of the government can bring divine intervention, both for blessings and for judgment.

Angels in World War II

One Sunday morning in September of 1940, Prime Minister Winston Churchill and some military advisers were in an underground operations room in southern England watching the lights on the electrical battle charts. There was a dangerous shortage of materials, and intelligence reports showed that German forces were preparing to invade England.

On that otherwise quiet Sunday morning, a sudden alert heralded the approach of Nazi aircraft from several directions—forty from one direction, sixty from another, followed by a formation of eighty planes. This was only the beginning. Aircraft continued to fill the sky from every direction.

> As each Nazi formation neared the English coast, a British squadron would rise to meet it. Since there were only 25 squadrons assigned to the 11th Fighter Command defending southern England, soon all of them were in the air. Tension grew in the underground shelter....
>
> Then inexplicably, the discs [markers] on the wall chart began to move eastward. The great Nazi air flotilla had turned back.

With 185 of their aircraft downed in flames, they were in retreat! Miraculously, against all logistical probability, the Royal Air Force had won the battle![6]

There was no natural explanation for the outcome of this Nazi attack during the Battle of Britain, but intelligence officers who interrogated downed Nazi airmen heard this question from at least three different men: "Where did you get all the planes you threw into the battle over Britain?"

The British force was inferior, but the Germans claimed that they were outnumbered by the British planes they saw.

Again, the British, as a nation, were praying for the safety of their country and their military forces. From 1940 until the end of the war, the people throughout the Commonwealth observed a silent moment of prayer at 9:00 p.m. each day.

An imprisoned Nazi intelligence officer told his captors:

> With the striking of your Big Ben clock each evening at nine, you used a secret weapon which we did not understand. It was very powerful and we could find no countermeasure against it.[7]

Evangelist Billy Graham in his book *Angels, God's Secret Agents* related an incident that reportedly occurred during the weeks-long Battle of Britain. He quoted reporter-author Adela Rogers St. John's story of a celebration some time after the war at which Chief Marshal Lord Hugh Dowding was present, along with many other dignitaries, including the king.

Lord Dowding told of British pilots who were badly wounded or even dead in their cockpits—yet their planes kept flying. On occasion, other pilots saw figures at the controls who were not RAF pilots. The air chief marshal believed angels actually piloted those planes.[8]

Roy Hicks Sr. wrote about a chaplain in the United States Armed Forces during World War II.

> During World War II, Chaplain Alex B. Cowie was stationed in the Pacific arena and riding in a United States transport plane when it was attacked by Japanese fighter planes. His plane was so badly shot up that the pilot said, "We can't make it. We're going down."

As the chaplain prayed, he looked out the window. The Lord opened his eyes, and he saw a mighty angel holding up the wing of the plane. He looked out the other side and saw another angel holding up that wing.[9]

After they landed, Cowie said everyone who saw the plane touch down marveled that it had made it back with everyone safe because it was damaged so badly.

Other Angelic Rescues From Attacks

Early in 1968 an entire village in South Vietnam is said to have experienced angelic protection. Cliff Custer told this story at the annual meeting of the Camps Farthest Out in May 1968, held at Oral Roberts University in Tulsa, Oklahoma.

Custer said he and a friend, Keith Swaggerty, were visiting a village where there were many Christians when a Viet Cong guerilla, who had spent time as a youth in this community, slipped into the village and warned they would be attacked the next day by a thousand Viet Cong.

The villagers had no weapons or ammunition and only a few men who could fight, so they decided to let the Lord be their defender. Instead of trying to escape or hide in fear, they prayed fervently and sang songs of praise and thanksgiving that filled their hearts "with a strange peace and courage."

The next day, while it was still dark, the first shots were heard. But then, just as suddenly, the firing stopped. There was nothing but silence the rest of the night, the next day, and in the days to come. A few days later some of the Viet Cong were captured by South Vietnamese forces and brought into the village.

> "Why did you halt your attack on our village?" they were asked.
>
> "As we opened fire," the Viet Cong prisoners replied in agitation, "all of a sudden there appeared all around the village men clad in shining white. We fired at them, but they wouldn't fall. They shone brighter than the sun, and we couldn't aim at them. We were terrified, and we ran."[10]

During the Boxer Rebellion in China in 1900, missionaries of several denominations in and around Peking fled to the British

Embassy. During one attack they saw their enemy abruptly stop and point upward. Suddenly, the attacking force fled.

Those who were captured said, "We saw the walls suddenly swarming with angels in white. Everyone began shouting that the *shen* (gods) had come down to fight for the foreigners, and our cause was lost."[11]

In his book *God, Satan, and Angels,* John MacArthur Jr. tells an incident about missionary John Paton. One night, natives known to be cannibals surrounded the lean-to on the South Pacific beach where Paton and his wife were living.

The couple dropped to their knees and prayed. Soon the attackers vanished into the jungle. A year later the chief of the tribe was converted, and Paton asked him why the group left so hurriedly that night. The chief described seeing "hundreds of big men" in shining clothes with swords in their hands.[12]

Coincidences?

Some may think the connection between prayer and angelic assistance or other miracles is just a coincidence, but William Temple, the late Archbishop of Canterbury, pointed out, "When I pray, coincidences happen, and when I do not, they don't."[13]

Many of these kinds of stories have been published, but many others have not. Some people have been too afraid of being laughed at to tell such experiences.

Few, however, seem to have any standard of measurement as to whether what they saw were truly angels or demonic beings appearing as angels or figments of their imaginations. Today's so-called angels are certainly not shy!

In the next chapter, we will see that knowledge about what angels are and are not is essential to judging an experience or a story. Not only individuals, but also millions of people have been affected eternally by beings the Bible calls "angels of light."

5

Angels of Light

One night a demon appeared to an old monk in his room,
saying, "I am the angel Gabriel, and I have been sent to
you." The monk responded humbly, "You must have the
wrong room. I'm not worthy to have an angel visit me."
Unable to tempt him to vanity the demon vanished.[1]

—Paul Thigpen

Many an arrogant person has received an angel of light and "come a real cropper," as equestrians say, which means tumbling head over heels off the back end of a horse. Some of the people we are going to talk about in this chapter would have been much better off to have done what the old monk did.

Thigpen says the lesson of the story is this: "Our best armor in spiritual warfare may be a humble heart."[2]

To whatever degree it exists, pride hinders discernment, and without discernment, we accept counterfeits.

An "angel of light" in biblical terms is not an angel that appears in a burst of light or looks radiant or has a halo around his head. An angel of light, regardless of what he looks like, says, or does, is a spirit who presents a gospel other than what is found in the Bible.

And no marvel; for Satan himself is transformed into an angel of light. Therefore it is no great thing if his ministers also be transformed as the ministers of righteousness; whose end shall be according to their works.

—2 Corinthians 11:14–15

But though we, or an angel from heaven, preach any other gospel unto you than that which we have preached unto you, let him be accursed.

—Galatians 1:8

The one real standard we have for knowing whether an angel is an angel of God or an angel of light is whether or not his words and actions match Scripture. In the last chapter of this book I'll give you a checklist for judging angelic visits. But at this point let me say that an angel of God is most concerned with furthering God's purposes on earth. Therefore, any other purpose or result of an angelic visit should cause immediate suspicion of the presence of an angel of light instead.

One young woman told how she was depressed from a traumatic emotional experience and cried out for divine help. Later she woke and saw the beams of her bedroom ceiling glowing in the shape of a large golden cross. A voice said, "Fear ye not, I am the Lord."

Later she began to have psychic experiences and dreams about what she described as her past lives (reincarnation).[3] The result of the woman's golden-cross vision was not a closer walk with God but an acceptance of "another gospel." Because of her experiences, she also started to give other people spiritual advice.

It is when we feel the most desperate that we must be on our guard against temptations from Satan. When this woman had an encounter with the supernatural, she accepted it as from God without judging the experience according to Scripture. I believe she was deceived by an angel of light.

What can protect us from being deceived? Bank tellers, learning to distinguish counterfeit money from the genuine item, do not major on the counterfeit. They study the real thing until they cannot accept a "dollar of light" as a real buck. In the same manner we need to study God's Word and learn His ways so we will recognize Satan's counterfeits.

In addition, there is no substitute for walking close enough to the Lord in prayer to be able to get what some Christians call "a check" or "a witness" from the Holy Spirit. These "red lights" and "green lights" tell us whether something we are hearing or reading is the real thing. Then we can investigate the matter further to find out what is right or wrong with it.

Angels of God often appear in the Bible as God's messengers. Angels of light carry messages, too, but they are not from God. Their lies started two major religions that are practiced today: Islam and Mormonism.[4]

The Angel of Muhammed

A young camel driver who was a member of one of the most powerful Arabian nomadic tribes married a wealthy older woman in the late sixth century. He had traveled widely with his uncle's caravans into Syria and Egypt and was familiar with many different thoughts and religions.

His people worshiped many gods, but because of his cosmopolitan cultural outlook, he began to question current practices and beliefs. As the husband of a wealthy woman, he no longer had to work, and he employed his leisure time in meditating and thinking on matters of religion.

While meditating in a cave, Muhammed began to have violent seizures and frightening visions, allegedly from the angel Gabriel. His first thought was that these were demonic, but his wife persuaded him that they were divine and that he should listen to "the angel." Out of these revelations, which lasted twenty-two years until his death in A.D. 632 at about sixty-four years of age, came the youngest major world religion—Islam.

Islam combines elements of the Bible with Muhammed's own doctrines, which often contradict the Bible. Muslims say in these instances that the Bible was changed by men or inaccurately translated. From Judaism they take the idea of God as one God. The trinity makes Christianity polytheistic, they say. They see Jesus as a prophet like Muhammed, but only a prophet.

Today Islam is spreading rapidly due to its strong cultural and political base and lack of racial barriers. It is the second-largest world religion after Christianity.

George Otis Jr. wrote in *The Last of the Giants*:

> As the world's fastest growing religion, Islam is predicted to double in size somewhere around the year 2020. If estimates hold up, Muslims will at that time number approximately 1.9 billion or 25 percent of humanity....

Muslims in the United States currently outnumber members of the Assemblies of God three to one, while in the U.K. there are now more followers of Allah than Methodists or Baptists combined. In France, Muslims represent the nation's second largest religious group, and boast more adherents than all Protestant denominations put together.[5]

Otis also says that Muslims are monitoring Christian activities. Given that fact, he points out that Christians should conduct themselves in a manner befitting Christ. At the same time, he says, we should recognize that "this daily observation extends to legions of unseen powers in the spiritual realm."[6]

A millennium after Muhammed and two continents away, another angel brought "revelation" for another new religion.

The Angel of Joseph Smith

In the early 1800s, a young man named Joseph Smith spent a great deal of time with his father looking for buried treasure and meditating on which religion was right, as did Muhammed. In the New England of that time, treasure hunters were considered "ne'er-do-wells." Their tools included shovels, pickaxes—and a "divining" tool.

In 1820 the fifteen-year-old boy related a vision in which both God the Father and God the Son told him that all churches were abominations. He said that he was called as a prophet to restore the true gospel. What developed over the years of Smith's pilgrimage through life, however, was not the true gospel restored but another gospel, as the apostle Paul warned against in Galatians 1:8:

> But though we, or an angel from heaven, preach any other gospel unto you than that which we have preached unto you, let him be accursed.

An angel of light (or angels of light) appeared to Joseph Smith in similar fashion as with Muhammed. Three years later another angel—or the same one in another guise—appeared calling himself Moroni. At times Smith said the angel's name was Nephi. This angel told Smith about some golden plates on which the "true gospel" was written.

Smith said he eventually found these buried in a hill near his home in Palmyra, New York. The writing, he said, was reformed Egyptian hieroglyphics. (Scholars say no such language exists.) He was able to translate them only by means of an angel-supplied pair of large spectacles called the Urim and Thummim (also the name of part of the breastplate of the Aaronic high priests in Exodus 28:30 and Leviticus 8:8).

In 1829 Smith founded the Church of Jesus Christ of Latter-Day Saints after saying he had received the Aaronic priesthood from John the Baptist in a vision. Most people who talk to John the Baptist or Napoleon end up being entertained at state expense. However, Smith had an angel backing him! Instead of being institutionalized, he was free to start one of the larger, and wealthier, pseudo-Christian religions in America. Today there are 8 million members in the Mormon Church worldwide, divided among six different sects that arose over various doctrinal disputes.

Mormon doctrines deny original sin and teach that the fall of man was not only good but necessary—a doctrine similar to that of some of the occult groups. Because of this, there is no imputed sin nature in children, who are born in complete innocence. However, everyone eventually sins when they reach the age of accountability.

This "other gospel" has some beautiful but misleading advertisements on television upholding family values and talking about Jesus, even calling Him "Savior," which Mormons do not at all believe He is.

Angels in Other Religions

Angels made Muhammed and Joseph Smith famous. The same could be said of Emmanuel Swedenborg, whom we mentioned earlier in this book. Swedenborg communicated regularly with "angels" whom he thought were the spirits of dead human beings.

One of his books, *Heaven and Hell,* contains an extremely detailed description of what he claimed was heaven and its inhabitants. His descriptions relied heavily on information from angels, whom he says have all the attributes of man, except bodies. In fact, Swedenborg wrote that "angels are men" and live together in societies as men do on earth. They exist in a more perfect state than man, he said.

Each angel's house reflects the degree to which he has received truth from God, Swedenborg wrote. He said angels are sent to earth to protect us from all error in thought and desire.

Swedenborg also said angels were not created in the beginning but are gradually brought into existence as human beings return to the Father. Every angel and demon began life somewhere on earth or on another planet, he wrote. According to his angelology system, angels and demons evolve from the spirits of the dead.[7]

Another elaborate hierarchy of angels developed in the mystic stream of Judaism—the Kabbalah (or Cabbalah). Writers say the Kabbalah would not be nearly as attractive to those interested in the occult or the esoteric without its pantheon of angels and demonic beings. There are many points of similarity between Kabbalah, Gnosticism, and Islamic Sufism (the mystic stream of Islam).[8]

Sophy Burnham says the Kabbalah guides believers with angelic assistance on the path to God through a series of heavenly halls and secret passwords by which they overcome demons on the way.

Is it not amazing how all of these angels of light know so much more about creation, heaven, and hell than the writers of the Old and New Testaments? Somewhere out there these angels and/or their boss are having a field day making up fantastic stories for the entrapment of gullible humans.

Parallel strands of doctrines run through all these religions. The same strands are in mythologies, Gnosticism, and so forth, and are distortions or perversions of basic Judeo-Christian truths.

Two basic differences from Christianity run through them all:

1. There is a God but not the one Christians believe in. They say God is a disinterested force (from Friedrich Hegel's "Absolute Idea" to *Star Wars*);[9] God is in everything (pantheism and environmentalism); or God is a woman, the Earth Mother, Gaia (white magic).

2. There was a Jesus, but He was not who Christians think He was.

These angels of light have said Jesus really is Lucifer, and the one we think is the devil really is the Son of God—which is the underlying principle of Freemasonry, as well. In fact, the five points of fellowship in Freemasonry and the five points of fellowship in

Mormonism are almost identical, which is not surprising, because Joseph Smith became a Mason in 1842, along with about twelve hundred other Mormons.[10]

I want to mention one more religion that started with an angel of light because it's different from the others in a key way.

The religion started about eight hundred years ago when a being that called itself the "Peacock Angel" appeared to a man in his twenties named Sheikh Adi Musafir, who lived in the Middle East. This angel of light called him to "proclaim the religion of truth to the world."[11]

Now there is a tribe in Northwestern Iraq named the Yezidi that worships the Peacock Angel. They are known as devil worshipers. The Peacock Angel is different from the "angels" of Islam and Mormonism in that he openly represents Satan instead of pretending to be a good angel of God.

One of the passages from the book that Musafir wrote describes other men in history who received the Peacock Angel:

> King Ahab and Amran were of us, so that they used to call the God of Ahab Beelzebub....We had a king in Babel (Babylon) whose name was Nebuchadnezzar...And Ahasuerus in Persia.[12]

In this chapter we looked at some angels of light and the monumental effect they have had on the history of mankind through their followers. However, we should remember not to throw out truth because it has been perverted, corrupted, or obscured.

There are credible accounts of angels who have appeared to people in recent years as guardians, messengers, or protectors, and who operated in line with biblical patterns. Some of these are in the following chapters.

6

Angelic Encounters in Modern Times

There is an ocean of difference between that which is "extra-biblical" and that which is "unbiblical." Extra-biblical is a yellow light that encourages passage with caution; unbiblical is a red light that requires travelers to halt in the name of the law and common sense.[1]

—George Otis Jr.

The subject of angels is one of several in the late twentieth century that requires spiritual common sense. George Otis Jr. gives good advice for these areas of modern Christian living that are not specifically spelled out in the Bible.

- If something—such as a foundational teaching—definitely is in the Word of God, that is a green-light doctrine or practice.

- If something is prohibited or obviously against the Word of God, such as angel-inspired religions without Jesus, then we have a red light and should stop.

- If something is not specifically a go or a stop, then we may proceed with caution until we find a definite answer.

Extra-biblical does not mean something added to the Bible but something that may fit into Bible principles and patterns even though it may not be specifically spelled out in Scripture.

For example, nowhere in the Bible do we have information about what car to buy, whether or not to use computers, or whether television is right or wrong. All of these things are extra-biblical. However, they are not unbiblical.

When God's ways are examined through the principles found in the Bible, guidelines about extra-biblical things can be found. For example, the number-one principle for any Christian is to do everything to the glory of God (1 Cor. 10:31). If something does not bring God glory or will bring shame to His name, then we should not have it or do it.

The second most important principle is to check your motives or attitudes. The reason we want something or want to do something is just as important as whatever it is we desire.

Cults are formed just as much from sloppy thinking as they are from angels of light. The problem with many Christians is that they leave their brains at the altar with their sins. Many think they are being spiritual by operating thereafter on emotions, or how they feel about something.

Right thinking is not to lay aside the mind but to have it renewed by meditating on and studying the Word of God (Rom. 12:2). The mind is like the software in a computer, which is the brain. Without a functioning mind, our brains could not operate any more than a computer could operate without software.

Our minds contain the sum total of our knowledge. And knowledge is comprised of everything we have heard, seen, or learned since we were in our mothers' wombs. Knowledge gained from the world is what has to be transformed by knowledge from the Word of God.

As Christians, we don't stop thinking. Our way of thinking is to be renewed through the "spirit" of our minds (Eph. 4:23).

We must measure everything by God's Word, not by how we feel or even how we think. For example, when movies were first invented, many Christians automatically were against them as being "of the devil." The same thing happened with radio and television.

Christians who first saw the potential of radio, television, and films for ministry were opposed and even persecuted by the majority of Christians. For that reason, it took the church about fifty years to catch up with the world in the use of these media.

The use of media was not unbiblical, but it was extra-biblical. Movies, television, and radio were simply new ways of communicating, and the Bible makes no objection to communication.

But some of the angel stories in the many books now on the market are obviously unbiblical and should be set aside immediately. These include:

- Angels who tell people, "You are the Christ."

- Angels who tell people they can be saved by their works.

- Angels who say that we have to be born again and again to work out karma.

- Angels who say that there is no hell and that everything after death is all sweetness and light—even if these angels are seen during out-of-body experiences.

- Angels who appear in the form of animals or birds.

- Angels who bring "new revelation" contradictory to the Bible—not just a deeper, expanded interpretation but added doctrines not previously mentioned.

The stories in this book have been examined closely and prayerfully to make sure they do not contain any unbiblical elements. Many of these encounters happened to me, to someone I know, or to people in churches where I have ministered and whose pastors vouch for their Christian lives and integrity. However, none of these stories directly parallel stories of angelic intervention in Scripture, so they are extra-biblical. Therefore, it is appropriate to judge and test them.

Angel Protects a Testimony

Anneice West, who helps with counseling at Agape Church in Little Rock, Arkansas, told of seeing angels several years ago. It happened at a Christmas party in 1990 when she was working with a ministry outreach to the homeless and needy.

During the party and ministry staff meeting, one of the staffers shared how he had felt strongly impressed one day to minister to a man on the street. He had gone out of his way to talk to this man and ask him how he was doing.

The man was not doing well at all. In fact, he was consider-ing suicide. He was not attending church anywhere, so the staffer could not send him to a pastor. Instead he talked to the man and encouraged him to turn his life over to God. Then he prayed with him.

Later the staffer saw the man again, who told him it was "phe-nomenal" how things in his life had turned around since he had given his life to the Lord. Problems and pressures that had seemed insurmountable were resolved. The man was so thankful that some-one had taken the time to stop and ask how he was.

West said that while she was listening to this story, she sud-denly saw an angel standing behind the man's chair. He was about six feet tall with powerful wings that were folded by his sides and reached all the way down to his ankles. West wrote:

> I remember feeling a sense of awe and fear at the sight of him and also feeling glad that he was not my enemy! The glory of God surrounded him, and a physical strength and power flowed out of him that went far beyond any human strength.
>
> Although he was standing only a few feet away from me, the angel said nothing to me, nor did he acknowledge my presence in any way. His entire attention was focused with deadly serious-ness on guarding the man who was speaking.
>
> At that point, I felt a keen awareness of danger that made my skin prickle. I knew unseen forces of darkness were waiting and watching for the slightest opportunity to come in and stop the words being spoken. I knew these forces were being held at bay by the presence of the angel.
>
> I knew they were unwilling to tangle with the fierce, powerful warrior of God. I also knew that, had the angel not been there, that testimony would never have come forth. I felt the Lord speak to my heart and show me that the angel had been sent specifically to guard that man while he delivered the words God wanted all of us to hear. The Lord made me aware that, at times, it is a mat-ter of life and death to reach out to those around us when He prompts our hearts to do so.

Angels Rejoice During Christian Worship

Sharon Abrams, a physician's wife who also attends Agape Church, told of seeing two angels during a church service. The angels were hovering over the congregation with their arms outstretched. They were light-skinned and had light-colored hair, and they stood seven or eight feet tall. Abrams wrote:

> Their faces were broad with high cheekbones and beautiful smiles. They looked like men except they did not have beards. There was an innocence to their faces, and the joy of their expressions was wonderful. They did not wear shoes, but wore long white gowns with gold braid. I cannot remember exactly where the braid was located on the gowns.
>
> I knew they were in the service because of our praise and worship...because Jesus was being lifted up and adored. I sensed there were many more beings present in the auditorium, but I was only able to see those two.[2]

Marilyn Cappo of Louisville Covenant Church in Kentucky says she has seen angels on a number of occasions. She reported seeing three angels dancing on the roof of a house where a home group was meeting. One of them was playing something like a small harp, perhaps a lyre. Later, during a church morning worship service, she saw a nine-foot angel standing behind the worship leader.

Most recently, she said she has seen two angels standing on the front platform of her church during several different services. She described them this way:

> They are a little over six feet tall and dressed in white. They do not speak but raise their wings when songs are sung of direct praise to the Father.
>
> They stand to the left of the pulpit, watching the congregation, and look at us expectantly. I have seen them off and on over a period of months and have prayed often to understand their purpose and mission at our church. One morning one of them walked over behind the pastor and spread his wings as our pastor was making

declarative statements about God to us. The angels appear to be waiting for us to do something and always watch intently.

Patsy Burton of Wethersfield, Essex, in England, wrote of hearing angels singing during a church service. She said the "clarity, pitch, and harmony was absolutely incredible. In fact, there are no words to describe how they sounded."

In *Somewhere Angels*, one of the best books that I have found on angels, author Larry Libby wrote about a worship meeting in Alaska.

> Outside, the winter wind moaned and hissed against the frosted church windows. But inside the little church, people were warm and happy and singing song after song of praise to God...something mysterious and wonderful happened that icy, starlit night. After one last praise song...people stopped singing. The musicians put down their instruments. But somehow, the singing kept going. Everyone heard it. The beautiful praise music kept rolling on and on for a little while, like a long, silvery echo.[3]

Angels Protect a Home During a Storm

Dawn Tallent told of angelic protection during a storm.

> My encounter occurred in 1976 when we lived in Missouri. It was the wee hours of the morning, and we had been having severe weather. We lived in a mobile home, and I was very fearful of storms. I remember waking up to a loud noise outside our bedroom window that sounded like a freight train. The window was shaking, and the whole house seemed to be moving.
>
> My husband was sound asleep next to me, but I was too scared to move or even wake him up. I began to pray fervently, asking God to spare my home and family because I knew that if He did not intervene, tragedy would hit. In that moment the Lord began to speak peace to me. I felt He wanted me to get up and look out the window so He could show me something. I eased my way up to the window and pulled open the curtains.
>
> To my surprise and shock, I saw a very bright light and figures of tall, broad-shouldered beings dressed in long, white robes. They had strong arms and hands and were holding hands, standing with

their backs to the wind and their faces toward me. However, I could not see their faces clearly because they were so bright.

At that moment I knew that angels were encompassing the mobile home and us. I sat on the bed, just gazing out of the window in awe for about fifteen minutes. All fear left, and I felt safe and secure. From that day on, whenever a storm comes my way, I know strong angels are there to protect me.

Angels Comfort an Evangelist

Joseph Morris of Mobile, Alabama, said the first time he saw an angel was in 1986 when he was crusade director for an evangelistic ministry and had some pressing financial needs.

He was in a hotel when an angel suddenly appeared in his room. Morris says the angel was about eight feet tall, masculine, had long hair down to his shoulders and was wearing a white robe. He appeared to be very strong and looked at him intently and, somehow, very businesslike.

At first Morris was shocked, but then somehow he "knew" the angel was there to hear him speak forth God's promise about his needs.

So Morris said, "My God supplies all my needs according to His riches in glory by Christ Jesus" (see Philippians 4:19), and the angel disappeared. Within a few days, Morris said, the finances were supplied.

A year later, Morris was praying at home one evening, but he was concerned about being away from his wife and family so much at other times. His wife was asleep in the bedroom when an angel walked into the living room where Morris was praying.

The angel said, "I was sent from the throne of God to tell you that I am to guard your wife and children and keep peace in your family." Then he disappeared.

"Thank God for His comfort at a time when I had to be away from home so much," Morris said.

Angel Appears in a Vision

John Bosman, senior pastor of Glad Tidings Assembly of God in Lake Charles, Indiana, told me about a vision that he had during a time of prayer.

> A bright light filled the room, and suddenly before my eyes the sanctuary of my church appeared (which seats about 1,500 people). At that same moment, I became aware that the sanctuary was full of people, and there was a huge angel standing in the middle of it. His shoulders and head seemed to be far above the balcony.

The angel showed him how some people in the church were full of God's anointing, while others were just full of religion. Those with the anointing spread life and sweetness, symbolized by honey bees, while those with religion carried death, like flies. It was a powerful call for discernment and gave him insight for pastoring.

Angels Rescue Man Stranded in Desert

A man named Bob Leech sent a story to my ministry's office in Great Britain about what he believes was angelic assistance rendered to him in Saudi Arabia. It occurred in 1977 (long before the Gulf War).

Leech was driving an American-made sedan, not a four-wheel-drive vehicle, from a construction camp to Dhahran on a seldom-used road with no nearby towns or villages.

At about 1:00 p.m., as the temperature soared to 120 degrees, Leech's vehicle hit a dip in the road that threw his car into soft sand. Immediately he was stuck, and for the first time in all his desert traveling, he had no water with him.

Trying to shovel the vehicle free only caused sand to slide in around the wheels. Leech knew that if he started out across the desert on foot, his chances of rescue were almost zero. The only recourse was to sit in the car and wait for passersby—if any.

He had been there for about an hour when suddenly three men who looked like Bedouins appeared seemingly out of nowhere. Leech wrote:

I had not seen them approach, although I had been keeping a constant lookout for the past hour. They were dressed as you might think the shepherds in the Bible might have looked. We greeted one another in Arabic, and they handed me a goatskin bag of water. That was the coolest water I ever tasted! They helped to move the car by vigorously bouncing it as I reversed onto the harder surface at the side of the road.

I thanked them and got into the car. I was at an angle and needed to complete my reverse, straighten up, and then continue. As I reversed and turned back onto the asphalt, I intended to wave one last time—but there was no one there.

The surrounding area was completely flat for miles, and there was no sign of them. *I never saw them come, and I never saw them go.*

Every time I think about, or relate, this event, I am overwhelmed by the understanding that God had His hand upon me even before I had a personal relationship with Him.

Little did I know that I, like Bob, too would experience angelic protection in the Middle East. God would allow me enter one of the most politically and spiritually volatile places—Iraq—but He also sent His "special agents" to watch over me.

7

Goodness and Mercy—God's Special Agents in the Middle East

Yea, though I walk through the valley of the shadow of death, I will fear no evil: for thou art with me; thy rod and thy staff they comfort me. Thou preparest a table before me in the presence of mine enemies: thou anointest my head with oil; my cup runneth over. Surely goodness and mercy shall follow me all the days of my life: and I will dwell in the house of the LORD for ever.

—David, in Psalm 23:4–6

Back in the late 1970s when I traveled with my music group Living Sound, I met Pastor Roland Buck. Pastor Buck shared with me some of his private conversations with angels. At first, I was skeptical, but then he told me specific information about the moment in time when I received my calling to full-time ministry (some of which I will share with you later in chapter nineteen). Nobody but God Himself could have known how I was feeling at that moment. Now Pastor Buck had my attention. Little did I know then how much his words would impact my life and my ministry almost thirty years later.

The Bible tells us that we are to test all things. I have never shared publicly what the angels said to Roland Buck about my ministry—until now. Those words were spoken almost three decades ago, and I think that, as the saying goes, "the proof is in the pudding."

Prophetic Words From the Father

The late Roland Buck shared with me a journal entry that he had written concerning a visitation with angels. The particular date in his journal was April 29, 1979. This is what the angel said:

> As Terry Law was concerned about his future and the seeming peril of his work in darkened countries, he asked if I was permitted to inquire of God concerning these things.

Normally questions seem so trivial to ask, but God somehow let me know that it was all right. Here was His answer:

> Terry Law has been chosen and prepared by God for a very special work, that of being in the forefront of his work in penetrating darkened countries with His life-giving light. The Father has interwoven a demanding urgency into all areas of his life. He has placed within him a persistence that refuses denial and a courage that accepts no defeat.
>
> God has opened to him long-closed doors and has accompanied him by His Spirit. He is a chosen messenger. The Father has given him guidance and protection. He has provided for him in ways he has not known by His Spirit by men and by angels of the Lord.

I remember some of my personal conversations with Pastor Buck in which he talked about the different kinds of angels. He talked about ministering angels who live among people. They ride in our cars, live in our homes, and are camped about us all the time. (See Psalm 34:7.) Their orders from God are to take care of us.

He commented that there are more angels on the earth than there are human beings. He talked about worship angels. These are the angels with six wings, and they dwell in the presence of the Lord. (See Isaiah 6:2–3; Revelation 4:8–9.)

He went on to speak about warring angels, whose job it is to defend God's purposes against the attacks of the enemy. Michael is the archangel of all the warring angels (Daniel 10:13).

He spoke finally about God's special forces, which are the messenger angels. Gabriel is the archangel of the messenger angels, and one of his chief purposes is in the unfolding of God's plan and the closing of one chapter of time and the opening of another. (See Daniel 9:20–23; Luke 1:19, 26.)

I was overwhelmed, to say the least, when Pastor Buck told me that God had assigned two bands of angels to travel with my music group Living Sound when we ventured into the darkened countries. He said a band of warrior angels went in before us to prepare the way and to protect us. Then he said when we went into darkened countries, there was a band of messenger angels that ministered with us under the power of the Holy Spirit.

The stories I'm about to share with you in this chapter, I believe, are powerful illustrations of words that were spoken almost twenty-seven years later to the date at the time of this writing. You be the judge and see what you think.

"…I Will Fear No Evil"

I was in Baghdad, Iraq, in the second week of December 2003. My traveling companions and I had just traveled over six hundred miles across the deserts of Jordan and Iraq in order to arrive in Baghdad. At times we were traveling at speeds of up to one hundred miles an hour through the Sunni Triangle, one of the most dangerous areas of Iraq, past the cities of Ramadi and Fallujah. They are famous to this day for their violence. We traveled through the night and arrived early the next morning. We were exhausted and went to our hotel in Baghdad.

About two o'clock in the afternoon, I was sleeping in my bedroom, totally exhausted, when the sound of gunfire awoke me. I jumped from my bed and rushed to the window, wondering if there was a revolution taking place in the city.

I looked down into the courtyard of the hotel, and I saw grown men standing with AK-47 Kalashnikov rifles, firing them into the air, and dancing wildly. Then I saw others across the square doing the same thing. They didn't seem to be angry; they seemed to be happy about something.

I pulled on my clothes and rushed downstairs to the hotel lobby. One of my Arab friends, who is an evangelist in the Middle East, had come with us on the trip into Baghdad, and he was standing in the lobby watching a television screen. The lobby was jammed with people who were talking excitedly in the Arabic language.

He turned and looked at me with wonderment on his face and said, "I think they've just captured Saddam Hussein." I couldn't believe my ears. The war with Iraq had begun on March 19, 2003, and was declared to be over by President Bush on May 1, 2003.

American forces had tried to pinpoint the location of Saddam Hussein. They had tried to destroy him with various bombing attacks, all of which had failed. For months our troops had been looking for him, following hundreds of leads.

I knew that the people of Iraq would never be totally free until Saddam Hussein had been captured, and now here it was. I was in Baghdad when the event occurred.

At three o'clock on the television screen, Paul Bremmer, the American administrator in Iraq, came on national Iraqi television, looked at the cameras, and said, "Ladies and gentlemen, we've got him!" I was shocked to realize that Saddam was found just a few miles from where we were situated. And then followed the pictures of the man who had terrorized the civilized world, captured in a spider hole outside of his hometown of Tikrit.

His head was straggly, his hair disheveled. Medical personnel were looking in his ears with medical instruments, compressing his tongue, and making him say, "Ahhh." The entire world gazed in amazement. It was one of those moments in your life that you never forget. The day was December 13, 2003.

I went to church that Sunday night, and I could see the relief etched on the faces of the people as they worshiped God. One brother told me that it was the greatest day of his life, second only to the day he received Christ as his Savior.

We were in the country to do ministry business and would be heading back to Amman, Jordan, a couple of days later. The airport in Baghdad had been put out of commission because of the war, so it was impossible to fly out of the country. The only transportation available was Suburban Chevrolet vehicles painted white to reflect the desert heat.

I was traveling with my associate, Joel Vesanen, and an Arab friend from Amman named Marwan. We were physically and emotionally exhausted because of the drama and danger in which we had been living.

We met in the hotel lobby at 3:30 in the morning and gathered our luggage. I looked out the door and realized that Baghdad was blanketed in a heavy fog. We left at about 4:30 for our journey across the desert of Iraq. It was dangerous driving through the streets of Baghdad because the fog was so intense.

There's something about the humming noise of tires on the highway that puts me to sleep. I don't know how many millions of miles I have traveled over land in the last forty years. I know I've logged about six million air miles on American Airlines alone.

As we left the outskirts of Baghdad, I fell into a deep sleep. I was sitting in the front seat beside the Arab driver, and I had slumped down in the seat with my knees up against the dashboard of the automobile. I was vaguely aware of the fact that he was driving at a rapid speed. But I was so bone weary that I didn't think a whole lot about it.

Suddenly, we crashed broadside into another vehicle. The noise of squealing tires skidding across the pavement and a loud curse from the Arab driver jolted me from a deep sleep. My first thought was, *This is a terrorist attack!* If there's one spot of danger on the highway between Baghdad and the border of Jordan, it is outside the city of Fallujah, which, for some time now, has been a center for al-Qaeda terrorism.

The pain from my knees being jammed into the dashboard was excruciating. At first I didn't know if I was going to be able to move my legs, but I climbed out of the vehicle into the fog, waiting for terrorists carrying machine guns to appear. I limped back and forth alongside the vehicle, which was a total wreck. I had blood on my left knee, but I was amazed that I could still move my legs.

At that very moment, the peace of God settled over my spirit. I remembered the words of Pastor Buck telling me that God had assigned warrior angels to protect us. I knew my legs were going to be all right, even though I was suffering temporary pain.

The terrorists did not show up; it was a traffic accident. It was about six in the morning, and dawn was breaking. All I remember is the squeal of tires skidding across the pavement, a loud curse from the Arab driver, the jolt from the impact of one vehicle hitting another, and the instant pain in my knees.

Apparently, another vehicle traveling in the opposite direction had run out of gas. It was a four-lane highway divided by a median. The travelers in the other vehicle had pushed their car across the median into our lane of traffic. Not being able to see them in the fog, our driver had no warning at all and hit the front quarter panel of their car broadside at about eighty miles an hour. I was startled when Joel later told me that we were traveling at speeds between eighty and one hundred miles an hour—in the middle of the fog.

While our driver was fighting with the other driver on the highway, we removed our suitcases from the vehicle and stood waiting to hitch a ride with another driver. About fifteen minutes later another driver with an empty vehicle stopped and picked us up, and we were on our way to Amman. We arrived safely, although a bit shaken, but very much thankful for the protection of the Lord's angels.

One of my favorite psalms came to mind, Psalm 91:11, which says, "He shall give His angels charge over you, to keep you in all your ways. In their hands they shall bear you up, lest you dash your foot against a stone" (NKJV).

Dr. Billy Graham, observing the plural in this text, included in his book about angels that each believer must have at least two angels whose assigned duty is to protect him or her. I believe Dr. Graham is accurate in that interpretation.

When I recount this story to people in my travels around the world, I often say in a humorous manner, "I have two angels that follow me. Their job is to look out for me, and I even know their names. One of them is called Goodness, and the other is called Mercy."

David wrote about this in Psalm 23:6, "Surely goodness and mercy shall follow me all the days of my life, and I will dwell in the house of the LORD for ever."

If I have ever sensed the presence of angels in my life, I sensed them that day on the highway outside the city of Fallujah in Iraq.

"…Thy Rod and Staff…Comfort Me"

In April 2005 I was ministering in the city of Irbil located in northern Iraq. We support a church in that region that now numbers somewhere between five hundred and seven hundred people. Every one is a former Muslim who converted to Christianity since the end of the war in 2003.

On that particular visit, we were invited to meet Massoud Barzani, president of the Iraqi Kurdistan region. President Barzani was a warrior chieftain and had spent more than twenty years of his life fighting Saddam from the Kurdistan Mountains in northern Iraq.

The Kurds, a forgotten people, are believed to be the largest homeless people group in the world. They currently number thirty to forty million people and are considered a minority group in Turkey, Iraq, Iran, Armenia, and Syria.

They do not have a flag in the United Nations. They are a non-Arabic people who speak Kurdish, a language related to Persian or Farsi.

My friend, General Georges Sada, whom I will refer to later, organized a meeting for us with President Barzani on this particular trip. (The same day of our appointment Donald Rumsfeld, the American Secretary of Defense, met with him for four hours in the morning.) We spent over an hour in his hideaway under the protection of his militia. I prayed for him on Kurdish national television and was grateful to God for the opportunity of talking to him about the freedom of Christians in his country.

I had a speaking engagement in Columbus, Ohio, the following Sunday, and there was no way to get to Baghdad to get out of the country. There was so much violence in Baghdad that Iraqi authorities had shut down the airport in Irbil. We had run into a major problem. I expressed my problem to the president, and he smiled and said, "[Abu Musab] al-Zarqawi would love to get his hands on you. They know about your presence here in Irbil, and they will be waiting for you on the road to Baghdad."

I was startled by the fact that he had intelligence from inside al-Qaeda. He later offered to send one of his cars to pick me up and to take me north out of Iraq up to the Turkish border. My journey would take me through southern Turkey, up to the city of Diyarbakir.

On Friday morning the bulletproof vehicle arrived at the hotel to carry me north three and a half hours through Iraq to Turkey. The highway out of Irbil quickly narrowed from four lanes to a pothole-strip of road about the width of one and one-half cars with a three-inch drop-off to rocks and gravel on both sides of the highway.

We were forced to stop at least five to six times for roadblocks, and each time I had to show my passport. There was real concern that al-Qaeda had penetrated the roadblock guards and would simply phone ahead to the next roadblock and tell them to capture me.

I did arrive safely, however, at the Turkish border. As I climbed out of the president's car with two big suitcases and a carry bag, I will never forget the sense of loneliness I felt. Here I was, alone, at a border with customs and immigration where not a single person spoke English.

It took four hours to process my way through customs and immigration. I found a taxi driver who spoke about four words of English and made me think that he understood our language. He was a surly, insolent kind of man, but I was encouraged that he spoke a few words of English. He loaded my suitcases in his car, spoke to the border guards, and got me out of Iraq, across the river-bridge, and into Turkey.

Customs checked our car thoroughly. They looked under every seat, in every cubbyhole, and in the trunk of the car for contraband. I was immediately relieved when we finally passed through the Turkish customs and were free to travel northward.

We stopped at the first town in Turkey for a rest stop. I went into a hotel up to the second floor while the driver remained in the car. When I went came down and walked up to the car, I found my driver pulling out drugs from under my passenger seat. He removed cartons of Korean cigarettes and was depositing them in a large, green garbage bag.

When I walked up to the car, he was startled. I think I came down faster than he expected, and I could tell by his eyes that he was angry that I had discovered his illicit drug operation. Some of the bags were filled with white powder. I will never forget the sick feeling in my stomach as he continued taking the contraband out of the various parts of the car.

He disappeared with the bag and came back fifteen minutes later with a fistful of money. As we continued our trip northward, I sensed that my life was in immediate danger. I checked my international cell phone and realized that I was picking up a signal from Syria. I placed a telephone call to my office in Tulsa, Oklahoma, and spoke to our business manager, Ben Dodwell. Of course, my driver could not understand my conversation.

"Ben," I said to him on the telephone, "I'm traveling north in South Turkey with a drug smuggler. I believe my life may be in danger."

I gave him the name of the town on the highway marker and the mile marker along the highway. I encouraged him that if I did not show up at the airport in Diyarbakir within five hours that he was to call Interpol, the European police, or anyone else who might be able to locate where I was.

It would be the easiest thing in the world to kidnap me, to murder me, or to try to extort money for my release. It did occur to me that perhaps the driver was associated with al-Qaeda.

As we traveled north on the highway, I began to pray quietly to myself in the front seat of the automobile. I realized that if he pulled off the highway that I could be in immediate danger.

We were traveling through a barren desert-like terrain. There were mountains with caves in the mountains that I could see. And, sure enough, he slowed down and pulled off the highway. I sat forward on my seat, my body tensed, wondering what kind of action I would take if he pulled out a weapon. But I soon realized he was taking a shortcut on a side road, and we soon pulled back onto the main highway again.

About a half-hour later, he received a telephone call on his cell. He handed the telephone to me and a woman began to speak in broken English. She said, "You go to Diyarbakir?"

I said, "Yes."

She said, "You fly to Diyarbakir, Istanbul?"

I said, "Yes."

She said, "You fly Istanbul America?"

I said, "Yes."

She said, "You buy ticket from me. I get you ticket. You got money?"

I will never forget the feeling in my stomach when she asked that question.

I quickly realized it was a setup. They were trying to find out if I had cash, especially enough to buy a $2,000 ticket back to America.

I said, "No, I don't need a ticket. My ticket has been wired from America."

There was a moment of silence, and then she said, "Let me talk driver."

I passed the cell phone back to the driver. He listened to what she had to say for a few moments, and I could see the anger on his face. I knew I had to do something at that moment, so I prayed, "God, give me wisdom." I was carrying a limited amount of cash in my wallet. I pulled out my wallet where he couldn't see it and extracted three hundred dollars from my wallet. I turned and offered him the money. I had contracted to pay him $120 for the trip to the airport, but I was now offering him over double the amount.

He looked at me and said, "Change?"

I said, "No change." And for the first time, he smiled, put the thumb of his right hand in the air, reached out, and shook my hand. I remember saying to myself, *This may just have saved my life.*

God's Goodness and Mercy Follow Me

I arrived safely at the airport at the scheduled time. I called Ben on my cell phone and told him that everything was all right. Then I walked over to the Turkish airlines to pick up my E-ticket. As I stood at the counter, I saw a young man out of the corner of my eye standing near me. And he said, "How are you doing?" in American English.

I looked at him and I said, "I'm doing well. How are you doing?"

He said, "Not very good."

I said, "Why is that?"

He said, "Back home in Houston, Texas, two young men looking for money to support their drug habit murdered my mother and father last night. I'm going back home to bury them." His eyes filled with tears, and he said, "I'm trying to make up my mind whether I want to live or die." This young Mexican-American was a military security guard from Iraq, and I knew that he had a weapon.

I prayed, *Lord, please tell me what to do.*

I looked at him and I said, "Can I talk to you for a moment?"

We walked over to a small restaurant in the airport terminal and sat down. As I tried to talk him out of committing suicide, I shared with him how I had lost my wife, Jan, in a car accident, and I understood the power of grief. I prayed with him.

About three hours later the plane arrived from Istanbul, and we boarded the airplane. God's grace and divine appointment placed me in the seat next to this young man on the plane that day. I continued to encourage him on the flight to Istanbul.

However, just before the flight took off, a group of Italian tourists came on the airplane just as the doors of the aircraft were closing. They crowded down the aisle of the airplane. I was sitting near the aisle.

The last tourist in the group was a beautiful young lady about thirty-five years of age. As she passed my aisle seat, suddenly she groaned and fell over backwards. I thought she was dead. Her eyes rolled back in her head. There was froth on her mouth, and she expelled her breath as though it were her last breath.

Someone called for a doctor, who rushed forward. They performed CPR and every effort was made to revive her. They got her into a semi-conscious state, picked her up, and sat her on the seat across the aisle from me.

I will never forget my feelings at that moment. I had a woman on one side of me who appeared to be dying. On the other side was a young Mexican-American who was contemplating suicide. I had just spent five hours in the desert with a drug smuggler. I remember whispering to the Lord and saying, "Father, if You have anything more for me in this twenty-four hours, please give it to somebody else."

Our plane arrived safely in Istanbul. I saw this young man off to Houston to his family. I went to my room, perhaps more exhausted than I had ever been in my life up to that point. I had been in my room for a short time when my telephone rang. It was my good friend Don Moen, the creative director for Integrity Hosanna Music. In the earlier years of ministry, Don and I had traveled together in my group Living Sound for about fourteen years.

Don's first words startled me. He said, "Terry, what were you doing eight hours ago?"

I responded, "Don, why do you want to know?"

He said, "Terry, what were you doing eight hours ago?"

I replied, "You wouldn't believe me if I told you. Why is this important?"

He said, "Laura and I were at home with friends, and I had an urgent burden to pray for you come over me. I spoke to Laura and our friends, and I said, 'We've got to pray for Terry Law.'" He continued, "Right there in our kitchen, we began to intercede and to pray for you."

And then he asked again, "What were you doing eight hours ago?"

I said, "Don, I was traveling across the deserts of East Turkey with a drug smuggler, wondering whether I was going to live or die."

When I told him the details, he began to laugh. Then I told him about the young soldier who was suicidal and the woman almost dying, and he laughed harder. Then I began to laugh, but it was a different kind of laugh. There were tears flowing down my cheeks as I laughed.

I remember thinking to myself, *God, when Your children are in danger, You look out for them. You put it on the heart of someone perhaps halfway around the world to pray at the precise moment of danger.*

I checked the timing when Don was urged to pray, and it was precisely at the time when I decided to pay the drug smuggler extra money in order to get me to the airport.

I thought about the story in Acts 12, when Herod placed Peter in prison and the church interceded for him in prayer, and how God sent an angel of the Lord to the prison to get him out of jail. When Peter showed up at the prayer meeting, they couldn't believe that he was really out of prison. They were amazed.

I thought to myself, *Just like with Peter, Don and Laura were praying for me, and the Lord sent His angels to protect me.* Not only did they protect me, but also the Holy Spirit allowed me to minister to someone who was about to take his own life.

When God tells you to pray for somebody, do what He says. Because when you pray, God sends His angels in response to your prayer to take care of His children who are in danger.

Since that moment, I have said to the Lord many times, "When You put a burden on my heart to pray for someone, I will pray. And I believe that my prayer will activate Your ministering angels on behalf of Your children somewhere in this great big world."

Angels: Our Heavenly Bodyguards

In April 2005, I was ministering at a Christian conference in northern Iraq in the city of Irbil. I received a phone call in my hotel room from a nun, who was the Mother Superior of the Sisters of the Sacred Heart in the country of Iraq.

She told me there were many Muslims in Iraq who wanted to convert to Christianity but did not dare because of the Quran and Sharia Law. She explained that both the Quran and Muslim law declares that if any Muslim ever converts to another religion, they're given three opportunities to repent. If they do not do so, they are called infidels, and their family is encouraged to kill them.

She said, "Terry Law, Iraq is in the process of creating a new constitution. Never before has there been an opportunity like this to introduce freedom of religion to our new constitution."

Then she explained that the universal declaration of human rights in Article 18 declares that people have the right to change religions without being persecuted or killed for that change. Only one Muslim country in the world, Afghanistan, has introduced the universal declaration into its constitution.

She asked me a question: "Terry Law, can you help us get this freedom of religion clause in the new constitution?"

I promised her that I would pray about it. When I returned home to my office in Tulsa, Oklahoma, I shared this request with my staff. We put together a petition directed to the prime minister of Iraq during this time, Ibrahim al-Jaafari.

In the petition we requested that the universal declaration of human rights and specifically Article 18 (which includes the changed provision) be included in the new constitution.

I then decided to invite citizens of the West, including America, the United Kingdom, and Canada to go to our Web site and sign up petitioning the government of Iraq to include this article into the constitution.

The response to my request was successful. Thousands of people signed up for the petition.

I have a good friend in Iraq whose name is General Georges Sada. Georges lives in the city of Baghdad, and God has placed him in a very special position. I regard him as a modern-day Daniel. He has a blockbuster book titled *Saddam's Secrets*.

General Sada is a deputy to the national security advisor of Iraq and has known the prime minister for many years. He arranged for me to present the petitions in Baghdad to the prime minister on June 21, 2005.

I flew to London in anticipation of my flight to Baghdad. I was staying at an airport hotel at Heathrow, when I received a phone call from the general, telling me that President Bush had just invited the prime minister of Iraq, Ibrahim al-Jaafari, to come to the White House. Therefore, my appointment with the prime minister would have to be canceled.

I was very disappointed, to say the least. I prayed in my hotel room, asking the Lord what I should do. Two hours later my cell phone rang, and as I looked at my caller ID, I was startled. It was a phone call from the White House. I answered the phone. The special advisor to the president for Iraq and Afghanistan, Meghan O'Sullivan, was on the line.

She said, "Dr. Law, I understand you are involved in Iraq."

I said, "Yes, I am."

She said, "I think we have some issues of mutual concern that we need to discuss. Would you be able to come to the White House?"

Two days later I arrived in Washington DC and went to the White House to see her. She asked me about our involvement in Iraq. I told her about our petition, and I was surprised to have her encourage us in our efforts to have the universal declaration of human rights included in the Iraqi constitution.

She said, "Our government has asked for this, but we cannot force the Iraqis to put something in their constitution. But you as an American citizen have a moral authority, and if you raise your voice, perhaps they will listen. I wish you luck."

I was greatly encouraged and spent the month of July raising thousands more petitions and garnering the signatures of concerned citizens.

In early August, just before the constitution was to be ratified, Joel and I flew to Baghdad to meet the prime minister. Our trip into Baghdad was one of the wildest rides of my life.

General Georges Sada met us at the airport and escorted us to his car accompanied by six Assyrian bodyguards carrying AK-47

(Kalashnikov) assault rifles and Glock pistols on their hip belts.

As I climbed into the passenger seat of Georges' automobile, he opened the glove compartment, pulled out a .38 Smith and Wesson Special, and said, "This will make sure we get into Baghdad."

The ten-mile stretch of highway between the airport and the city of Baghdad is considered one of the most dangerous highways in the world. I remember looking at his gun in disbelief and then sensing something deep in my spirit. I remembered the words of Roland Buck. He said, "Remember, whenever you go into a country of danger, the ministering angels are there taking care of you."

I never said anything to anybody in the car, but I knew in my heart that they would never have to use those weapons. I knew that God would get us into Baghdad safely. The angels would bear us up, lest we dash our foot against a stone.

The general immediately accelerated the car to a speed of one hundred miles an hour and began to move in an S formation from one side of the highway to the other. When I inquired as to why he was doing that, he said, "There's a lot of RPG rocket fire on this highway. We want to make sure we miss any incoming missiles."

Just before we arrived in Baghdad, the bodyguards in the car behind us passed us at a speed in excess of one hundred miles an hour. They had been running interference for us from the rear. Now they were moving to the front.

When we arrived at our first stoplight, the bodyguard's vehicle jumped the curb and moved into the traffic of the oncoming lane. They beeped their horn and flashed their lights, and we followed them at speeds of up to forty miles an hour.

When I inquired of the general as to why we were doing that, he said, "The suicide bombers wait at the red lights, looking for Americans or government officials in order to blow themselves up."

Again, I remember saying in my heart, *They'll never get a chance to do that because God's angels are taking care of us.*

The one overwhelming impression that I have concerning my visit was the fact that Baghdad is the most violent city in the world. At night we would hear machine gun fire. When I called the White House from the roof of General Sada's home, I had a man standing fifteen feet away from me with a machine gun in hand watching for snipers on the rooftops.

And yet I have never felt so safe anywhere in my life. I believe I am safer in the will of God in Baghdad than I am in Main Town, USA, out of the will of God.

I remembered the words of Paul when he was on the ship in the middle of the raging storm in the Mediterranean:

> For there stood by me this night the angel of God, whose I am, and whom I serve, saying, Fear not, Paul; thou must be brought before Caesar: and, lo, God hath given thee all them that sail with thee. Wherefore, sirs, be of good cheer: for I believe God, that it shall be even as it was told me.
>
> —Acts 27:23–25

The next five days are a blur in my memory. We met with most of the major leaders of Iraq: President Jalal Talabani; National Security Advisor Mowaffak al-Rubaie; Minister of Planning Barham Saleh; the Ayatollah of Baghdad, Hussein al-Sadr; and then finally with Prime Minister Ibrahim al-Jaafari.

We presented thousands of our petitions to Prime Minister Jaafari, and I posed a question. "Sir, when Muslims come to America, we allow them freedom of their religion. We let them build mosques and share their message to anyone who wants to listen. Are you willing to guarantee Christians the same right in Iraq?"

I said, "If an Iraqi citizen should decide to change to another religion and is persecuted or killed for changing religions, is that not the most basic abuse of human rights possible?"

Then I said, "Would you include the universal declaration of human rights in your new constitution?"

He avoided my question and began to talk about the American Constitution. Forty-five minutes later, I brought up the same question again. Again, he avoided the issue.

When we walked out of his office one hour and twenty minutes later, I thought that our visit had been futile. However, when the new Iraqi constitution was published in October 2005, Articles 39–41 and 43 grant all Iraqis the freedom of religion:

> Iraqis are free in their commitment to their personal status according to their religions, sects, beliefs, or choices. This shall be regulated by law. *Each individual has freedom of thought, conscience and belief.*

First: The followers of all religions and sects are free in the:

A. Practice of religious rites, including the Husseini ceremonies (Shiite religious ceremonies)

B. Management of the endowments, its affairs and its religious institutions. The law shall regulate this.

Second: *The state guarantees freedom of worship and the protection of the places of worship.*

Article 43:

First: The State shall seek to strengthen the role of civil society institutions, to support, develop and preserve its independence in a way that is consistent with peaceful means to achieve its legitimate goals. This will be organized by law.

Second: *The State shall seek the advancement of the Iraqi clans and tribes and shall attend to their affairs in a manner that is consistent with religion and the law and upholds its noble human values in a way that contributes to the development of society.* The State shall prohibit the tribal traditions that are in contradiction with human rights. [1]

Today twenty-seven million people in Iraq have the right to make their own choices in terms of their religious preference.

There are many other stories that I could recount of God's faithfulness in protecting my life over these last years since the angel spoke to Roland Buck.

As I said earlier in the chapter, the proof is in the pudding. Did the angel of the Lord speak the right words to Roland Buck? I believe that he did. And I can promise you that I will continue to do God's work in the most dangerous areas of our world because I am protected by the ministry of God's guardian angels.

8

Guardian Angels

I saw an angel in white—very luminous—hovering in a corner of the room. He seemed to stand in the air and was actually taller than the room. Suddenly, I felt a peace come over me and a great comfort. I knew the Lord was still watching over me, even though my mother had gone to heaven to be with Him.

—Scot Law

One of the most common questions I hear about angels is this: Do I have a guardian angel? One poll showed that 46 percent of Americans believe they have guardian angels.[1]

The idea of guardian angels comes from two passages in the Bible. One is in Matthew 18:10 where Jesus said the angels of little children always behold the face of the Father in heaven. The other is in Acts 12 when the believers praying for Peter's release thought his angel had arrived unexpectedly at their door—not Peter himself.

Whether or not everyone has a guardian angel and whether or not only Christians have them is a subject on which theologians are divided. Personally, I believe everyone has a guardian angel assigned at birth. Otherwise it would seem capricious for God to pick and choose who has one and who does not. Many unbelievers have reported being rescued from danger by angels; however, this is not specifically spelled out in the Bible.

Early church fathers who generally accepted the concept of guardian angels include Origen, Jerome, John Chrysostom, Basil, Cyril of Alexandria, and Ambrose. Some of them thought that only Christians have guardian angels while others thought that angels are assigned to children and relieved of duty when the children commit "mortal sins."

This doctrine of guardian angels is extended by some to include not only people but also nations, churches, and other groups. Certainly this would mean "an innumerable company" of angels must exist.

Adler noted that if each human being is assigned a personal angel, and if they are drawn from heaven's lowest rank, then the population of heaven or the number of heavenly beings must exceed Earth's population.[2]

Some believe that guardian angels are involved in escorting the righteous dead to their final destination. Marilyn Hickey believes her guardian angel strengthened and encouraged her when her father died.

> It was then a light and warmth came into the room. With fascination I watched as it moved toward me. I felt the touch of the light and warmth as it permeated my own chest. Instantly, my grief disappeared, and I realized that my guardian angel had touched me. I knew then, as never before, that not only had Jesus carried my sins, but He had also carried my griefs and sorrows. I fell asleep again, but this time, it was in peace and with an indescribable joy. Once more that night, I felt the same angelic touch.[3]

The comfort brought by this visitation dispelled her grief and depression. She pointed out that an angel ministered to Elijah when he became depressed over the threats of Jezebel. Apparently angels can minister to our emotional and mental health as well as our physical well-being.

Hickey adds, "Depression is one of Satan's tools to take our eyes off the promises of God and to put them onto the circumstances around us."

While working on the original version of this book I had made a ministry trip with my two sons into my native Canada. One night we camped out with relatives, and as we sat around the campfire, they asked me about angels. I shared some of the stories and facts from my research.

As we left the group, my oldest son, Scot, said, "Dad, can I tell you something?"

He shared an incident that he had never told me about, something that happened in 1982 on the night his mother was killed in an automobile accident. I was preaching in England when Jan was killed. After the accident, Gordon and Stella Calmeyer, friends of ours, took my three children, who weren't with me, into their home until I could get back to the United States.

At that time, the Calmeyers lived near Oral Roberts University, adjacent to the home of Richard and Lindsay Roberts. Scot was eight years old at the time.

He told me of being put to bed about 10:00 p.m. at the Calmeyers, feeling so empty, alone, and terrified. His mother was gone, and his father was preaching somewhere in England. He could not go to sleep, so he lay there crying quietly for hours. He said that at about 2:00 a.m., Lindsay Roberts came over to the Calmeyers' home and into Scot's room. Apparently she had been impressed by the Holy Spirit to check on him.

She sat down by the bed and prayed for Scot to have peace and for the Holy Spirit to comfort him. She also prayed that God would have Scot's guardian angel watch over him, especially now that his mother was gone.

Scot said, "Dad, after she got up and left, I saw an angel in white—very luminous—hovering in a corner of the room. He seemed to stand in the air and was actually taller than the room. Suddenly, I felt a peace come over me and a great comfort. I knew the Lord was still watching over me, even though my mother had gone to heaven to be with Him."

In all the years since then—and Scot is now a grown man—he had never told me or anyone else of that incident. I thank the Lord so much for letting a little boy see his angel and be comforted after he had just lost his mother.

Protected in a Train Wreck

I was cofounder of the Living Sound musical ministry team at Oral Roberts University in 1969, and we launched into a worldwide ministry the following year. Our ministry had been very successful in Eastern Europe where the Lord had given us a specific call to take the gospel behind the Iron Curtain.

In 1974 Yugoslavia was still a nonaligned country but was considered a part of the communist world under the dictatorship of

Tito. At that point we had two ministry teams and had been working in Protestant and Roman Catholic churches in Zagreb, in northern Yugoslavia.

I had to get back to the states to minister at the Full Gospel Business Men's convention in St. Louis, and it was impossible to get a plane out of Zagreb. Therefore, I traveled by train through the high mountains of northern Yugoslavia and southern Austria to Vienna.

I had been fortunate enough to get a sleeper car for the eighteen-hour journey. At about 1:00 a.m., I sensed a presence in my room that awakened me. I had been lying on the edge of the bed about a foot away from the wall in my sleeper car.

Suddenly, I felt I should change my position on the bed and put my back against the wall. About thirty seconds after I did that, we had a head-on collision with another train. After a tremendous, grinding crash, our train came to a halt. There is no question that I would have been thrown into the wall and severely injured if I had not already been lying right up against it.

Immediately, I leaped out of the bunk, pulled on my clothes, and ran out into the corridor to see if there was anything I could do. The man in the next car had his nose smashed and blood was running down his face. People all around me were screaming and wailing. I found out later that six people were killed.

I jumped off the train and began to run through the darkness toward the front where the worst damage was. Rail cars were lying on their sides everywhere. I could hear people talking excitedly, but not understanding the language very well, I could only make out one word, "Sabotage! Sabotage!"

I heard someone in front of me bark a command, but not understanding, I kept moving forward, wanting to help people I could hear crying in the darkness. Several train cars were scattered around the track, mangled horribly, but my car was one of the few left standing on the track.

Suddenly, one of the men from the train spoke to me in English and asked if I understood English. When I answered yes, he said, "Don't move another step." Of course I asked why, and he said, "The guards have their guns trained on you and have ordered you to stop. They suspect sabotage in this wreck."

Again, I sensed the same presence that I had felt in my compartment immediately before the wreck. I sensed that an angel was with me. I quickly got back on the train, where I was ordered back to my sleeper car. We waited seventeen hours before another train came to clear the track.

I arrived in Vienna twenty-four hours later—late but unharmed thanks to the intervention of an angel of God.

A Constant Companion

One of the leaders of the underground church in the former Soviet Union with whom I have worked for many years says that "his" angel always took care of him. He was in constant danger on many occasions because he ran the underground network and was instrumental in smuggling Bibles and overseeing most of our ministry's operations in Russia and other Soviet republics.

He will not talk much about the danger. In fact, he is very humble when it comes to talking about the sacrifices he has made consistently for many years for the sake of the gospel.

His daughter, who attended a university in the United States, told me that for years she lived in fear for his life. However, he had told her not to worry because he was aware of the constant presence of a guardian angel.

He knows that this angel protected him from police roadblocks and many other incursions by the secret police in his life.

Rescued From the Chinese PSB

A man who assisted our ministry in China wrote to us about being stopped by Public Security Bureau (PSB) police as he attempted to pick up a large bag of Christian literature in another city. A few weeks before, five Chinese Christians had been arrested, abused, and beaten for conducting Christian fellowship activities. Our associate was understandably nervous on his next trip.

He was late in leaving for his own city with the literature. No public transportation was still running, so he hired a motorcycle and driver. As they traveled a dark road, floodlights suddenly surrounded them. They were confronted by about twenty PSB officers in uniform with weapons who began to inspect the motorcycle and asked the driver for his license. The driver did not have his license, and there were irregularities with the vehicle registration form. To make matters worse, our ministry associate did not have his passport with him. This was a sure recipe for instant arrest and perhaps worse.

However, just as they were being accused of stealing the motorcycle and before the bag of literature was opened, someone intervened. The officers were hitting and kicking the hired driver when an angel appeared to our associate.

The angel said, "Stand firm and witness the mighty power of God to deliver you through this!"

As the angel spoke, one of the officers walked up to our friend, unaware of the angel. The officer shoved his flashlight under our friend's nose and then began to shout to his companions, "No, no, you cannot do this! This man is my wife's uncle. He is a very respectable man. Besides, my wife would kill me if she learned of this!"

Then he very gently begged our friend's pardon for not immediately recognizing him. He told him to take his bag and go quickly, and our friend did just that!

My friend ended his story by writing:

> As I passed through the cordon of the PSB, the beautiful angel tapped my shoulder, smiled and disappeared. Believe me, the next six or seven kilometers of dark road ahead of me I walked through in sheer joy, singing and praising the Lord. Indeed, He is our only Light amidst all the darkness!

Missionary Protected During Prayer

The late Frank Laubach was a missionary in the Philippine Islands in 1929. One day he walked up to a hilltop on Mindanao, looking for a place to pray. He was unaware that he was being followed by a band of Moro headhunters.

They told him later, rather shamefacedly, that they would have killed him, but he was never alone. A big man walked beside Laubach, and the Moros were strangely afraid of him. Laubach's prayer vigil on that hilltop was extremely important, because there he made the commitment that resulted in his missionary and literacy work with impoverished people—"each one teach one"—that affected almost a million lives.[4]

Oral Roberts Tells
of Assassins Stopped

A similar story of protection was told to me by Oral Roberts when I interviewed him in May 1994 on the subject of this book. He told me that he believes God dispatches angels on the "wings of the prayers" of God's people. He said that during the many years when he traveled with a big tent and held crusade meetings, he was aware of the presence of angels all the time.

"I am always praying, and I'm never without angels. I'm aware of their presence every day of my life," he said.

Roberts told me there have been at least a dozen attempts on his life over the years. He believes angels were constantly protecting him.

One major attempt occurred in Tulsa, Oklahoma, in June 1947, a month after Roberts began his healing ministry. He was holding a tent meeting with about one thousand people in attendance. A man stood on the sidewalk outside the tent at an opening where he could see Roberts, aimed a gun at him, and pulled the trigger.

The bullet flew over Roberts's head and punctured the tent above him. Roberts is convinced that angels deflected the bullet. The wire services picked up the story, and it became national news. When the man was arrested, he said he had no idea why he did it.

"Something came over me, and I felt I had to kill Oral Roberts," he said. (Evil angels can actually influence our thoughts, which I'll describe in more detail in chapter sixteen.)

However, what the devil meant for evil, God turned for good. Because newspapers coast to coast carried the story, the public—religious and nonreligious—knew for the first time that a major healing evangelist was working in America. That particular event launched Roberts's healing ministry.

Roberts also told me, "I think all of us have seen 'angels unawares.'" In other words, angels will appear in the form of human beings so that we don't know we are seeing them. This often occurred in Scripture.

Angel Gives Message to Kenneth Hagin

The late Kenneth Hagin Sr. was a well-known radio Bible teacher and founder of Rhema Bible Training Center in Tulsa, Oklahoma. I have the highest regard for him as a man whose ministry and credibility have been proven over the years. He once told me about an angelic encounter that changed the way he thought about the ministry of angels for today's Christian.

In 1963 he was conducting a meeting in a church in Houston. One night after everyone left, he said Jesus appeared to him as he prayed on the platform. Standing to Jesus' left and about three feet behind him was a very tall angel. Hagin told me that Jesus seemed to be about six feet tall, and the angel was much taller. His head nearly reached the beams of the church ceiling.

When Hagin would look at the angel, he would open his mouth as if he were about to speak, but when Hagin looked back at Jesus, the angel would close his mouth. Hagin's first question to Jesus was, "Who is that fellow?"

He says that Jesus answered very specifically, "He's your angel."

Hagin asked, "What do you mean, he's my angel?"

He said Jesus quoted Matthew 18:10, the foundational verse for most belief in guardian angels. In that verse, Jesus told the disciples that the angels of "these little ones" always behold the face of God.

Hagin said that Jesus added, "You don't lose your angel just because you grow up."

Hagin's next question was, "What does he want?"

Jesus replied, "He has a message for you from almighty God."

Hagin asked why Jesus Himself could not give him the message and pointed out that the Bible also says we are to be led by the Spirit (Rom. 8:14). At that point, Hagin felt that angels did not lead or instruct God's people under the new covenant.

He said Jesus simply smiled and asked him if he remembered the story of Philip in the Bible (Acts 8:26). An angel told Philip where to go to meet the Ethiopian eunuch. He reminded Hagin of the angel's instructions brought to the apostle Paul when his ship was about to wreck (Acts 27:23). He also reminded Hagin that many times in Scripture angels brought directions from God to man.

After Jesus finished speaking, Hagin looked back at the angel, and then the angel spoke to him: "I am sent from the presence of almighty God with instructions for your ministry."

At that time, Hagin's ministry was operating out of a garage. Three Texas businessmen had offered him wonderful office space free of charge if he would move his ministry from Tulsa to Houston. Someone else had offered to duplicate his tapes for nothing.

The angel said to Hagin about the businessmen: "Don't do it. They will end up controlling your ministry, and you must stay in control of your own ministry."

He also told him not to let the man take over the tape duplication, and he called the man by name.

He said: "God has provided the money for your office and for your tape duplication operation. In fact, I already have dispatched the ministering angels to bring in the money for you." And he named a specific amount of money—several thousands of dollars—that Hagin would receive within a specified period of time in order to set up his offices.

Hagin told me the money did come within the time set by the angel with only about fifteen dollars left over.

I have heard several accounts of angels who helped to supply needed finances.

Angel Frees Christian From Prison

Denver Bible teacher Marilyn Hickey tells of a man she knows who was rescued by the same angel in two different countries. (She says she calls the man Louis for her book, though that is not his real name.) The first time Louis encountered an angel was when he was imprisoned in his own country, and his fellow believers were praying earnestly for him.

One night a man dressed as a military police officer came and unlocked the door of Louis' cell. He said, "Follow me." Louis noticed that, as he followed this "man," some unusual things happened. The man never unlocked the doors before him; they just popped open. The man had unlocked his cell, but he did not unlock the doors on the way out of the prison. When they finally got outside, the man said, "Go home"; then he disappeared. Louis realized he had seen an angel of the Lord![5]

Later he left his country to come to America, ministering in small groups all across the nation. One night in Colorado, when he was to be at a place across the mountain to minister the next day, it looked like he would be stopped by a blizzard. Forecasts said all roads were impassable. But Louis knew if he did not get over the mountain that night, he would be missing his assignment from God.

A few minutes after he began the long, cold drive over the mountain, he spotted a hitchhiker and felt the Lord tell him to stop and give him a ride, so he did. As they talked, the man spoke to him about future things. When they passed under a highway light, Louis saw that it was the same "man" who led him out of prison.

When they got across the mountain, the man disappeared out of the car.

God's Ways Work Well

Many more stories have been told and will be told about guardian angels. Believing that there are guardian angels may be extrabiblical, but it is not unbiblical. And the fact that there are so many examples of angelic protection gives this belief added validity.

But, of course, the question always arises about the times when guardian angels don't intervene and tragedy occurs. I wish I could answer that question now, but I believe we'll have to wait and ask God when we get to heaven. Scripture simply does not speak directly to the issue.

There's another ministry of angels that has been getting attention in recent years. Many people believe that God brings healing in response to prayers. Some people are now saying that angels may be involved in some of those healings. In the next chapter, we'll look at the evidence.

9

Angels and Healing

If angels can strike people with sickness as they did in the Old Testament when God's judgment was carried out, then why can't angels assist with healing or removal of diseases?[1]
—Roy Hicks Sr.

There is an aspect of angelic intervention in the affairs of men that receives cautious attention in both the secular and Christian world. That is the involvement of angels in healing.

Obviously, Jesus provided the way for us to receive healing (Isa. 53:5; Matt. 8:17; 1 Pet. 2:24), and the Holy Spirit provides the enabling power through His gifts (1 Cor. 12:4–11; Acts 10:38) and in answer to our faith or to the laying on of hands (Mark 16:17; Heb. 6:2; James 5:14–15).

But do those facts rule out the possibility of angels assisting in healings?

I am including these stories for at least prayerful consideration, as I have had a couple of incidents in my own ministry where angels seemed to be involved in healings.

These events fall into the category of extra-biblical, but they are certainly not unbiblical. We know that angels ministered to and strengthened various people in the Bible, including Jesus Himself. Healing perhaps is just an extension of that ministry.

Angels in the Healing Line

Oral Roberts told me in a personal interview that he particularly felt the presence of angels in the healing line when the anointing of the Holy Spirit was on him and he was praying for the sick.

"I could feel them brush me," he said. "There were times when I wheeled around on the platform to see who was there." He never actually saw the angels, but he began to understand they were present in his healing meetings.

People in the audience would see angels and tell Roberts what they had seen.

Angelic Healing After Serious Accident

Roy Hicks Sr. shares a story told to him by relatives of a man who was involved in a very serious automobile accident.[2]

The attending physician had led family members into the hospital room and told them that there was no hope. When he left, they gathered around the bed and began to pray. Suddenly one of them saw a large angel enter the room and lay both of his hands on their loved one's face. The doctor returned a few minutes later and immediately noticed a change. He said that perhaps, after all, there was some hope.

He left the room, and they continued praying. Again, the angel appeared and repeated his action. When the doctor came in the next time, he marveled at the change in the man's condition.

In the end, the severely wounded man fully recovered, and the family is still thankful and gives praise to God for sending an angel in their time of need.

Two Angels Open Deaf Ears

Two incidents involving angels and healing occurred in my own meetings shortly after the Lord had moved me into a healing ministry.

The first was in Baker, a small town not far from Baton Rouge, Louisiana. I was ministering in a large church pastored by Larry Stockstill, also an ORU graduate. The volume of praise was high at the close of the Sunday morning service, and the presence and blessing of the Lord obviously had come upon the people.

I noticed a lady off to my right jump as if she had been scared by something, but I could not see any reason for her action. At the end of the service, when others were testifying of healings during the praise and worship, I called this lady forward and asked her what had happened.

She began to tell me how she had contracted a disease nine years prior that had fully deteriorated her eardrums. For at least eight years she had been completely deaf, absolutely unable to hear anything.

She then looked up at me with incredible excitement and said, "Did you see them?"

I asked her what she meant, and she said, "Did you see the angels?"

When I told her I had not seen anything except her sudden jump, she said, "Well, there were two huge angels, one standing on either side of me. I felt one of them working on one eardrum and the other one on the other."

She said both ears began to work simultaneously as if someone had pushed an "on" switch. The sudden burst of sound startled her, which is why she jumped.

"My ears are perfect," she said. "I can hear everything you are saying."

I had someone from the audience whom she did not know come up and whisper in both of her ears, one at a time as the other ear was covered. There was no question she had been healed, and there were many people in the audience who testified that she had been totally deaf for a number of years.

Personally, I saw no angels, but I saw the results of their presence, according to the woman's testimony. At any rate the Lord got the glory and honor for the healing.

An Angel Touches an Asthmatic Child

Several months later, I was ministering in Dallas at a fairly large church not long after my wife, Jan, had been killed in an automobile accident. Initially, I had been overwhelmed, but the Lord taught me the power of praise and worship during the trauma of that time.

He had let me know that if I would lead people into His presence with praise and worship, He would heal the sick. This particular Sunday night, about a thousand people were in the audience. My procedure had been to have my associate at the time, Don Moen, lead a congregation into praise and worship at the close of a service; then God would sovereignly begin to heal people. I did not lay hands on anyone but just prayed a healing prayer.

This particular night, during the healing prayer, I saw a small boy about eight years old suddenly jump out of his seat and run down the center aisle toward the back door. He disappeared through the door and was gone for about fifteen minutes. I thought this a little unusual, so I noticed when he returned.

He walked back in breathing heavily. I called him to the front and asked what had happened.

"I was born with asthma, and I have had it so bad that I have never been able to run and play like other kids," he said. "I could not play soccer or football. After taking a few steps, I could not get air into my lungs, and I would fall flat on my face. Then I would think I was going to die because I couldn't get my breath."

He said other kids made fun of him and called him a sissy.

His face then lit up with a smile as he said almost the same thing the woman had said in Louisiana: "Did you see them tonight?"

I said, "What do you mean, did I see them?"

"Did you see the angels?" he said.

When I asked where, he pointed up toward the speakers suspended from the ceiling and said there were "a whole bunch" of angels up there. He continued, "A great big one came down and stood in front of me. He put his hand on my chest, and when he did, my chest started to burn. Then I started to breathe deep, and I knew my asthma was gone. As soon as the angel left, I jumped up and ran down the aisle and out into the parking lot.

"I've been running around the parking lot for the last fifteen minutes," he said, and I could see the perspiration on his forehead. "I can breathe perfectly," he continued. "Listen!" He began to breathe in and out, and his lungs were obviously healed, apparently through the ministry of an angel.

I asked if his parents were present, and his mother came forward weeping for joy. She testified that what her son said about his asthma was correct and that he undoubtedly had been healed.

Other than these two incidents, I am not aware that angels have participated in any other healings in my services. However, we cannot see them very often, so we do not really know what they do in our meetings.

Judging by Scripture

Earlier in this book I wrote about how important it is to judge our experiences. The question is, how do we do that? For Christians, the answer is to look in Scripture to see how God has used angels among His people in the past. While no experience will match Scripture exactly, we can compare experiences we have and stories we hear with the accounts of angelic activity in Scripture.

If you've never looked at the Bible specifically to see how often angels appear, you're going to be very surprised. Many of the most commonly told stories from the Old Testament have angels as principle players. There are dramatic stories of angels in the New Testament as well.

10

Angels in the Bible

*The fact that angels exist is as certain as the fact that God
exists. The Bible reveals the certainty of each. Though angelology is not a cardinal doctrine, its acceptance opens the
mind to a better understanding of the Bible, God's plan of
the ages, the Christian life and ministry, as well as world
conditions and course of affairs.[1]*

—C. Fred Dickason

In biblical accounts an angel cooked meals for a prophet, and
the Israelites ate angels' food.

A donkey saw an angel, and a prophet acted like a donkey—
and almost got killed by an angel.

Angels fought battles for men, and a man wrestled with an
angel all night.

An angel saved one man from sacrificing his son of promise,
and angels were present when that man's true Son of Promise was
to be sacrificed.

An angel was involved in a jail break, and the man who escaped
was mistaken for an angel.

Angels brought prophetic messages about the far future, yet
angels do not know the day or the hour of the Lord's return.

Four categories seem to cover most of the ways angels, mankind, and God interacted in the Bible.

1. Angels ministered to people.

2. Angels brought messages to people from God.

3. Angels helped deliver individuals in danger and nations
   in trouble, sometimes fighting—and winning—battles.

4. Angels administered the judgments of God.

(In chapter thirteen we are going to look at assignments of angels in more detail.)

God can send angels either to show compassion and mercy or to execute wrath and judgment. However, the reason behind all of God's actions is to forward His plans and purposes in the earth.

The best way to know that angels will be dispatched if you should happen to need them is to cry out to God in prayer, to remain humble, and to make sure that you are fulfilling God's purpose for you. Bible teacher Norvel Hayes says the best way to "put angels to work [ministering] for you" is to obey God.[2]

Three sure ways to see an angel of light instead are:

1. To seek angels, not God.

2. To seek beyond what has been told us in the Bible (curiosity and speculation) as Swedenborg did.

3. To seek "another" way than what has been given in Scripture, as Muhammed and Joseph Smith did.

It's important to look at the angelic visits in Scripture to give us a standard to use to judge the angelic visits of today. Angelic visits always had a purpose, and they brought people closer to God and His plan for them.

Angels Who Ministered to People

Abram, patriarch of the Hebrews (whom God later renamed Abraham), had been promised a son of his own for many years. Yet Sarah, Abraham's wife, did not get pregnant.

Sarah decided to help God out by observing a custom of the time, which was to give a wife's maidservant to the husband to bear a child when the wife was unable to conceive.[3] However, when Hagar the maidservant became pregnant, Sarah was not happy. She mistreated Hagar, who ran away, apparently very discouraged. An angel appeared to Hagar at a fountain and told her to return to Sarah and that a nation would be born of the son she was carrying (Gen. 16:9–11). The angel named that son Ishmael, who did go on to have many descendants now known as Arabs.

Ishmael was fifteen when the promised son, Isaac, was born. Once again Sarah persecuted Hagar, who fled into the wilderness, this time with her son. When their water was gone, they lay down under some bushes to die. An angel again appeared to her and showed them a well of water. They remained in the wilderness near Beersheba, living off the land (Gen. 21:14–21). Even though Ishmael was not the son God promised Abraham, God still provided for his needs through the ministry of angels.

When Abraham's son Isaac needed a wife, Abraham sent his servant to find the right girl, saying, "The LORD God of heaven . . . shall send his angel before thee" (Gen. 24:7). The servant received a supernatural sign that identified the girl (Gen. 24:10–67).

An angel actually built a fire and cooked bread for the prophet Elijah, who cried out to God for help as he fled from wicked Queen Jezebel. That food sustained him for forty days and nights (1 Kin. 19:5–8).

When Abraham's descendants came out of Egypt after spending 430 years in exile, an angel led them through the wilderness to the Promised Land (Exod. 14:19; 23:20,23; 32:34; Num. 20:16). In the wilderness, angels' food, or manna (Ps. 78:25), was provided daily for the Israelites and ministered to their nutritional needs (Exod. 16:14–18).

God also said the angel would drive out the pagan tribes from the Promised Land ahead of Israel (Exod. 33:2). However, Israel disobeyed God by making treaties with the pagans and by not pulling down and destroying all of their idols. The angel was then not allowed to help (Judg. 2:1–4).

Angels Who Brought Messages

The first person who entertained angels "unawares" was Abraham (Heb. 13:2). Three strangers came to the door of his tent, and Abraham immediately asked them to sit down and visit for a while. Then he had Sarah and his servants prepared a meal out of their best provisions (Gen. 18:1–8).

Two of these "men" were angels and many believe the third was the Lord Himself. (See Appendix C.) They delivered two important messages.

- Abraham and Sarah would at long last have the promised son, "at the set time" (a year from then).

- Judgment was to fall on the towns in the valley where Abraham's nephew Lot had chosen to live with his family.

Just before the cities were destroyed, two angels led Lot and his two daughters to safety (Gen. 19:15–22).

More than fifteen years later, at the direction of God, an angel brought a message to Abraham while he was preparing to offer up his only son as a sacrifice (Gen. 22:1–19).

Angels brought messages to Isaac's son Jacob three times. The first time, he saw angels climbing up and down a ladder into the heavens. At this place, called Bethel, the Lord confirmed that His promises to Abraham and Isaac would continue through Jacob (Gen. 28:10–15).

Later Jacob saw angels as he returned to his parents' home after twenty years of exile (Gen. 32:1–2), but at that point the visit is not explained. Years later, however, as he was dying, Jacob told his eleventh son Joseph that the "angel which redeemed me from all evil" would bless Joseph's sons (Gen. 48:16). (Was Jacob possibly referring to his guardian angel?)

The night before Jacob was to be reunited with his brother, Esau, after twenty years, an angel wrestled with him all night long. Jacob refused to let him go until he received a blessing. In the morning, the angel touched the hollow of Jacob's thigh, causing him to limp for the rest of his life. An encounter with an angelic messenger from God will change you for a lifetime (Gen. 32:24–32).

More than four hundred years later an angel appeared to Moses as a flame of fire out of a bush. It was God who spoke to Moses out of the bush and called him to lead Israel out of Egypt (Exod. 3:1–4).

A prophet named Balaam got a message from an angel that almost cost him his life. Balaam was on his way to pronounce a curse over the nation of Israel when an angel got in his way. He did not see the angel, but the donkey he was riding did. The animal tried to avoid the angel three times and finally fell down. The Lord "opened" Balaam's eyes, and he saw the problem—an angel with a drawn sword waiting in ambush (Num. 22:1–35). After that, Balaam fell down!

Angels had something to do with giving Israel the law through Moses. This is recorded in the New Testament where Stephen said in his great speech before the high priest that Israel had "received the law by the disposition of angels, and have not kept it" (Acts 7:53). Paul also said the law was "ordained by angels" (Gal. 3:19).

In the days when Israel had judges but not kings, an angel appeared to Gideon, a fearful man who was hiding from Israel's conquerors.

Much to Gideon's surprise, the angel told him, "The LORD is with thee," and he called Gideon "a mighty man of valour" (Judg. 6:12). Gideon informed this visitor that his family was poor, and he was "the least" of his family.

But God was calling things that were not as though they were, as He had with Abraham (Rom. 4:17). God spoke of Gideon's future potential as though it were already reality. We must learn to see ourselves as God sees us and speak of His plans for our future in faith.

Gideon finally believed the angel and led Israel to victory over Midian. He later served as one of fifteen men and women who judged Israel (Judg. 6–8). He became what the angel called him.

An angel also was involved in the life of another judge of Israel: Samson, a man known for his "might." This angel also appeared to be a man when he brought a message to Samson's mother that she was to have a child. However, she knew he was a "man of God" because his face "shone like the countenance of an angel." Later, he appeared to both prospective parents with instructions on how to bring up their baby to fulfill his part in God's plan (Judg. 13:2–14).

Angels delivered messages to Ezekiel, Daniel, Zechariah, and the apostle John concerning God's people and events of the End Times.

In the New Testament, a Christian evangelist named Philip was in the middle of a citywide revival in Samaria when an angel told him to leave and go south. As Philip obeyed, he met an Ethiopian official who had been seeking to understand the gospel (Acts 8). That one man's salvation meant the turning of an entire nation.

An angel appeared to a Gentile army officer named Cornelius and told him to send for Peter, who would give him instructions. This officer prayed to God always and gave much alms to God's people (Acts 10).

In both of these examples, non-Christians had been sincerely seeking the Lord, and He sent an angel to be a part of the answer to their prayers.

An angel brought a message to the apostle Paul just before the catastrophic shipwreck he and other Christians underwent en route to Paul's trial in Rome (Acts 27:23–24). The angel told Paul that if he and all on board followed orders, they would be saved, although the ship and its cargo would be lost. Events unfolded just as the angel had said (Acts 27).

Angels also heralded the births of Jesus and John the Baptist, as we'll see in the next chapter.

Angels Who Delivered People From Danger

During Israel's exile in Babylon, three young men who followed God were thrown into a fiery furnace for refusing to worship the king. To the king's amazement, however, a fourth "person" appeared in the furnace with them. The youths and their "friend" were not touched by the flames, which were so intense that those who threw them in were burned to death. The fourth figure may have been an angel or Jesus Himself (Dan. 3:19–30; see Appendix C).

Another youth taken into exile with the other three became a prophet and a great leader of the people. Daniel experienced angelic intervention in his life several times. The first time was when he was thrown into a den of lions for refusing to worship the king (the same "crime" that got his friends in trouble earlier). This was a different king but the outcome was the same: Daniel was untouched. He told the authorities that God had "sent his angel" and shut the lions' mouths (Dan. 6:22).

In the New Testament, the apostle Peter was delivered from prison by an angel. Peter was asleep when a light appeared and an angel "smote" Peter on the side and told him to get up, put on his cloak, and follow him. The chains immediately fell off his hands. At that time, "many were gathered together praying" in the home of John Mark's mother. Peter followed the angel, and when they reached the iron gate leading into the city, it opened by itself (Acts 12).

For years many people prayed together in the Soviet Union and the Eastern bloc, and then the "iron gate" opened by itself. I wonder how many angels were involved in that?

Angels Who Administered Judgment

Almighty God also dispatches angels to carry out His judgments on nations and people whose "iniquity" is full (Gen. 15:16; 2 Thess. 2:7). God's mercy is forbearing and long-lasting. However, there comes a time when judgment can no longer be withheld, and God remains just.

Pharaoh ran head-on into God's judgment when he refused to let the Israelites go. The final and tenth plague was the angel of death passing over Egypt and killing all of the country's firstborn, both people and animals (Ps. 78:43–51).

One time an angel killed seventy thousand people because King David had counted the number of fighting men in Israel in disobedience to the Lord's command. It could have been worse, but God stopped the angel before Jerusalem was destroyed (2 Sam. 24:1–17).

As we saw in chapter four, sometimes innocent people suffer because those in authority disobeyed God.

Another Old Testament occasion when angels brought destruction—this time on Israel's enemies—during the time of Elisha.

At one point, Elisha and the residents of a town called Dothan were besieged by the Syrian army. Elisha may have had peace in the middle of the siege, but his servant was overcome by fear (2 Kings 6:17).

Elisha reassured him, "They that be with us are more than they that be with them" (2 Kings 6:17). After Elisha prayed, his servant's eyes were opened to see horses and chariots of fire between them and the enemy.

I wonder how many Christians would see angels if their eyes were truly opened? There are more good angels with us than bad angels. At the very most, the Bible tells us, only a third of the angels followed Satan (Rev. 12:4).

The great Sennacherib, king of Assyria, got his comeuppance at the hands of an angel when he defied God by sending letters to other nations, boasting that God could not deliver Judah from his hand (2 Chron. 32:17). But God sent one angel who alone "cut off" (killed) 185,000 soldiers in the Assyrian camp (2 Chron. 32:21).

The other side of the story is that when King Hezekiah of Judah received that threatening letter from the Assyrian king, he "went up unto the house of the LORD, and spread it [the letter] before the LORD." Then he proceeded to really "lay hold" of God (Isa. 37:14–20). He told the Lord what the Assyrians were doing to His people and the land. After that, Hezekiah appealed to God's honor and good name not to let the Assyrian boasts prevail.

Hezekiah did not "pray the problem," nor did he identify the problem as his. The first words out of his mouth acknowledged that God is sovereign Commander and Ruler over all of the earth. According to Marilyn Hickey, Hezekiah "prayed the bigger picture."[4] The angelic intervention came in response to that prayer.

In the New Testament, Herod was smitten with disease by an angel of the Lord because he accepted worship instead of giving glory to God (Acts 12:20–23). He was "eaten of worms" and died.

The last time angels are shown carrying out God's judgments is in the Book of Revelation, where angels are mentioned more often than in any other book of the Bible. There are angels of the seven churches in Asia, angels in heaven, angels controlling the elements, angels standing around the throne, angels blowing trumpets, angels showing visions to John, and angels overcoming the devil and his angels. Last of all, there are the angels who bring the plagues and disasters to earth, and there is the angel who binds Satan and later throws Death and Hades into the lake of fire.

Biblical Patterns

So what standards does Scripture provide for judging angelic appearances? Here are some of the conclusions we can draw.

- Angels can come in answer to sincere prayers from believers and nonbelievers.

- Angels sometimes appear to be human at first, which is why we can be unaware of who they are. They often reveal their true identity before the visit is over.

- Angels bring messages that further God's plans on earth.

- Angelic intervention always has a purpose. Angels don't come to build relationships with humans or just socialize.

- God will withhold angelic assistance because of disobedience.

- Angels carry out God's judgments against wickedness.

In chapter twenty-one I will go into more detail about judging stories and experiences with angels.

In the next chapter, we are going to take a look at what must have been one of the happiest times for angels since the creation of the earth: the birth, ministry, death, resurrection, and ascension of Jesus Christ. Surely they must have wondered at the Son of God becoming a baby in a manger and living on earth with men.

11

Angels and Jesus

The road was like any other road in Palestine. The snapping of grasshoppers in the olive groves was a steady rhythm in the heat....A shepherd boy piped somewhere on the hill, playing a maddening little tune without beginning or end....It was, as I have said, like any other road in Palestine. But one thing marked it out from all other roads in the world. It was the road to Bethlehem.[1]

—H. V. Morton

The road to Bethlehem.
The road to Jerusalem.
The road to Nazareth.
The names of these roads are evocative of something beyond natural reality to almost everyone who has lived during the past two thousand years. As few others in history can do, their very names cause thoughts of events and people larger than our own small worlds to pop instantly into our minds.

The Great Silk Road from Italy into Cathay (China) was once a road whose very name meant romance, adventure, and treasure—but not like these three roads in what once was Palestine. These three roads denote matters beyond romance. They denote life and death, matters of eternal importance, and events that turned the world upside down.

Daily traffic on the roads to those three places that collectively could have been called the "Golden Triangle" of Palestine, the Grand Central Station of the universe, or the crossroads of the spiritual world must have been closely observed by angels, at least from the time of Abraham.

Angels did not necessarily watch because they knew in advance everything that would take place on those roads. They watched because the Lord God Himself assigned "watchers" over the land so important to His plan (Eccles. 5:6; Dan. 4:13, 17, 23).

Hal Lindsey has written that once man was created, he was watched by both angels of God and angels of light.

> Fantastic thought, isn't it? We believe that we can take ourselves to a remote Pacific island or an isolated mountain retreat and get away from everybody and everything. However, we are still being watched by angels. We know this from many passages in the Bible.[2]

The road to Bethlehem is where the main event in God's plan for the redemption of mankind began.

The road to Nazareth is where the ministry of His Son unfolded the reality of that plan.

The road to Jerusalem is where it seemed to have ended—for three days—until the grave broke open and the plan of redemption was completed.

Angels were observing or actually involved in many of the events of those thirty-three years of Jesus' life, a short lifetime that did not end on Earth but extends throughout eternity. The true reality of space with no time is something we cannot understand, but it is the home of multitudes of angels.

The noted nineteenth-century astronomer, Camille Flammarion (1842–1925), upon finally catching a glimpse of the immensity of God's universe, said:

> Then I understood that all the stars which have ever been observed in the sky…do not in the infinite represent more than a…city in a grand total of population. In this city of the limitless empire, our sun and its system represent one house—a single house among millions of habitations. Is our solar system a palace or a hovel in this great city? Probably a hovel. And the earth? The earth is a room in the solar mansion—a small dwelling, miserably small.[3]

Billy Graham pointed out that in Scripture when angels appear as angels, humans react in awe or even fear. He believes the reason is because angels represent the immensity of God and space. We are suddenly aware of how small we are compared to God and how small the earth is in relation to the universe.[4]

Somehow, our small "room in the solar mansion" has been of central importance to the universe. God has a purpose and a plan for mankind, but we are not pawns in a divine demonstration of good triumphing over evil. God created us to have a destiny in Himself.[5]

Jesus, the only begotten Son of God, paved the way for us to live in His presence with the Father and all of the holy angels forever if we simply receive Him in our hearts and confess Him with our mouths (Rom. 10:9–10).

Angels and the Birth of Jesus

Confessing Jesus with their mouths was not just "a choice" to the angels who appeared that night to shepherds watching over the flocks of their masters. Perhaps it was an assignment, but most of all it was a joy, a triumph, a privilege, and a sign that marking time on Earth was over. Time still had millennia to go before it was no more. But the time of waiting for the Redeemer, the Messiah, to be born on Earth as a child ended that night.

That night the focus of all of those angelic watchers was on a specific place: Bethlehem. Luke's Gospel gives the clearest and most lyrical account of the events on that momentous evening (Luke 2:8–14).

Imagine several shepherds huddled around a small campfire in the middle of the fields. They are wearing coats made of camel's hair for warmth, and they are huddled in the lee of a hill to get out of the wind. The Holy Land gets chilly once the sun goes down.

Some of them talk softly while others are curled up in beds they made by piling rushes in the middle of oblongs outlined by stones. It is quiet except for an occasional tinkle of a bell around a lead sheep's neck or someone's cough or the sound of a stick crackling in the fire. It's hard to imagine how quiet the night must have been at that time and in that place—no cars, no planes, no boom boxes blaring the latest hits. When Luke wrote, "And, lo," he was saying, "suddenly, all at once, without any warning signal," an angel "came upon them." It must have been something like a jet breaking the sound barrier right above them.

Perhaps it was at the very moment of Jesus' birth that the skies split open in that quiet field and there was light, sound, and an unbelievable sight! The light was the glory of the Lord, the sound was celestial voices raised as one, and the sight was not just one angel but multitudes—perhaps millions! I believe all heaven was in a tumult of rejoicing and excitement at this fulfillment of God's purpose and plan.

No wonder Luke says the shepherds were "sore afraid." That means scared-out-of-your-wits afraid or perhaps the kind of fear that results from a sudden earthquake. One angel immediately reassured them by saying, "Don't be afraid. I have good news!"

The news brought by angels was the best news mankind could have had. The only news comparable for those born again will be when the sky splits open in a second, and Jesus appears for the final time. Angels will be involved in that as well, and we are told it will be just as sudden—"in the twinkling of an eye" (1 Cor. 15:52).

After the angels returned to heaven, the shepherds left their flocks and made their way into the village to find the baby who had been heralded by angels. Do you think they were so excited that they left the sheep unattended and ran off to Bethlehem? Perhaps they left one of their number to watch the sheep.

The shepherds may have been youths because younger sons usually were assigned the duty of tending the sheep. We do not know how old they were, exactly how they were dressed, or how many there were. But we can be sure of one thing: For the rest of their lives, those shepherds never forgot the angels and the baby. They never had any question about the reality of angels and probably dated everything in their lives as "before we saw the angels" or "after we saw the angels." The Bible says they went back to their sheep glorifying and praising God for the things they had heard and seen (Luke 2:20).

The shepherds then took over from the angels in telling the good news, the message of hope. The Bible says that "they made known abroad the saying...and all they that heard it wondered at those things." In essence, they became the first evangelists (Luke 2:17–18).

Did you ever wonder why it was in God's plan for uneducated men of a lowly profession to see multitudes of the heavenly hosts? Why were shepherds chosen to be the first to hear that the King of kings and Lord of lords had been born?

Was it simply because God wanted the birth of Jesus announced to commoners first and then to kings in order to reach a broad spectrum of humanity?

Was it simply that the angels were so bursting with excitement they had to tell someone to "go and see" this wonderful thing that God had done?

Was it coincidence that Jesus, born of the lineage of David in the town of David, was first worshiped by shepherds? David, His ancestor, began as a shepherd and rose to become a king.

Many questions about angels have no answers in our realm, as with other mysteries of God. What we can understand is what is spelled out for us in Scripture:

Angels were messengers at the birth of Jesus.

Angels ministered to Jesus after a forty-day fast.

Angels ministered to Jesus as He prayed in the garden of Gethsemane the night He was arrested.

Angels were there at the cross and at the grave when the stone was rolled away.

Angels announced His resurrection and later spoke to the disciples after Jesus ascended to heaven to sit at the right hand of the Father and await the time of His return.

A Busy Time for Angels

The years of Jesus' life were a busy time for messenger angels. As the "fullness of time" drew near, the time when all things were in place and ready for the birth of Jesus, an angel was sent with a special message.

He appeared to the young girl whom God had selected as the mother of the promised Messiah. Not just any angel got this assignment, but a most important one—Gabriel. Gabriel appeared not only to Mary but also to Joseph. The man who would act as an earthly father to the Son of God needed to be told that it was all right to marry his fiancée, who was pregnant but not by him.

Even before that, Gabriel appeared to a priest officiating in the holy place. He brought this priest a message similar to that which Abraham received from God. The priest and his wife, both aged, were to have a son. This son was "Elijah," the forerunner of Jesus. Just as an angel had named Abraham's first son Ishmael, the angel named this baby John.

Marilyn Hickey calls such "birth announcements" a part of the ministry of angels.[6] During this particular year, angels were busy bringing lots of birth announcements!

Zacharias was an ordinary priest taking his turn at executing the priest's office, but his family had been priests for generations, as was the custom. It might be understandable if uneducated shepherds had been skeptical of angels, but a priest should have known Gabriel had to be exactly who he said he was. A fallen angel, an "angel of light," would have been unable to manifest in the holy place before the veil.

You would think Zacharias would have been happy to experience a visit from an angel. However, Zacharias apparently walked by sight and not by faith. Unlike Abraham who "considered not" the condition of his and Sarah's flesh but believed God (Rom. 4:19), Zacharias was skeptical. He was not excited, honored, or happy. Instead, Luke writes he was "troubled" and "fear fell on him."

Instead of thanking the angel for this wonderful gift from God, he said, "Whereby shall I know this? for I am an old man, and my wife well stricken in years" (Luke 1:18).

The angel replied, "I am Gabriel, that stand in the presence of God" (Luke 1:19).

The implication was, "You ought to know by seeing me here in this place that I come from the presence of God. How dare you question my word! You are doubting the Lord God Almighty, not me."

Zacharias "provoked" Gabriel, but he was only struck dumb until the baby was born. Remember Balaam? He was the prophet in the Old Testament who almost got himself killed by provoking an angel.

Can you imagine how angels must have walked through the streets of Jerusalem and watched from the heavenlies above Bethlehem, wondering how the people could be so oblivious to the great event about to burst upon them?

Did Mary and Joseph feel the presence of angels as they traveled the dusty road from Nazareth to Bethlehem when she was ready to give birth? I am sure angels hovered around them.

Did they hear the brush of angels' wings over the cave-stable—the only private place they could find? I can imagine angels surrounding the birth scene and the baby in the manger.

Angels must have been near Jesus throughout His life. However, the only other mentions we have of them before the resurrection is after He observed a forty-day fast (Matt. 4:1–11) and when He prayed in the garden of Gethsemane the night of His arrest (Luke 22:43).

The forty-day fast not only was spent without anything to eat, but it also was spent in the wilderness with wild beasts. Next a "beast" wilder than any on earth came and tempted Him. After He resisted Satan—who handled the temptation in person then left Him "for a season"—Jesus must have been totally exhausted and very weak.

Matthew and Mark mention the angels almost as an aside, as if to say, "So, of course, angels came and ministered to Him." (See Matthew 4:11; Mark 1:13.) The word *minister* in both references is the Greek word *diakoneo*, from which we get the word *deacon*. Strong's concordance says it means "to be an attendant" or "to wait on someone."[7]

We are not told this, but the angels may have fed Jesus just as the angel fed Elijah. If the angel did not feed Jesus, he strengthened and encouraged Him in some manner. We are told that He "returned in the power of the Spirit" to Galilee and began to minister so that His fame spread throughout the region (Luke 4:14).

Jesus spoke of angels often during His ministry. He also ran across plenty of Satan's minions, who will be discussed in a later chapter. The authors of *The Foundations of Pentecostal Theology* say:

> Demon-possessed people were brought to Jesus. He dealt with them as those who were possessed by casting out the demons (Matt. 8:16; 9:32–33; Mark 5:2–13).

Jesus most certainly believed that He cast the demons out of those individuals. He pointed out that this fact of His ministry was part of the proof of His divine mission (Matt. 12:26–28).[8]

Angels at His Death and Resurrection

At the close of Jesus' three years of ministry, as time drew near for the awesome, incomprehensible conclusion of God's plan for the redemption of mankind, angels again became active in the natural.

As Jesus took the road to Jerusalem for the last time, can you see in your mind's eye the unseen legions of angels that must have hovered over Him? Perhaps they were strengthening Him for the coming ordeal.

As Jesus neared the city of Jerusalem to eat the Passover meal with His disciples, there was a "spontaneous" outburst of welcome from the throngs gathered from all over the known world for this high feast.

Is it possible that angels orchestrated this outpouring of love and welcome? (The crowd's welcome had been prophesied in Scripture.)

Were the angels shouting for joy again as Jesus was received this way? Or were they quiet, knowing what was ahead? During His arrest, Jesus remarked that, if He so prayed, His Father would give Him more than twelve legions of angels (about 72,000) for a rescue (Matt. 26:53).

As the time drew near for His trial and crucifixion, Jesus' heart was heavy and sorrowful. In Gethsemane, He left the disciples at one place and asked Peter, James, and John to pray at a place farther on. Jesus prayed alone some distance away. Instead of praying, however, Peter, James, and John did what many of us do—they fell asleep. While Jesus was waking the disciples for the second time, soldiers came to arrest Him (Matt. 26:45–46).

By being asleep, the disciples missed the opportunity to pray with Jesus, which probably caused them remorse in times to come, and they missed the visit of an angel. Luke wrote that an angel appeared to Jesus from heaven as He prayed, strengthening Him (Luke 22:43).

On the third day after the crucifixion, women came to Jesus' tomb with spices and ointments. They wondered who they could get to roll away the stone from in front of the grave, which had been carved out of the rock of a small hill. Estimates are that this "tomb-stone" may have weighed as much as four thousand pounds.

When they reached the grave, however, the stone was rolled away, and Jesus' body was gone! The women were quite puzzled and, I am sure, wondered if the high priest or perhaps Pilate had ordered His body taken elsewhere for some wicked reason.

Suddenly, two "men" stood before the frightened women,[9] and again, the first thing the angels said was, "Don't be afraid" (Matt. 28:1–7; Mark 16:2–7; Luke 24:1–8).

The angels asked, "Why seek ye the living among the dead?... Remember how he spake unto you when he was yet in Galilee" (Luke 24:5–6).

At that point, Luke writes, the women "remembered his words." They had forgotten what Jesus had told them would happen.

I wonder if angels can understand how people can forget the words of Jesus, or just not believe them. Angels must shake their heads many times, thinking, *How can people do this? How can they not know that God is real, Jesus is real, and angels are real?*

After His resurrection, Jesus appeared to His disciples and other followers and spent a period of about forty days with them before He ascended into heaven. On His final day with the disciples, Jesus led them out as far as Bethany. Apparently they had no warning this was the last time they would see Him on earth. After He had talked with them a while, He was taken up into the heavens where a cloud hid Him.

At this point, we have the last message delivered by angels during Jesus' time on earth. Two "men" suddenly appeared and asked a question, as if wondering why Jesus' closest followers did not understand what was going on (Acts 1:9–11).

However, they added words of assurance that caused them to hope—words that have brought hope to His disciples throughout the ages.

> Ye men of Galilee, why stand ye gazing up into heaven? this same Jesus, which is taken up from you into heaven, shall so come in like manner as ye have seen him go into heaven.   —Acts 1:11

As Christians, we believe Jesus will be returning for us again in the same way that He left. What will the angels do to announce His Second Coming?

Dick Mills wrote:

> It is my firm conviction that before the second coming of our Lord, there will be as much angel activity as there was during His first coming.[10]

That is all the more reason for us to understand what angels are.

How are they different from human beings?

How are they similar?

How do they fit into God's purposes for the earth?

12

What Are Angels?

Millions of spiritual Creatures walk the Earth unseen, both when we wake, and when we sleep....For God will deigne to visit oft the dwellings of just Men, delighted, and with frequent intercourse thither will send his winged Messengers on errands of supernal Grace.[1]

—John Milton

To some people, the very existence of angels is in question. To them, no proof may be possible, though evidence may abound. Yet if you place confidence in Scripture, it is clear that the angels who appear from beginning to end are not symbols, figures of speech, or mental illusions. They are individual beings created by God, and they share in His plan for mankind or oppose it with Satan as their leader.

Accepting the existence of angels raises many other questions about them.

- Where did angels come from?

- How many are there?

- What is their nature?

- What do they look like?

- How much power and authority do they have over the earth and its inhabitants?

- What is their position in relation to mankind?

- What is their position in relation to Jesus?

The word *angel* simply means "messenger." The Hebrew word is *malakh*, and the Greek is *angelos*. Depending on the context these words can indicate a human messenger (1 Sam. 6:21; Isa. 44:26; Matt. 11:10; Luke 7:24; James 2:25) or the supernatural heavenly beings we call angels (Luke 1:11; Ps. 104:4; Matt. 4:6; Rev. 16:1).[2]

The Origin of Angels

The psalmist understood that God created the angels (Ps. 103:20–21; 148:2).

In the New Testament, the apostle Paul wrote to the church at Colossae in what is now Turkey:

> For by him [Jesus] were all things created, that are in heaven, and that are in earth, visible and invisible, whether they be thrones, or dominions, or principalities, or powers [which are understood as angels]: all things were created by him, and for him.
>
> —Colossians 1:16

One of the errors Paul was writing about to the Colossians was the worship of angels. Some scholars think this was part of a Judaistic Gnosticism, a forerunner of the full-blown Gnostic religion of the third century.

Also, it is obvious from this verse that Jesus is not the first and highest angel, as some New Age and other non-Christian systems teach. Paul wrote that by Him were all things created, and that includes angels.

Paul told them that it was misguided humility to bow down to angels (Col. 2:18). Angels are created beings, not divine.

There are differences of opinion as to exactly when the creation of angels took place in relation to the creation of man. Here are two different ideas.

1. Angels were created before man when God created the heavens and the earth (Gen. 1:1). This involves the "gap theory" or the "ruin-reconstruction" theory, which presents the idea that there is an indefinite time gap between verses 1 and 2 of Genesis 1. This theory, or doctrine, says God created a perfect world some time in the unknown past. When Satan rebelled (Isa. 14), the inhabitants of

that world fell with him. Judgment, or warfare, resulted in the earth becoming chaotic. According to the theory, the plants, animals, and beings of that time whose fossils are found today are genetically unrelated to today's earth or to human beings.

2. Angels were not created before the universe but during the "hexaemeron"—the six epochs or eras of creation represented by six days in Scripture. Only God existed before the creation of the universe (Gen. 2:2–3).[3]

After studying Scripture and the various theological positions on this, it seems to me that angels must have been created before the universe when there was only God Himself. One verse in the Bible literally spells out that angels were already there when God created the earth.

> Where wast thou when I laid the foundations of the earth…when the morning stars sang together, and all the sons of God shouted for joy?
>
> —Job 38:4–7

The phrase "sons of God" is used several times in Scripture to refer to angels. Also, it is obvious that Satan existed before God created Adam and Eve, and that he is an angelic being.

All angels were created holy, because God said that everything He had created was "good" (Gen. 1:21). God could not be all good and directly create anything wicked.

Angels were not only holy in nature (Mark 8:38), but everything and every influence in their surroundings were good. They had great privileges—one of them being direct, personal fellowship with God.

However, God granted angels the ability to make choices, and some angels chose to rebel with Satan.

According to the Bible, those angels who followed Satan cannot be redeemed (Matt. 25:41). Some theologians suggest the rebellious angels may have had a period of probation when they could have repented.

But why would God provide redemption for the sons of Adam but not for angels? Theissen wrote:

Because angels are a company and not a race, they sinned individually, and not in some federal head of the race (like Adam). It may be that because of this, God made no provision of salvation for the fallen angels.[4]

Why Did God Create Angels?

Thomas Aquinas, a medieval scholar who was called the "angelic doctor" because he wrote about angels so much, suggested that angels had to be created in order to "perfect" the universe. In other words, if everything that could exist was not created, then creation would not be perfect, which would be impossible for God.

Another theory is that God is a God of "order," and an unfilled gap would upset the order of the universe. This is called the "great chain of being" theory. This thought, carried to the extreme, led to the idea that God had to be approached through intermediaries.

A third idea is that God created angels to praise Him, show Him honor, and bring Him glory.

The very name for this order of beings—messengers—also seems to imply that they were created for a certain function.

However, it seems to me that all of the theories about why God created angels can be put to rest with one statement: He did it because He wanted to! It really is not necessary—and may not be our business—to understand why He wanted to.

One thing we can observe is that each angel appears to have been a direct creation of God, says Robert Lightner of Dallas Theological Seminary.[5] In contrast, for the beginning of mankind, God created an original pair that could reproduce. Men and angels have different natures because they were created in different ways.

The result of this, according to the late Henry Clarence Theissen, first dean of Wheaton College, is that angels are a company, not a race, and are considered an "order" of creation. That means angels do not procreate—at least, they do not procreate in their natural state. (See Appendix A.) They are called "sons of God" in the sense of having been created by God, but they are never called "sons of angels."[6]

Angels do not die (Luke 20:36), so the number God created has, and will, remain the same.

How Many Angels Are There?

The number of angels that exist was a popular subject for theologians during the Middle Ages in spite of the fact that they never did argue over how many angels could stand on the head of a pin.

Jewish mystics in the Middle Ages came up with 301,655,722 angels, a number arrived at by a complicated formula of assigning numbers to letters, then translating the letters back to numbers and counting them.

Author and publisher John Ronner wrote that no matter how many there are, angels "outnumber us like the Sioux nation did Custer at the Little Big Horn!"[7]

One Scripture verse mentions "ten thousand times ten thousand," which would be a hundred million in that one place (Dan. 7:10). The bottom line of these allusions seems to be that angels are innumerable (Heb. 12:22). Or, as Elisha told his servant, "They that be with us are more than they that be with them" (2 Kings 6:16).

However, Job had the perfect answer to questions about the number of angels: "Who is able to number his hosts of angels?" (Job 25:3, TLB).

If we cannot know how many angels there are, can we know what angels are like? What kind of natures do they have, since each one is a separate creation and not a race with inherited characteristics as is man?

The Nature and Appearance of Angels

It is generally recognized that there are three elements or attributes of personality, all of which are possessed by angels.

1. Angels have intelligence, which is expressed through a desire to look into the salvation of humans (1 Pet. 1:12) and by the ability to communicate intelligently in speech. In fact, they apparently have their own languages (1 Cor. 13:1).

   Writers of all systematic theologies, both Protestant and Catholic, call angels "rational" beings. Angels have wisdom, as well as knowledge that is beyond man's about many matters. Second Samuel 14:20 says, "My lord is wise, according to the wisdom of an angel of God to know all things that are in the earth."

We also can infer that angels render intelligent worship to God from passages throughout Scripture and especially in the Book of Revelation. However, there is nothing in the Bible that would lead us to believe that some angels are more intelligent than others. Apparently, they were not created with all the knowledge they ever would have, but from inferences in Scripture they are growing in knowledge (Eph. 3:9–10; 1 Pet. 1:12).

2. Angels have emotions, which we see by their rejoicing over a sinner who is saved (Luke 15:10) and their exuberant celebration at the birth of Jesus.

3. Angels have wills. They have the ability to choose from various courses of action and to follow through. In the case of Lucifer and the angels who followed him, some angels exercised their wills by rebelling against God.

It seems evident from the examples of angels in the Bible that they definitely have personalities. But what does the Bible say about what angels look like?

In spite of being individually created (which means God could have created them exactly alike), there seem to be differences between certain orders of angelic beings. Messenger angels do not look like cherubim and vice versa.

Roland Buck, my friend who described many personal incidents of angelic visitations, said:

Everyone seems to be interested in knowing something about the physical appearance of angels. No two of them look alike! They are different sizes, have different hairstyles, and completely different appearances.[8]

Angels' bodies are not discussed in the Bible. However, this question has been the subject of much discussion and debate over the years in the church, particularly during the Middle Ages.

Do they have bodies at all? Or are they pure spirit beings?

In stories we have collected, there have been angels with wings and angels without wings, angels who appear as angels and angels who appear as human beings.

It seems likely to me that angels who appear to us as men, not as angels, would look like whatever people to whom they are appearing. In other words, if the angel who appeared to Samson's mother had not looked like an Israelite, would she have called him "a man of God" as if he were an Israelite prophet (Judg. 13:6)?

If angels "appear unawares" (Heb. 13:2), then angels are appearing as Chinese to Chinese and African to Africans, as well as American to Americans. That would mean there are angels appearing as blacks as well as whites—probably as every nationality of the world.

The Bible does not tell us that all angels have wings. This idea of wings comes from a verse in Daniel where it says an angel "was caused to fly swiftly" (Dan. 9:21). However, as angels do not move through space and time as we do, we do not know that they need wings to fly. The fact remains that people who report seeing angels often observe that they have wings.

Other orders of heavenly beings called cherubim, seraphim, and living creatures are described with wings (Ezek. 1:5–11, 1 Kings 6:27). In medieval art, many angels were drawn with wings, but they were based on the Greek goddess Nike, as I've mentioned earlier. Therefore, I believe many angels probably do not have wings.

Both the Roman Catholic Church and Protestants agree that angels do not have material bodies. They are "pure spirits, not composed of matter and form, but composed of essence and existence, of act and potentiality," wrote Aquinas.[9]

In non-Christian religions, the idea of how angels look varies, particularly with specific angelic personalities as they are perceived or imagined by different groups.

We are not usually aware of their presence because angels do not make visible appearances the majority of the time. Hope Price quotes a Suffolk, England, minister as saying:

> Angels tend to be shy creatures. They are messengers and so do not flaunt themselves. If at all possible, they do not appear.[10]

Are they shy? Or are real angels concerned that people might focus on them?

Are angels aware of the human propensity to worship creatures instead of the Creator?

Do they realize that the glory of their appearance can cause such fear that their message is overshadowed?

Billy Graham was asked, "What would I see if I saw an angel?" His answer was:

> God is forever imaginative, colorful, and glorious in what He designs. Some of the descriptions of angels, including the one of Lucifer in Ezekiel 28, indicate that they are exotic to the human eye and mind. Apparently angels have a beauty and variety that surpass anything known to men.[11]

Angels in Scripture appear in masculine form, and the word *angel* is always in the masculine gender. Nowhere in the Bible do we read of a feminine angel. Even when they appeared to people as humans ("angels unawares"), it was always in the form of men, not women.

The Power and Authority of Angels

Angels are greater than mankind in might and power (2 Pet. 2:11). They are not all-powerful as God is, but unusual strength is attributed to them (Ps. 103:20; Matt. 28:2). Certain elements of nature are under angelic control at certain times (Rev. 7:1; 14:18).

Their powers are derived from God and exercised in accordance with the laws of the material and spiritual world:

- They rolled back a stone that could have weighed two tons (Luke 24:2–4).

- They closed the mouths of lions (Dan. 6:22).

- They opened prison doors and loosed chains (Acts 12:7–10).

Dickason commented that even though angels have powers that are different from ours, God limits what they can do. Yet He does permit them some latitude in how they deal with the people to whom they are sent. Apparently, the higher the rank, the more delegated authority they have on which to act.[12]

I believe one example of an angel exercising the authority God gave him is in the meeting between Gabriel and the priest Zacharias. It is unlikely that God had told Gabriel to strike Zacharias dumb for months if Zacharias responded with unbelief. Gabriel had the latitude to handle such things as he saw fit. In the end, when the baby arrived and they named him what the angel had said, Zacharias's speech was restored (Luke 1:20, 64). The result was much glory and honor given to God, which is always the aim of the angels.

Apparently, even the fallen angels have limits beyond which God will not allow them to go, and there are conditions under which they operate. However, I do not believe God assigns them to do evil. This is something we discuss in chapter thirteen.

The Relationship of Jesus, Angels, and Man

Both people and angels are responsible to obey and serve God, and all will be held accountable to Him. We may look at the greater wisdom, knowledge, and power of the angels and think of ourselves as inferior. Yet, angels are curious about us.

- They want to understand redemption (1 Pet. 1:12).

- They observe the affairs of the redeemed (1 Cor. 4:9; 11:10; 1 Tim. 5:21).

- They are to gain a better understanding of God's wisdom as it is displayed through the church (Eph. 3:9–10).

- They know when the lost become "found" by God and rejoice over their salvation (Luke 15:10).

- They apparently stay busy ministering to people in various ways (see the following chapter), yet we do not have to do anything for angels.

In Jesus' future kingdom, there is no mention that angels will rule and reign with Him, yet we will (2 Tim. 2:12; Rev. 5:10; 20:6; 22:5).

Chafer said angels are called "sons of God" in the Old Testament, while men are called "servants of God." This is reversed in the New Testament. He says this may be because in the New Testament, saints are seen in relation to "their final exaltation into the likeness of Christ compared to which estate, the angels are inferior."[13]

It seems the bottom line is that both angels and born-again human beings were designed to be servants of God, but only man is called a "child" of God through a blood covenant. In the Old Testament angels are called "sons of God," but the relationship is quite different from being a child of God through the blood of Jesus (Heb. 9:14–15).

Jesus Compared to Angels

The Book of Hebrews contrasts the relative positions of Jesus and angels very carefully. Angels were held in high regard by the Jews of Jesus' day, which is why the author of Hebrews addressed this question.

Hebrews 1:5–14 demonstrates that Christ is superior to angels in the dignity of His position.

- He is God's only begotten Son.

- He is the Son of David, who inherited and fulfilled God's promise to David.

- He is the reigning Son of man.

- His throne is higher than the angels.

- He is eternal and not a created being. Although angels do not die, they have not always existed, as the Bible tells us Jesus has.

- He is the victorious King and Priest, while angels are "ministering spirits" assigned to render service to those who accept the salvation provided by Jesus.

- He is ruler of the kingdom of God, while angels are not assigned dominion. We see that only the begotten Son of God could overcome Satan and his fallen angels. On the cross, Jesus defeated and judged all the evil angelic forces arrayed against God (John 12:31–33; 16:11; Heb. 2:14).

Because of that, Jesus is declared Lord over all, and every knee in heaven, on earth, and under the earth will bow to Him, and every tongue will confess that He is Lord to the glory of God (Phil. 2:9–11). Angels will join with all of creation in worshiping Jesus.

If all of the knees in heaven will bow to Him, does that mean angels live in heaven? And where is heaven?

If angels are a company and an army, is there an organization to their activities?

Does an angel have a "name, rank, and serial number"?

In the next chapter, we will look at some answers to these questions.

13

What Do Angels Do?

Angelic beings are continually ministering to people in many ways in these present days. Many seeming coincidences are really angels on the job! We haven't fully realized God's use of heavenly hosts to get His job done, because of our limited information concerning angels.[1]

—Roland Buck

Angels appear to mankind on Earth.

Angels minister to the saints on Earth.

Angels protect people on Earth.

Angels deliver God's judgment on nations and people on Earth.

However, angels do not live on Earth. This planet probably is a place they visit, but they would not want to live here! So where do angels live?

The authors of *The Foundations of Pentecostal Theology* wrote:

While angels are often depicted as ministering on God's behalf to saints here on earth, it seems their main abode is in heaven (Matt. 22:30; John 1:51).[2]

While heaven seems like a simple answer, many scholars believe the Bible speaks of three heavens. Gaebelein pointed out that heaven in the Hebrew is plural—"the heavens."[3]

The first heaven would be the atmosphere above the earth.

The second heaven is the stellar realm of stars and planets.

The third heaven is the realm where God lives, beyond the dimension of a telescope.

Within the various levels of heaven, it seems that the angels have a special place in which to dwell. Jude wrote of the angels that "kept not their first estate, but left their own habitation" (Jude 6). I believe these angels may have fallen from the third heaven to the second heaven. Paul warned against angels "from heaven" who would preach a false gospel (Gal. 1:8). These were probably angels from the second heaven.

All angels probably had their original abode in the third heaven, but since the time when some of them fell, opinions vary on where angels live. Perhaps the answer is that there are good angels in both the second and third heavens. However, no evil angels can be in the third heaven because they could not tolerate God's presence. (The exception is Satan, as we see in Job 1:6 and Rev. 12:10.)

The seraphim, the living creatures, and Gabriel are spoken of as being in the presence of God, so we can assume they are in the third heaven (Isa. 6:1–6; Rev. 4:6–11; Luke 1:19).

The "heavenly hosts" or the multitudes of angels who live in the heavens are also spoken of in military terms. As such, they are an extension of the power and providence of Jehovah of hosts. God is pictured as the "sovereign commander of a great heavenly army, who works all His pleasure in heaven and in earth"[4] (1 Sam. 17:45; Ps. 89:6, 8). It seems then that angels live in the heavenlies and "work" there and on the earth.

Admiration, Not Adulation

It is easy to see how the theologians and populace of the Middle Ages became fascinated with the whole idea of angels and their functions. Today we must still be careful not to get carried away with the subtle fascination of the godly supernatural, or we could lose our focus on Jesus.

We should see angels not as having a "mystique" but as being servants, warriors, and messengers of the living God. In fact, the angel who appeared to John said, "I am thy fellowservant, and of thy brethren the prophets, and of them which keep the sayings of this book" (Rev. 22:9).

If we can keep the perspective that angels serve God in the unseen realm and we serve Him in the visible realm, it will help us treat the subject of angels with only the respect due "fellowservants."

Those angels who have remained in their "first estate" are more loyal, obedient, and trustworthy than we can possibly imagine. They deserve our admiration but not our adulation.

Andrew J. Bandstra, a professor at Calvin Theological Seminary, wrote in an article in *Christianity Today* that "one theologian has suggested that when we speak of angels we should do so only 'softly and incidently.' He meant that Christ, not angels, stands at the center of the biblical message."[5]

Timothy Jones, writing in the same issue, commented, "The Bible cares more about what angels say or do than what they are."

In earlier chapters we have seen some of the things angels do, but how do they know what to do?

Who organizes them and makes their assignments?

Does God personally make out a daily agenda for each angel?

Billy Graham wrote that angels cannot be studied without realizing that there are ranks among them. He said evidence shows "they are organized in terms of authority and glory."[6]

Name, Rank, and Serial Number

Angels not only have rank, but they apparently have proper names, too. We are only told the personal names of three: Gabriel and Michael, and Lucifer, who was one of the cherubim. Jewish and medieval Christian writings give the names of many more angels, but these are not in the Bible and may or may not be accurate. We do not know whether every angel has a proper name or not, although it is very probable that each does.

The word *angel* is a transliteration of the Greek word for "messenger" (*angelos*), that being one of the major functions or assignments of angels. Some of the generic terms used for angels often indicate their assignments or functions.[7]

- *Leitourgos* (Greek) and *mishrathim* (Hebrew), sometimes used to mean "angels," are the words for "servant" or "minister."

- *Host* is the Hebrew word *sava*. This encompasses the whole array of God's heavenly army—a military force to fight His battles and accomplish His will.

- *Watchers,* as in Daniel 4:13 and 17, define angels as supervisors and agents employed by God in the affairs of the world. Perhaps this rank of angel is involved in decision-making and carrying out God's decrees in earthly matters.

- *Bene elim,* or "sons of the mighty," is translated "O ye mighty" in Psalm 29:1. It is descriptive of the great power of angels.

- *Bene elohim,* or "sons of God," defines angels as a certain class of being. This term includes Satan.

- *Elohim* by itself is sometimes applied to angels. It pictures angels as a supernatural class of beings higher in strength than natural man. When the angels appeared to Jacob at Bethel, the term used is *elohim* (Gen. 35:7).

- *Stars* is a symbolic term for angels, implying their residence in the heavens (Rev. 12:4).

In Jude 9, Michael's "rank" is mentioned. He is an archangel, which means he has a high rank. We see him as the leader of an army of angels who overcome Satan (Rev. 12:7). Some believe there are three archangels, as I do, but only Michael is specifically called that in Scripture. He is also called "one of the chief princes" in Daniel 10:13, which is evidence there may be other "princes," or archangels. However, Michael is called *the* archangel in Jude 9. His name means "who is like God?"

Gabriel, the angel who "stands in the presence of God" (Luke 1:19), appears to be God's special messenger. Whenever he appears, it is to communicate revelation and interpretation concerning God's kingdom development. His name means "mighty one of God." In Scripture, he appeared in the form of a man, spoke with a man's voice, and had the power of touch as humans do. He has great strength and is the angel described in Daniel as flying swiftly. Nowhere is he called an archangel (which means it may not be "Gabe" who blows the trumpet on that "great gettin' up mornin'!")

The Bible lists eight major levels among angels, both angels of God and fallen angels. These apparently are governmental levels, which again shows organization and rank. They are thrones, dominions, principalities, authorities, powers, world rulers, wicked spirits, and archangels (Rom. 8:38; 1 Cor. 15:24; Eph. 1:21; 3:10; 6:12; Col. 1:16; 2:10, 15).

What we can see from these brief mentions is that, yes, angels do have names and ranks; identification is as definite in the heavenly army as dog tags with serial numbers are in the United States military. These ranks obviously are not the three "choirs" developed in the Middle Ages, but there are definitely levels of authority. God is the originator of order and organization and not of confusion (1 Cor. 14:33).

Cherubim, Seraphim, and Living Creatures

The Bible also gives us names of special classes of beings. They have certain characteristics, duties, and what we might call "serial numbers" that separate them from "ordinary" angels. Some people view these beings as separate classes from angels—not as other types of angels.

At any rate, the apparent highest-ranking class is mentioned eighty-five times in the Bible and never called "angel." These are the *cherubim*, who definitely have wings. Dickason wrote:

> As is the case with many heavenly realities, their character and appearance is so far beyond human imagination and present comprehension that they must be described in earthly terms obviously designed to convey something surpassingly supernatural. (Ezek. 1:5,14; 28:12–14).[8]

Cherubim guarded the Garden of Eden with flaming swords after Adam and Eve were evicted, teaching us that sin and paradise are incompatible (Gen. 3:24).[9]

Cherubim were the golden symbols God directed Moses to put on the lid of the ark of the covenant. In this case, each had a face and two wings that covered the ark. They were designed to look down on the ark rather than across at each other (Exod. 37:9).

Seraphim also have wings; in fact, they each have six of them. Two cover their faces, two cover their feet, and they fly with the other two (Isa. 6:2). They are seen in connection with the glory of God, along with the cherubim.

Their "name" or designation means "the burning ones." In Isaiah 6, they were seen hovering above and on both sides of Jehovah on His throne.

Ezekiel describes the *living creatures* who each have four faces and four wings with hands under the wings, and the noise of their coming is "like the roar of rushing waters, like the voice of the Almighty, like the tumult of an army." (See Ezekiel 1:24, NIV.)

The living creatures mentioned in Ezekiel and Revelation may actually be cherubim because they fit the description in Ezekiel. Or they could actually be seraphim. It is not possible to ascertain this with certainty.

Assignments Among Cherubim, Seraphim, and Living Creatures

Cherubim appear to be the highest ranking of the heavenly beings. One reason cherubim are never called angels may be because they are never messengers. They are never used in Scripture to carry revelation or instruction from God to men. They are used to protect God's glory and proclaim His grace.

Likewise, seraphim are never messengers. Their function seems to be showing forth the holiness and transcendence of God. When the prophet Isaiah confessed his sinfulness and uncleanness, a seraphim flew with a live coal to touch Isaiah's lips and purge his sin (Isa. 6:6–7). This is a priestly type of service for God whose holy standards demand that believers be cleansed before serving Him.

The purpose of the living creatures—whatever they are—seems to be to worship God directly, to witness the worship of God by redeemed men, and, in Revelation, to direct the judgments of God.

Job Assignments of Angels

Chafer wrote that the chief assignment of angels is not so much to carry messages and deal with God's people as it is to praise and worship Him.[10] This is the "first and most obvious work of angels," says

James Montgomery Boice, pastor of Tenth Presbyterian Church in Philadelphia.[11]

Michael, the only one specifically called "archangel" in the Bible, apparently has an assignment as a military leader. This probably makes him head of the warrior angels.

Michael stands up for God's people and opposes God's enemies but always under the authority of God. When the devil challenged him over Moses' body (Jude 9), he did not handle matters on his own. He said, "The Lord rebuke thee."

Gabriel, who most people believe is an archangel although he is never called that in the Bible, is God's leading or highest-ranking messenger.

Other angels are also identified by the service they carry out. These are:

- Angels of judgment (Gen. 19:13; 2 Sam. 24:16; 2 Kings 19:35; Ezek. 9:1; Ps. 78:49).

- Angels designated as "watchers" (Dan. 4:13, 23).

- Angel of the abyss (Rev. 9:11).

- Angel over fire (Rev. 14:18).

- Angel of the waters (Rev. 16:5).

Angels in general—apparently the lowest ranking in the heavenly hierarchy—are messengers. As we saw from biblical examples:

- They deliver messages *and* deliver people from danger when God ordains it.

- They protect and defend God's people, even helping to fight battles when it is within His will.

- They minister to God's people in various ways.

Will angels still minister to the saints after the resurrection?

Lester Sumrall wrote in his Indiana Christian University course on angels:

Angels are not short-term missionaries in God's eternal program. The time will never come when He will turn to them and say,

"Sorry, I have no further use for you." Angels will certainly continue their work of praising and worshipping God throughout eternity. They will always be standing by to serve God in any way He desires.[12]

Angels in John's Revelation

In the Book of Revelation there are angels of the seven churches, angels who stand before God, angels who blow seven trumpets, and angels who administrate the last seven plagues (Rev. 8:2).

Some people believe the twenty-four elders in Revelation 4 and 5 are angelic beings who attend God along with the cherubim, seraphim, and the living creatures. Other scholars believe these twenty-four elders may actually be the twelve patriarchs of Israel and the twelve apostles. There is not enough evidence to prove either view.

There are angels with the key to the abyss and with a great chain to bind Satan for a thousand years (Rev. 20:1–3).

Last, but not least, are the angels in charge of death and hell (Rev. 6:8; 20:14). In chapter eighteen I will describe why I think that there is actually an angel named Death and an angel named Hell.

There is another angel in the Old Testament called the angel of Jehovah, who some think was Jesus Himself appearing on Earth from time to time.[13] (See Appendix C.)

Angels minister to believers by revealing, guiding, providing, protecting, delivering, strengthening, encouraging, assisting in answering prayer, and attending the righteous dead. In Luke 16, Jesus told a story in which a beggar named Lazarus died and was carried by angels to "Abraham's bosom" (v. 22). Many people on their deathbeds have spoken aloud of angels appearing to escort them home to heaven, and some of these angels have been seen by friends and loved ones.

Other people have testified to receiving angelic protection. Boice wrote that, from a practical standpoint, becoming more aware of such protection would cause us to be less fearful of circumstances and enemies. Being convinced of angelic protection would loosen the fears haunting many of God's people. Reformer John Calvin thought that God cares for us through angels, not because He needs them, but because we do!

What Angels Cannot Do

We think of angels as mighty and powerful and without limits. However, there are certain things they cannot do.

1. Angels cannot call God "Father," only "Creator."

2. Angels cannot preach the gospel in the same way as those who have been saved by the gospel can. Marilyn Hickey wrote:

   Have you noticed that in the Bible, humans always preach the gospel to other humans? Although there are perhaps millions of elect angels and although God could send angels to share the gospel with people all over the earth, the Lord has seen fit to entrust the Great Commission to humans, not angels.[14]

3. Angels cannot be redeemed or conformed to the image of Christ.

4. Angels in God's service cannot indwell men. Only the Holy Spirit can. Billy Graham wrote:

   The Holy Spirit seals them [men] and indwells them when He has regenerated them. The Holy Spirit is all-knowing, all-present, and all-powerful. Angels are mightier than men, but they are not gods, and they do not possess the attributes of the Godhead.... So far as I know, no scripture says that the Holy Spirit ever manifested Himself in human form to man.... We know the Holy Spirit as spirit, not flesh. But we can know angels not as spirits alone, but sometimes also in visible form.[15]

5. Angels of God do not act on their own power or out of their own wills.

6. Angels can appear as men, but they never "become" human beings; and human beings never "become" angels. Angels are not glorified human beings. In Hebrews 12:22–23, angels are distinguished from the "spirits of righteous men made perfect."

7. Angels do not judge men, but righteous men will judge angels (1 Cor. 6:3).

8. Angels cannot be everywhere at the same time. Only God is omnipresent.

9. Angels of God do not command or receive worship; only "angels of light" do that as a perversion of their first estate. The late Roland Buck said:

> Angels are never to be worshipped. They are so ordained and created that there is no place in their entire being for praise or honor. They are called "the hosts of the Lord," and their purpose is to serve the eternal God.[16]

Buck said that his angelic visitors told him they had a list of seven priorities about what they are to communicate to us from God. They are: (1) the blood of Jesus; (2) fellowship and communion with God; (3) "Jesus is alive!"; (4) the promise of the Holy Spirit; (5) "Go tell the world"; (6) "The atonement of Jesus is everlasting"; and (7) "Jesus will return."[17]

Angels are creations of God, and under the discretion of the Holy Spirit they help us carry out our assignments as believers.

However, not all angels are on God's side, nor do all angels have good intentions toward mankind. There is another realm of angels to be considered before we can get a complete picture of these beings. This realm is the dark kingdom of Satan.

14

The Rise and Fall of Lucifer

One of Satan's greatest assets in opposing the work of the Lord is his deceptiveness. Down through the centuries he has posed in roles that have caused men to think of him in any way other than his true character, thus making it easier for him to lead them from God.[1]
—The Foundations of Pentecostal Theology

Do you believe in the existence of Satan? Fallen angels? Demons? A *Time* poll showed that 49 percent of Americans believe that evil angels exist.[2] So the other half believes either that there are no supernatural beings or that supernatural beings are only good. Some Christians believe that bad angels exist but that only good angels can impact their lives.

Unfortunately, belief does not make anything true or false. All belief does is influence the way you deal with a truth or a falsehood. Sincerity is no substitute for truth. To the question, Does Satan exist?, the Bible answers affirmatively.

Seven books of the Old Testament and every writer in the New Testament refer to Satan. Of the twenty-nine specific references in the New Testament, Jesus is speaking in twenty-five of them. To reject something as false that Jesus Himself accepted as true, including angels, is to deny the authority of the Bible and to impugn the person of the Lord Jesus Christ.[3]

The reason why Christians today tend to discount Satan is because of the delusion caused by the stereotypical images of him developed since the Middle Ages. Greek mythology has strongly influenced the image Christians have of the devil and angels. According to Boice, the church in the Middle Ages developed a symbolic image of Satan to convey biblical truths to a mostly illiterate population.[4]

The result was a translation of the pagan satyr—a half-human, half-beast figure—into the Christian devil. Instead of becoming a symbol, however, that caricature became our image of Satan—a figure in a red suit with horns, a tail, cloven hooves, and carrying a pitchfork.

In the twentieth century, the devil has been transformed into the sophisticated Mephistopheles of the eighteenth-century German play *Faust*. This image became the modern stereotype. In this persona, the devil usually is very good-looking, has dark hair, a suave manner, and a debonair mustache. Neither stereotype fits the biblical picture of Satan, and both are easy for people to discount as unbelievable.

The authors of *The Foundations of Pentecostal Theology* wrote that this tendency to speak of the devil as a figure of speech, a metaphorical personification of evil, or a delusion of unsound minds only occurs in Christian lands.[5] People in non-Christian lands have no problem believing in wicked supernatural beings.

It is important to understand the reality of Satan and just who he is: the father of lies and essence of evil. He is the first and chief sinner.

Chafer wrote, "The fall of this mighty angel was not a compromise between good and evil. He *became* the embodiment of evil and wholly void of good." What's more, we should not elevate him to an evil equivalent of God.[6] The Bible shows that Satan is very limited, and he is never given a position equal to God.

God knows all things, but Satan does not. Nor does Satan know the future. His one advantage over man is having observed human nature for millennia. Therefore, as long as man acts out of the flesh—the Adamic fallen nature—Satan can predict and influence what we do. The way to keep the devil from knowing our business is always to follow the leading of the Holy Spirit. The redeemed nature of man is something Satan has never been able to understand.

Satan cannot be in more than one place at one time as God can. He has to delegate assignments to his followers.

Satan's power is limited to what he was given when he was created. It is nothing compared to God's. Much of Satan's "power" always has consisted in influencing people to do his evil works. However, he has absolute sovereignty over fallen angels and demons.

The Problem of the Origin of Evil

There is a classic problem with the origin of evil: God is wholly good and cannot have created anything that is not good. This leads to the questions most of us have asked at one time or another.

How could a perfect, holy being fall?

How could the first unholy affection arise in an angelic being?

Where would the will get its first impulse to turn from God?

Theissen wrote, "It is helpful to remember that the creature originally had what the Latin theologians called 'ability *posse peccare, et posse nonpeccare*,' that is (the ability) 'to sin and not to sin.'"[7]

We call that ability freedom of choice, or the ability to choose. We are not told when this "fall" occurred. However, it had to have been before the Fall of man because Satan already was a deceptive, wicked being in the Garden of Eden. (See Ezekiel 28:11–19; Isaiah 14:4–17.)

Augustine dealt with the problem of the existence of evil in his fifth-century book, *The City of God*. His conclusion was that good may exist on its own, but evil cannot. Therefore, evil is simply a perversion of something that was originally good.[8]

That is why Satan has never created anything. He perverts, distorts, copies, and destroys. Evil cannot stand alone but must have good as a beginning foundation. Therefore, Augustine reasoned, evil is a choice, not an original part of the nature of creation.

Another "question of the ages" accompanies any discussion about evil: Why does God allow it? All evil must exist only by divine permission. Therefore, evil is under divine limitations—or the human race would have been destroyed in Noah's day when the "end of all flesh" came before God (Gen. 6:12–13). The flood only cleansed the earth of those whose natures had been corrupted by their choices. Evil had destroyed the earth, except for Noah and his family.

I have found Chafer's explanation of why evil exists to be the best:

> It becomes clear that Satan's determination—which constituted his initial sin—to build a vast structure of independent relationships around himself as the center and wholly autonomous with respect to the Creator...was permitted of God to be tested experimentally to its bitter end...

God could have hindered him, but He rather allowed Satan to take the course he desired to follow, and to allow that course to become, in the end, the ground of its own universal condemnation.

When Satan and his theory come up for final judgment and execution, "every mouth will be stopped" (Rom. 3:19) and all will be guilty...in the light of the colossal failure of the whole enterprise. *The lie will be conceded to be a lie.*[9]

Apparently God, out of respect for man's free will, feels it is important to demonstrate for all eternity that any way but His way does not work. In the end, the presence of evil will never again affect the universe: no more sickness, poverty, sin, warfare, or death. The father of evil will have become a sneer and a byword to all creation (Isa. 14:16–17).

In the meantime, we must live in a world affected by Satan, so we need to be able to answer these questions: What kind of character or nature does Satan have? What is his personality?

The Names of Satan

The more than forty names by which he is called in Scripture give us glimpses into Satan's character and personality.[10] However, the "root" of his identity is pride, self-will, and rebellion intertwined. Together these characteristics spell "independence" from God, or a spirit of lawlessness.

Names that concern aspects of his position are:

- Anointed Cherub Who Covers and Lucifer, "son of the morning" (past)

- Prince of Demons (present)

  Names that concern his character are:

- Devil, which signifies slanderer, or "one who trips up," used thirty-five times

  - Old serpent, meaning "subtle or crafty"

  - Great dragon—a terrifying and destructive beast

- The evil one—in Greek this name means "one not satisfied to be corrupt in himself, but who seeks to corrupt others."

- Abaddon, which means "destroyer"

- Murderer and liar, the father of lies, and the father of unbelievers, by inference (John 8:44)

- Beelzebub, which originally meant "lord of the flies" but later was changed by the Jews to "lord of the dunghill," where flies like to congregate (Matt. 10:25)

- Wicked, evil, or lawless one

- One who comes "as" a roaring lion—in other words, one who attempts to paralyze you with fear by his roar so he can overtake and devour you.

  Names that convey a sense of his activities include:

- Satan, the opposer of God's program, God's will, and God's people, which is used some fifty-six times, accentuating his activities as the chief adversary

- Tempter, accuser, deceiver, spirit that works in the sons of disobedience

- Angel of light, the greatest deceptive role Satan plays

Other names referring to him show his present dominion.

- Ruler of this world, meaning his power over the world order or the world's systems (John 12:31; 14:30; 16:11). The Greek word *archon*, translated "ruler," literally means "a political ruler."

- Prince of the power of the air, suggesting his rulership over the fallen angels. Ephesians 6:12 shows that there is a highly organized army behind the world's systems.

- God of this age. "Age" is the Greek word *aion*, which often means the prevailing thought of a certain era. So the implication of this name is "god of culture."

How did Satan acquire these titles?

In *The Triumphant Church*, Hagin wrote that if people could understand Satan is the "god of this world," it would clear up a lot of confusion about why evil exists! Hagin said evil has become so prevalent that some people think the universe is fundamentally evil and that God created evil. Hagin and others believe that the following steps occurred to make Satan "god of the cosmos" for a limited time.[11]

1. God gave mankind, through Adam, "dominion" over the earth as recorded in Genesis 1:26 and 28. The Bible does not say that God gave mankind the earth, only the rule over it (Ps. 8:4–6). The earth and its fullness belong to God (Ps. 24:1; 50:12). Chafer pointed out that though creation itself was affected by the Fall, it still remained under God's ownership.[12]

2. At the Fall, Adam's dominion was forfeited to Satan (Rom. 5:14). We know Satan did not have authority over the earth before Adam "gave" it to him, because in Ezekiel 28:16–18 and Luke 10:18 we are told that Satan lost his authority when he rebelled against God.

Even after Jesus defeated Satan on the cross, Satan was still called the "god of this world" (2 Cor. 4:4). Satan retains the authority he usurped from man until God establishes His kingdom on the earth.

If Satan were not the god of this world's systems, his offer to give Jesus the kingdoms of the world would have been no temptation (Luke 4:5–7).

Jesus, as all man and all God, now owns the earth and is the real King of kings and Lord of lords (Rev. 17:14). However, He will not take over completely until Adam's lease runs out. Then Satan's dominion will end.

Until the ultimate restoration of all things, we must live amid Satan's world systems. How long will that be? We do not know exactly.

We do know, however, that God has already predetermined a limit. Perhaps Derek Prince explained best this idea of Satan's time of rule:

> Time is directly and inseparably related to our present world order. With this world order, time came into being, and with this world order, time will once again cease to be.[13]

There was a beginning to evil, and there will be an end to evil. The "reality" we know as time is a temporary lease that will run out, releasing the earth from bondage to darkness.

The *Cosmos Diabolicus*: All of the World's Systems

In order to understand the difference between the earth itself and dominion over it, we need to understand the meaning of the Greek word *kosmos*. Transliterated, *kosmos* means "order, arrangement, adornment, or ornament."[14] It is used 187 times in the New Testament, with Jesus using it more than anyone else.

Cosmos literally refers to the economic, political, cultural, educational, social, and even "religious" systems that operate in the world. It is the orders or systems man has developed that conform to the ideals, aims, and methods of Satan. This would include all of them, not just the ones that are overtly evil such as Nazism. As Chafer says, "It is civilization now functioning apart from God."[15]

I agree with Hal Lindsey that not every government is totally evil or immoral. However, every government—even Israel under the kings of the Old Testament—is a mixture of God's ways and the world's ways. The world's ways usually are Satan's ways. Lindsey wrote:

> Satan is not the man below, heaping coals into an eternal furnace. He is the original "jet-setter"; he is "right on" with the latest cause....What a picture! Satan "trucking" all over the earth, constantly "doing his thing" in every spot he can! He's working in our world's systems through governments, education, business, and culture. You name it, he'll tame it!
>
> Extremes of criminal behavior are not the only ways in which Satan works. His control of the atmosphere of thought in the world

system is more deadly than the cold steel of a gun in your back. His modus operandi has been so successful that even Christians are constantly being lured from the divine viewpoint of life into Satan's web of deceit.[16]

Both the way to keep from being caught up in this *cosmos diabolicus* and the way to be able to live in the world but separate from it (2 Cor. 6:17) begin in our minds.

Every action, philosophy, or system began with thoughts, which are under the authority of Satan (more on this in chapter sixteen).

Even after salvation, our minds are not instantly transformed to the thoughts of Jesus (Rom. 8:29, 12:2). Nearly everything that we think about or believe in this world must be overhauled in the light of the Bible.

The Foundational Lie of the Satanic Cosmos

One specific lie is the foundation for all other falsehoods and antichrist ideas and practices, and the devil is the father of it. *The lie* is the denial of God as God and the deifying of the created being.

This is the essence of Satan's character, and its cause is found in Isaiah 14:12–17, summed up in two words: "I will," with the emphasis on "I." Actually there were five "I wills" in Satan's original declaration of independence, summed up in the last one: "I will be like the Most High." Everything Satan does or tries to do is an attempt to turn the lie into reality.

C. Peter Wagner, professor of church growth at Fuller Theological Seminary, wrote of this lie as being the thing that seems to upset God the most: serving the creature rather than the Creator (Rom. 1:25). He wrote that God especially hates it when human beings use visible creation to glorify Satan and other evil demonic beings.[17]

In the Garden of Eden, Satan began to brainwash mankind into accepting his lie as truth and God's truth as error. I believe the most recent form of this subtle perversion is so-called political correctness. Political correctness calls for tolerance of other cultures, which seems good. But Wagner has pointed out that Christianity by nature is "intolerant." Christians believe that only through Jesus can we regain a relationship with God; therefore, "Christianity is anything but politically correct."[18]

God loves the people who live under the world's systems, but He hates the systems. The vast world order always has been based on the devil's character, and it fulfills his purposes.

"But I see good in some of these systems!" some say.

"What about democracy?"

"What about good social programs?"

"What about the part where environmentalists are right?"

Next to *the lie* itself, Chafer wrote:

> The greatest delusion Satan imposes...is the supposition that only such things as society considers evil could originate with the devil....Satan has always adapted his methods to the times and conditions. If attention has been gained, a complete denial of the truth has been made, or, when some recognition of the truth is demanded, it has been granted on the condition that that which is vital in redemption should be omitted. This partial recognition of the truth (part-truthism) is required by the world today.[19]

In light of all of this, where does Satan operate now?

Satan's Present Position and Power

Satan and his leaders, the fallen angels, dwell in the second heaven. However, Satan still had access to the third heaven in Job's day, and by inference, he still does in ours (Rev. 12:10–11). At least at one point he had a throne on earth at Pergamos (Rev. 2:13). So we see two things:

- Satan is permitted access to heaven (Job 1:6).

- Satan's main sphere of operation is the earth (Job 1:7).

One doctrine that has become quite popular is that Satan already is in the lower regions, if not in hell itself. Nothing in the Bible, however, supports this. All of the references to the lake of fire are future tense. (References are only in the New Testament.)

There is to be a time when Satan is first bound in the abyss (Rev.

20:2–3) and then, a thousand years later, finally cast into the lake of fire forever. That is the final "prison" of wickedness, but he has not been sent there yet (Rev. 20:10).

As "political ruler" of the earth and through his fallen angels, Satan influences governments to make laws and allow things that oppose God. He influences man to develop religions that range from worshiping him in disguise to putting something—a person, establishment, or doctrine—between mankind and God. In other words, he sets up substitutes for God.

Throughout history, the church was a check on Satan's activities, according to the degree in which the church operated in God's truth. The more truth the church had, the more it could check Satan's activity. Today, the church as a whole appears to have little influence.

Education is one place where Satan has moved in to fill the vacuum. References to and even belief in God have been eliminated in schools. History has been rewritten to take out Christian references, and ungodly philosophies have been substituted for truth.

In cultural affairs, Satan has been more subtle and progressive. Culture includes religion, the arts—music, drama, literature, visual arts—and social habits and trends. We can see films and television as being part of the *cosmos diabolicus,* but do we realize what has happened to our music as well?

Satan was created as the ultimate musician. When he fell, his musical ability was not taken from him, but it was corrupted.

The information about Satan's musicianship comes from Ezekiel 28:13:

> The workmanship of thy tabrets and of thy pipes was prepared in thee in the day that thou wast created.

Pipes apparently were built into his very body. Notice that *pipes* is plural, meaning more than one. He was a master musician. I am inclined to believe that God created him with a harmony of sound and chord in the wind instruments (pipes) that was the basic structure for melody as we know it.

Tabrets are what we understand to be percussion instruments. They would give him the ability to give rhythm to the music he played. In Isaiah 14:11 there is mention of the "noise of thy viols," which are six-stringed instruments. This could represent all of the stringed instruments, from violins to guitars to pianos.

We see in this being created by God a musician who not only is able to lead others but also is himself a living orchestra. Satan had been given a special, very distinctive commission from God to minister unto Him and cover His glory with music through worship and praise.

Brad Young, associate professor of biblical literature at Oral Roberts University, specializes in the Hebrew language. He is recognized by a rabbinical school in New York as one of the top Hebrew scholars in the United States.

Because some versions of the Bible eliminate references in Ezekiel 28:13 to musical instruments in favor of "settings and mountings" for precious stones, I asked Young to give me his opinion on Satan's musical equipment. I quote from his letter to me:

> While I understand well why many modern translations have preferred to render the Hebrew words *melechet, tupechad, unkavechah* as being a continuation of the precious stones described in the immediate context, I tend to feel that the KJV, which sees these as musical instruments, is preferable. The Hebrew text is somewhat unclear and could be rendered either way. Nevertheless, I believe that greater accuracy is found in some type of musical instrument resembling drums and flutes.
>
> My analysis is based in part on the meaning of the root words in Hebrew and partially upon medieval Jewish commentators who were outstanding scholars for all time. The word *tof* from *tupechah* refers to a drum. The other term, *unkavechah,* is more difficult but seems to be derived from the root *nakav,* which means "to pierce." It may well refer to the holes which were pierced into a cane or reed, to fashion a flute-like instrument.
>
> The famous commentator Rashi explains it like this: "drums and flutes which will produce the melodious sounds, like a drum." And the great Hebrew scholar Radak described them (tabrets and pipes) as "drums...for dancing and pierced instruments for music, which have holes made in them."

LaMar Boschman, a well-known musician and teacher on praise and worship, wrote in his book *The Rebirth of Music:*

The day Lucifer fell, music fell. Music that was once used to worship almighty God became music of an earthly nature. He still has that same powerful ministry to create worship, but now...Lucifer uses that ministry to get worship for himself, because he craves it.[20]

Music is used in advertising to make us feel a certain product will change our lives.

Music is a means for communicating, influencing, and controlling our spirits, minds, and bodies.

Music is a powerful vehicle for achieving positive or negative goals.

When Lucifer fell from heaven, a vacancy was created. However, I believe God has a plan for replacing the "anointed cherub" who fell. I believe it is the church who is going to bathe God in the glory of worship. The church is going to sing "love songs" to the Father. The church is going to make the universe ring with praise and worship of God, and the time to begin is now while we are still on Earth.

Satan's second major vehicle for gaining influence in today's cultural affairs is in the area of sex—from widespread pornography to legalized abortions.

I once heard Jack Hayford, pastor of The Church On The Way in Van Nuys, California, address the question of the devil and sex in his Sunday morning service.

Hayford said he believes the reason Satan has set out to so pervert our relationships in the sexual area is because he does not have the ability to procreate, and he is angry that we can do things he cannot, despite all of his original beauty, abilities, and power.

Therefore, Satan has done what he usually does with our good gifts from God. He has perverted sex, making substitutes for it or destroying what he cannot pervert. Obviously, his anger at God is turned on God's creations, and he hates mankind with a vengeance. As Mark Bubeck wrote in his book, *The Adversary:*

> The understanding of our foe also entails an awareness of the powers of darkness that work with him in his kingdom.[21]

These powers of darkness do exist, as we will see in the next chapter.

15

The Reality of Demons

There are two equal and opposite errors into which our race can fall about the devils [demons]. One is to disbelieve their existence. The other is to believe and feel an unhealthy interest in them.[1]

—C. S. Lewis

If angels are real—both angels of God and evil angels—and if the devil is real, then demons also must exist.

Are demons and fallen angels the same?

Are demons the spirits of deceased wicked men?

Various groups of people have different explanations for demons.

What do demons look like? Are they like men, animals, half man and half beast, the figures that introduce *Tales From the Crypt*, spiders, flies, Mutant Ninja Turtles, gremlins, the weird little aliens associated with UFOs—or all of the above?

If this world order over which Satan is said to be ruler and prince is going to end with time, when will time end? What will happen to the present wicked rulers of darkness and their troops?

The natural roads to Bethlehem, Nazareth, and Jerusalem really were only *one* road in the invisible realm of eternity. That road came from eternity, flowed through this world, and ended up back in eternity. Jesus not only blazed and traveled the road, but He is also the road—"the way, the truth, and the life" (John 14:6).

It took only one, *the* One, to make Himself a road for our sakes, but it takes multitudes of the enemy to keep us from traveling that road.

According to the Bible, there is only one *diablos* (devil), but there are many fallen angels and apparently multitudes of demons.

In the *Jewish New Testament Commentary*, messianic Jew David H. Stern says that Paul was speaking of "elemental spirits of the universe" when he wrote we "were in bondage under the elements of the world" (Gal. 4:3).

> We, both Jews and Gentiles, were slaves to them. Gentiles served these demonic spirits as gods. Jews, though knowing the one true God, were sometimes led astray by demonic spirits, including the demonic spirit of legalism.... That Jews too were bound by demonic spirits is indicated in Ephesians 2:3.[2]

The origin of demons is even more of a mystery than that of angels and Satan.

Nowhere in Scripture does it tell us specifically what demons are, where they originated, or when. However, demons cannot be metaphors or figures of speech because they are treated as realities in the Bible, particularly by Jesus. A legion of "figures of speech" could not cause a herd of pigs to self-destruct (Mark 5:1–13; Luke 8:26–33).

In writing of the "equal and opposite" errors into which we can fall, C. S. Lewis said demons are "equally pleased by both errors and hail a materialist or a magician with the same delight."[3]

The only thing we can be sure of is that because God created the beings now called demons, they were created good. At some point they must have rebelled against God.

It is difficult, indeed almost impossible, to say with certainty how demons originated. Each theory has its difficulties and its support.

Here are the four principle theories that have been developed by Christian scholars:[4]

1. Demons are disembodied inhabitants of a pre-Adamic earth. This perspective is based on the gap theory, which I described earlier. According to this theory the world that was created before Adam was under Lucifer's rule. When Lucifer fell, the inhabitants of this world rebelled against God as well. These rebellious spirits are the demons that operate in the world today.

2. Demons are the offspring of angels and women (Gen. 6:1–2, 4) who came together before the flood. The offspring

were destroyed in the flood, but their spirits remained on the earth as demons.

3. Demons are the offspring of the sons of Seth and the daughters of Cain (Gen. 6:1–2, 4). This is a variation of theory number two. It's main weakness is that everywhere else in the Old Testament where the term "sons of God" is used, it refers to angels.

4. Demons are fallen angels. This theory comes from the number of scriptures that refer to a great host of spirits designated as under the authority of Satan, Beelzebub, or the prince of demons (Matt. 12:26–27). Why some of these fallen angels would be cast down to hell or kept in chains of darkness (Jude 6) and others left free is not made clear.

Even if the origins are difficult to ascertain, we can know for certain that demons do exist and are active in keeping people from trusting in Christ, in pulling Christians into error, or in hindering victory in the lives of God's people.

Personally, I believe demons probably are the disembodied inhabitants of a pre-Adamic earth (theory number one above). One reason is because demons are apparently desirous of being embodied in human beings (or sometimes even animals). Fallen angels already have their own bodies, so it wouldn't make sense that they would have such a strong desire to inhabit other bodies. But because the majority of people believe fallen angels and demons are synonymous, I will be sensitive to that point of view throughout this book.

The Nature and Character of Demons

We can assume that demons have names because Jesus asked one his name (Luke 8:30).

Demons are able to speak and hear.

Demons have intelligence in varying degrees and are able to amass knowledge.

Demons have emotions; they exhibited fear and trembling in Luke 8:28 and James 2:19.

Demons exercise their wills. The "legion" of demons appealed to Jesus to cast them into the pigs, not the abyss "before their time" (Luke 8:32).

Demons, like Satan, seem to crave attention. Angels of God shun attention. Many church leaders warn against too great an emphasis on demons since talking about them seems to attract them. A balanced approach is to deal with them when necessary but to focus primarily on Jesus. Any victorious dealing with demons will be based on the foundation that both Satan and his followers were defeated by Jesus.

Demons cannot be in more than one place at a time. But because there are so many of them and because they all do Satan's will, they enable his influence to be felt in many places simultaneously. Physical barriers or space limitations do not hinder demons any more than they do angels.

Demons can have supernatural strength, which makes them stronger than people.

Demons can cause various physical ailments and afflictions.

Demons can possess people. (For a more in-depth discussion of oppression, obsession, and possession by demons, see Appendix B.)

Demons are apparently comforted when they are embodied— living in the soul, flesh, or spirit of human beings.

Demons have a twofold purpose: (1) "to hinder the purposes of God," and (2) "to extend the power of Satan."[5]

Demons are very shrewd and knowledgeable about human nature. They are able to adapt to the cultural environment of a place or an age. In some societies, demons manifest themselves in hideous forms, but in an educated and highly cultured community, they do not reveal the grosser aspects of their natures.

Sometimes demons may appear to be "ministers of righteousness" (2 Cor. 11:15), encouraging personal or self-promoted righteousness, endeavoring to sell the lie that the creature is greater than the Creator. Angels and humans were created to be God-centered. Therefore, becoming self-centered is a violation of the basic law of creature existence.

Satan's Foundational Lie Manifested in Pharisaism

The essence of the believer's covenant with God through Jesus is that our sins were imputed (credited) to Jesus, and His righteousness was imputed (credited) to us.

Self-righteousness is a form of rebellion against God. It is the "seed" or root of legalism in secular or religious thinking. Legalism is what we see in the present "politically correct" movement. Legalism was in full flower among the Pharisees of Jesus' day.

Self-righteousness carries with it an almost tangible "high." It is addictive. You might call it a counterfeit anointing because it can literally be felt and can be mistaken for the anointing of God.

Self-righteousness in Christianity can result in a great zealousness for the Lord's work. Those who have accepted Satan's lie that works are more important than faith will even "kill" others—either physically or by reputation—who do not agree, thinking they are doing God a favor. The apostle Paul, who was a Pharisee and son of a Pharisee, persecuted Christians "unto the death" before his conversion (Acts 22:3–4). I believe demons encourage Pharisaism because of the harm it does in the church.

William DeArteaga pointed out in *Quenching the Spirit* that Gnosticism and Pharisaism are heresies on opposite sides of the truth:

> The early Gnostics believed, among other things, that the created world was evil and in opposition to the world of the spirit, which was good. As a result, the Gnostic way of spirituality accepts visions, prophecies and spiritual experiences without any restraint. In effect, the Gnostics do not discern between the activities of the lower demonic spirits and the inspiration of the Holy Spirit.
>
> Pharisaism deals with spiritual experiences exactly opposite to the way Gnosticism does. Unlike the Gnostics, Pharisees restrict the flow of spiritual experiences until religion becomes purely a theological exercise, and the Spirit is quenched.[6]

Someone has said Christians tend either to operate in wildfire or no fire at all. Many demons are assigned to pull Christians off that middle ground of balanced truth.

In essence, self-righteousness is putting the works of the creation (man, even Christian man) over the works of the Creator.
Those caught in this deception are usually very sincere, and they see
those who operate in the flow of the Holy Spirit as in error because
they do not conform to past traditions.

Since the victory of Jesus on the cross, the primary motivation
of Satan, fallen angels, or demons seems to be hatred. Pride got
them into this mess, and hatred of God and His people is sustaining
them in their present realm of influence—the *cosmos diabolicus.*

The misery of demons or fallen angels is on the same level as
the joy of angels who serve God. Yet they can only blame themselves
for their state. Augustine wrote:

> When we ask the cause of the evil angels' misery, we find it is the
> just result of their turning away from him who supremely is, and
> their turning toward themselves, who do not exist in that supreme
> degree. What other name is there for this fault than pride? The
> beginning of all sin is pride.[7]

What we see in the latter half of the twentieth century is Satan
adapting and incorporating man's new inventions and activities,
even man's hunger for spiritual realities, into his *cosmos diabolicus.*

The Present Realm of
Demonic Influence

I see the present realm of demonic activity as a fulfillment of 2
Timothy 3:1–5, which says that in the last days men will be lovers of
themselves, covetous, boasters, proud, blasphemers, disobedient to
parents (lawless), ungrateful, unholy, without natural affection, truce
breakers, false accusers, despisers of those who are good, and loving
pleasures more than God although having a form of godliness.

Paul called people with these natures "men of corrupt minds"
and those who "resist the truth."

The New Age movement is a prime example of truth being
turned into Satan's lie right before our eyes.

- The belief in God as sovereign Lord and Creator is being transformed into belief in a "supreme energy force" or "super-consciousness."

- Christians are being called "antichrist" by New Agers because the church says there is only one way while New Agers say it is obvious there are many ways to God.

- The power of Satan is being compared to the power of God. It's similar to the way Pharaoh's magicians said, "Look, we can do what Moses did" (Exod. 7:11). Through demonic power, New Agers are saying, "We can do what you Christians do and more. Look at us!"

Rick Renner, a friend of mine from Tulsa who is an author and Bible teacher, has written:

> What's happening today is that the devil has gotten smart, and he no longer is coming with the pitchfork and horns on his head. Today he looks like godliness. He has disguised himself.
>
> Do you know what the primary byword of the New Age movement is? Are you ready for this? [It is] Christ in you, the hope of glory. That is what New Age leaders say when they start their occultic seminars.... That sounds like godliness, doesn't it? Except we're talking about a "different" Christ.[8]

In his 1988 book, *Seducing Spirits and Doctrines of Demons*, Renner described watching a secular television talk show that featured a whole panel of New Agers. He said they kept saying, "God is love. God is love. You don't need to be afraid of the 'walk-ins.'"

The term "walk-ins" means spirits who walk in and become part of you. In other words, this is an open invitation for a demon to enter not just your life but your person.

Renner says a Unity pastor on that same talk show called Christians "primitive" and said Christians must be done away with because they believe there is only one way.

In 2 Timothy 3:13 it says that "evil men and seducers shall wax worse and worse, deceiving, and being deceived." Renner says this means that a worldwide impact of sorcery will come upon every area of life all over the earth. He pointed out that even our homes are being invaded with this counterfeit via television programs (including children's cartoons), books, films, and children's toys.

In 1988, channeling was the latest craze; today, it is angels. Obtaining your own "angel" to personally guide you through life and become part of your own personality is a far cry from the protection of God's angels. Those who open themselves up to these "angels" will find, just as mediums or channels have discovered, that soon their wills will be overridden.

A demon will find ways to bully or coerce a person and override his or her will. But an angel of God will never violate man's free will—his right to choose.

Is it possible for a believer to give heed to seducing spirits and doctrines of demons?

Renner answers, "Absolutely. It happened all the time in the New Testament. Most of Paul's epistles were written to correct doctrines of demons."[9] Paul's epistles were written to believers, not to the world.

In the epistle to Timothy, Paul described deceptive doctrines and counterfeit signs and wonders that demons would plant within the church in the last of the last days (1 Tim. 4:1).

Another development within the New Age movement that gives yet another name to demons is the story of "starseeds." Following Satan's propensity for being up to date, this probably is riding on the interest in space travel and possible space beings. According to one New Age book, these "light workers" or starseeds have been scattered among earth's population.[10]

This author says the archangel Michael or other masters speak through him. He warns that earth is on its last legs and about to be transformed into a new earth in a catastrophic and devastating process. Those who are ready to ascend, mostly starseeds, will be taken out in waves, but he hopes some humans will be prepared to go. The third wave of rescue was to occur before earth's destruction in a polar shift sometime in the 1990s, which never materialized.

Some of the rescues were to take place in spaceships, according to the "angel" presenting this material. Some ships were to be counterfeit from the "wrong" beings. The way to know the difference is to "simply ask your heart or 'feeling nature' if you feel a Christ vibration."[11] Those are the "right" ships.

The same book says fundamentalist Christian churches are so

violently against New Age because they are "afraid of losing their power." If everyone experiences God individually, this "angel" said, there would no longer be a reason to go to a particular church.

His advice was:

> If you feel a fundamentalist bent in someone's nature, love them unconditionally but silently for your own protection. The Christ is love. The Christ is the presence that we are and the presence that we share.[12]

The false is being presented as true, and truth is being transformed into a falsehood—Satan's essence of the lie.

Renner wrote that what Paul was saying in his epistles to Timothy was:

> In the last days demons are going to become so seducing that people will not realize they are witnessing demonic activity. And the demons are going to begin to operate in such a tantalizing way that it will actually cause people to stop, look, and turn their heads to listen and look in a different direction—rather than curse and rebuke the demons.... Turning from the faith and opening up their minds to new ideas and new revelations will be the first step to being deceived. Revelation that is so new you can't find it in the Word is not from God. You can be sure of that.[13]

Many Christians may think this could not happen in our day, yet it *is* happening now. Several recent surveys show that a significant number of Christians think New Age beliefs are compatible with Christianity.[14]

A stunning example is the furor over an essentially New Age book that was selling like hotcakes in Christian bookstores until Christian writers exposed it. Written by a Mormon woman who is a former hypnotherapist, the book reveals "truths" given to the author in heaven during an alleged after-death experience.

Some of these so-called truths contradict the doctrine of the Trinity, promote universalism (everyone will eventually be saved, even those who already have died), and argue that every religion is "necessary and precious" to God.[15]

Even though all three of these and other ideas presented in the book are not only unbiblical but anti-Christian, *Charisma* magazine received numerous letters saying nothing in the book contradicts the New Testament and taking the editors to task for calling the book New Age! Also, it remained near the top of the secular best-selling books lists for some time.

In this decade, we can see the *cosmos diabolicus* gearing up for a mighty challenge—if not the final challenge—to the church. Sometimes we lose sight of the fact that the church is now the primary target.

What is still to come before Satan's lease runs out is a glorious triumphant church that truly knows its blood-bought condition and walks in victory. This is the manifestation that will prove to the principalities and powers God's wisdom in creating man and in allowing Satan's lie to run its course (Eph. 3:10).

In terms of warfare, what the demons are doing at the instigation of their lord is called camouflage and propaganda and, in terms of the old Soviet regime, "the big lie." Here's some of their best work:

- Killing unborn babies is right, but killing animals for food is wrong.

- Satanism and witchcraft can be taught in public schools, but Christianity is illegal.

- Pornography, even involving children, is free speech, but preaching on street corners is disturbing the peace.

Most of us could compile a list of similar lies that already have replaced truth in our society. Peter Jones wrote that the "intelligentsia" (educators and media specialists) already have opted for "the New Age creed of globalism which denies sin, idealizes human potential, and is so profoundly politically correct."[16] Idealizing human potential again is the lie, elevating the created over the Creator.

What we must remember as the tide of darkness begins to look overwhelming is that we not only know our own destinies as Christians, but we also know what is going to happen to Satan, fallen angels, demons, and wicked humanity. Christian men, women, and children of all races, nationalities, and classes have a common destiny, and Satan's followers have a common destiny, also.

The Destiny of Satan, Fallen Angels, and Demons

What will happen to these beings who have developed a counterfeit world system when Jesus establishes His kingdom in its fullness?

Where will they go? And for how long?

Can we even imagine what a world will be like without evil?

The first thing to keep in mind is that Satan has already been judged and defeated (John 16:11; Col. 2:15; Heb. 2:14). All that is lacking is the final sentencing and consignment to "prison."

Satan is yet to be cast out of the second heaven and confined to earth (Rev. 12:9–12).

Satan is yet to be cast into the bottomless pit for a thousand years (Rev. 20:1–3).

Satan is yet to be consigned eternally to the lake of fire created for him and his angels (Rev. 20:10).

Where Satan goes, so go the fallen angels, the demons, and the people who did not receive Jesus' redemption for their iniquities and sins.

The question of where these evil spirits go is answered for us, but the question of exactly when it will happen is not.

In the meantime, we must continue to live in this world. We are to "walk by faith, not by sight" (2 Cor. 5:7). That means living according to the principles of the "invisible" kingdom of God while literally dwelling in the visible cosmos of the devil. By conforming to Jesus and not to this world, we can make sure that Satan has no foothold in our lives (Eph. 4:27). The Bible also tells us to "be vigilant" (1 Pet. 5:8).

Jesus did not leave us without armor or weapons; they are described in Ephesians 6:10–18. Nor did He leave us without power and authority against the realm of dark angels or demons.

Throughout the earlier chapters in this book, I have discussed the angelic world, both good and evil. These facts demand a response on our part.

Will the ministry of angels be a part of our lives?

Will we allow demons to harass us and interfere with our relationship with God?

Remember at the beginning of this book how I talked about

heaven meeting earth? I believe the angelic realm touches our lives much more often than we realize. In the remaining chapters of this book, you'll learn about the personal side of angelology, when angels become a part of our experience.

16

Evil Angels and Thought

*If an angel strengthened our Lord Himself after His agony
in the garden, His people also may experience the support
of angels; and if evil angels tempt to sin, good angels may
allure to holiness.*[1]

—Charles Hodge

If every action begins with a thought, where do thoughts come
from? Is every wicked or every good thought solely of man's
production?

Is there any truth to the cartoons we have seen over the years
showing an imp whispering in one ear of a person and an angel
whispering in the other?

The late John Wimber, author, pastor, and founder of the
Vineyard churches, said our minds are "the landing fields" for
demons. Can good angels also influence our thought patterns?

Many theologians believe we are influenced by outside "inspi-
rations" as well as by thoughts and imaginations that arise within
our minds and hearts. Hodge suggested that good angels not only
execute the will of God in the natural world but also act upon the
minds of people.

> They have access to our minds and can influence them for good,
> in accordance with the laws of our nature and in the use of appro-
> priate means. They do not act by that direct operation which is the
> peculiar prerogative of God and His Spirit, but by the suggestion
> of truth and guidance of thought and feeling, much as one man
> may act upon another. If the angels may communicate one with
> another, there's no reason why they may not, in like manner, com-
> municate with our spirits.[2]

When I interviewed the late Kenneth Hagin Sr. for the original edition of this book, he told me the Holy Spirit taught him years ago how demons operate in influencing the minds of people. He commented:

> If demons and evil spirits can influence people's thoughts for bad, then angels must also have access to the thinking processes of people, and they can influence people for good. Angels can suggest thoughts to people in line with the direction of the Holy Spirit.

Both Hodge and Hagin, as well as other theologians, pastors, and teachers, have indicated in their teachings that angels—good and bad—can affect the thinking processes of mankind. However, this may be one of the best-kept secrets in the Christian world today!

Does the Bible give us any specific indication that angels can influence the thoughts of mankind?

Paul's words in 2 Corinthians 10:4–5 are very interesting.

> (For the weapons of our warfare are not carnal, but mighty through God to the pulling down of strongholds;) Casting down imaginations, and every high thing that exalteth itself against the knowledge of God, and bringing into captivity every thought to the obedience of Christ.

In those two verses Paul linked the word *strongholds* directly with imaginations and thoughts, and connected spiritual weapons to pulling down these strongholds. He indicated that imaginations and thoughts can be evil strongholds established by demons even in the minds of Christians. We can see Satan's modus operandi from his first attempt at this (Gen. 3).

Biblical Examples of Satanic Brainwashing

Satan asked Eve the question that is the heartbeat of all sin: "Hath God said?" Notice that Satan did not make a dogmatic statement declaring God's Word was not true. All he did was ask a question carefully designed to begin a process in her mind of questioning and distrust. That ploy worked so well that he still uses it today. He has mastered and perfected the business of temptation by injecting thoughts into our minds.

Can Satan actually put thoughts into our minds?

I believe he can. I believe he cannot force us to think anything, but he is a master of suggestion. Evil spirits fire suggestive thoughts into our minds like the "fiery darts" that Paul wrote about to the Christians in Ephesus (Eph. 6:16).

In fact, we have specific examples of this in the Bible, not just passages that can be applied to the possibility.

In John 13:2, Jesus was eating the Passover (the Last Supper) with His disciples, when...

> Supper being ended, the devil having now put into the heart of Judas Iscariot, Simon's son, to betray him [Jesus].

The Bible explicitly states that the devil put the concept of betrayal into Judas's heart. That means the devil had the ability to influence Judas's thinking processes. When two members of the early church, Ananias and Sapphira, lied to Peter about the price they had received for their property, Peter said:

> Ananias, why hath Satan filled thine heart to lie to the Holy Ghost, and to keep back part of the price of the land?
>
> —Acts 5:3

Peter had no doubt that Satan had filled this man's heart with a lie. The only way that could happen was through thought attack.

At one point in Jesus' ministry, He asked the disciples who men said He was. Peter answered, "Thou art the Christ, the Son of the living God" (Matt. 16:16). Jesus replied that this truth had been revealed to Peter by the Father in heaven. However, only six verses later Peter rebuked Jesus when Jesus began to talk of what was going to happen to Him.

Jesus' reply was very different:

> But he turned, and said unto Peter, Get thee behind me, Satan: thou art an offense unto me: for thou savorest not the things that be of God, but those that be of men.
>
> —Matthew 16:23

It is obvious that Jesus was not calling Peter "Satan." Rather, He was dealing with the fact that Satan had dropped a thought into

Peter's mind. How interesting that at one moment Peter makes such a powerful declaration of truth and faith that Jesus commends him for it, only to be rebuked a few moments later for a thought from Satan that was a subtle attempt to hinder Jesus.

There is a truth here that all Christians should keep in mind: even at the times of our greatest faith, our minds are still susceptible to the thought attacks hurled at us from Satan.

Thought Attacks

Not only can evil spirits apparently drop suggestions into our minds, but they can also take thoughts out of our minds. In the parable of the sower, Jesus told of seeds falling on good soil, rocky ground, and by the wayside. He interpreted the seeds that fell "by the wayside" as the Word of God that someone hears and does not understand. Jesus explained that the "fowl" that devours the "seed" of the Word is the wicked one (Matt. 13:19).

In what ways can evil spirits push thoughts out of our minds?

It is possible for someone sitting in a church service or even reading the Bible to allow his or her mind to wander.

It is possible for a young mother to be planning meals for the coming week while listening to a sermon.

It is possible for a businessperson to be planning corporate strategy while sitting in a church pew.

Notice, these are not wicked thoughts; they are simply thoughts planted by the enemy to gently tug our attention away from the Word.

I believe evil spirits are more active on Sunday mornings than at any other time. If they can divert our attention from the sermon, they can "catch away" the Word that was sown into our hearts.

> When any one heareth the word of the kingdom, and understandeth it not, then cometh the wicked one, and catcheth away that which was sown in his heart.
>   —Matthew 13:19

Jesus accentuated this possibility again in the parable of the two kinds of builders, the wise man who built on a rock versus the foolish one who built on sand (Matt. 7:24–27). It rained and the floods came while the winds blew and beat upon both their houses.

One house stood, but the other fell. Why?

Jesus pointed out that one man was a "doer" of the Word and the other was not. Notice that both men apparently heard the Word. In modern terms, let us suppose that both men attend your church faithfully every Sunday morning.

However, one leaves the church with a commitment to do the Word that he has just made an effort to hear and understand. The other man is simply a listener. He has not really heard and understood what was said. He probably goes home, turns on the football game, and promptly forgets everything. His spiritual house is built on sand, while the other man's is set solidly on the Rock that is the Word of God.

These examples show us the commitment of Satan and his evil spirits to affect the process of our thoughts. An undisciplined thought life leaves one vulnerable to the enemy. A passive mind, a lazy mind, or an undisciplined mind makes it easy for the wicked one to drop in thoughts or to steal those dropped in by the Holy Spirit or good angels.

Romans 8:7 says that a carnal mind, one operating on fleshly motives, actually is at enmity with God.

Judson Cornwall has written that Satan even aims his attacks at us when we are children. Satan knows that early training determines the course of one's life (Prov. 22:6).[3]

The Battlefield Is the Mind

I believe that many Christians have no idea that evil spirits are dropping thoughts into their minds because they accept them as their own. We badly underestimate the influence that thoughts have on our lives. Yet the Bible has many verses about thinking only on good things and avoiding evil thoughts (Josh. 1:8; Phil. 4:6–8).

In 1993, I was invited by Baroness Cox, a deputy speaker of Great Britain's House of Lords, to accompany a fact-finding mission into a small, nominally Christian country called Nagorno-Karabakh in the southern part of the former Soviet Union. We were to take Bibles and medicines into this war zone through our ministry, World Compassion.

We flew on a Russian-built military helicopter from Yerevan, the capital of Armenia, into the Caucasus Mountains. Our route covered more than three hundred miles, some of which was over hostile territory and put us in range of the Scud missiles from their enemy Azerbaijan, a Muslim republic that surrounds them. When we arrived, we had to travel by military jeep to an area where we were close enough to the front lines to hear the boom of artillery and the chatter of machine-gun fire. Five people had been killed by an incoming missile the day we arrived at the medical unit with our supplies.

In preparing for the trip, I thought it would be a good idea to increase my life insurance since I have a family. However, the only insurance company that would cover me going into a war zone was Lloyd's of London, who said I was insane for doing this!

But the warfare that was the biggest threat to me was not missiles in the air or cannons on the ground. The real battlefield was in my mind as I was interviewed for the insurance policy. The usual questions were asked:

Is there a history of heart attacks in your family?

Is there a history of cancer in your family?

Is there a history of any other major diseases or conditions?

As I began to detail the family members who had died with heart problems, my mind began to get ready for a heart attack. When I enumerated those who had died of cancer, I sensed a knot in my stomach.

But praise the Lord, I had learned to watch out for such thoughts of the enemy.

I knew angels had been assigned to protect me on these missions. So I began to think on that and to remember what an angel had told my father when I first went into Eastern Europe and Russia.

My father, a former pastor with the Pentecostal Assemblies of Canada, had been very concerned for my well-being and went into prayer. He said an angel told him not to worry, that I was doing the work of the Lord behind the Iron Curtain and that "they" (the angels) were looking out for me. Our trip to that war-torn country was a success, and we were protected while there.

When the City of Faith medical center was operating at Oral Roberts University, I asked Jim Winslow, chief surgeon and director of the hospital, if thoughts had anything to do with disease. He said most doctors would agree that about 70 percent of all disease originates in the human mind. An article in the *New England Journal of Medicine* some years ago placed it higher than that—at 80 percent. The article said that about half of the remaining 20 percent would get well by themselves!

That does not mean all of these diseases are imaginary, but many of them began with a thought or a belief and developed into a physical condition. Many of us have heard self-fulfilling prophecies such as, "My grandfather had a heart attack at forty, my father had a heart attack at forty, and I probably will, too."

I am not talking about mind control or mind over matter.

I am talking about thoughts that allow the Word of God to be stolen out of your heart so that your faith is hindered or erased by doubts and fears.

In Romans 12:1–2, Paul wrote of two things Christians need to do:

1. Present our bodies a living sacrifice.

2. Be transformed by the renewing of our minds.

This means living according to God's moral principles and bringing our bodies into subjection to Him. Renewing our minds requires meditating on the Word of God, which means to actively read, think on, speak about, and dwell on the Bible.

This is the only way to defend ourselves against the thought attacks of evil angels or demons. The present invasion of predominately evil angels into society foretells major thought attacks that are about to come against the church.

If you know the Bible well enough to know the principles and thoughts of God, then thoughts that run against God's Word will immediately stand out as alien. If you have the real in your heart, the counterfeit or the false will be easily recognized.

If you have a mind actively fixed on the Word of God, it will not be easy for the enemy's thoughts to take root.

Victory over the devil does not mean constantly casting out demons. The most enduring victory comes from getting your mind so transformed that your spirit so agrees with the Holy Spirit that it will not accept the ideas of the world.

Neil Anderson, chairman of the Practical Theology Department at Biola University, calls this method of opposing Satan "truth encounters" as opposed to "power encounters." Certainly there are times when demons need to be cast out of some people, but demonic attempts at thought control are aimed at everyone. Not every person has a demon to be cast out. (See Appendix B.) Anderson wrote:

> If Satan can place a thought in your mind—and he can—it isn't much more of a trick for him to make you think it's your idea. If you knew it was Satan, you'd reject the thought, wouldn't you? But when he disguises his suggestion as your idea, you are more likely to accept it. That is his primary deception. . . . Since Satan's primary weapon is a lie, your defense against him is the truth. Dealing with Satan is not a power encounter; it's a truth encounter. When you expose Satan's lie with God's truth, his power is broken. That's why Jesus said: "You shall know the truth, and the truth shall make you free" (John 8:32).[4]

In one of my services, I received a word of knowledge about a man who was planning to kill his wife. When the Lord exposed those demonic thoughts, the man came forward and was converted to Christ. I later shared that story on my national radio program. Afterward I received a letter stained with tears from a man living in Phoenix, Arizona, who had been harboring the same thought but gave his heart to the Lord while listening to the broadcast.

Expose the lie, and you can defeat the liar.

Demons have no right to override a human being's free will. But they fool us into thinking that these thoughts and desires are our own, and somehow that makes them valid and credible to us. We then accept the thought, act on it, and even defend it as our own.

That battle extends beyond the devil's ranks, making us susceptible to our own flesh and the world around us, the *cosmos diabolicus.*

The World, the Flesh, and the Devil

Believers can yield to alien thoughts and be defeated.

Believers can yield to the carnal desires of the flesh and be defeated.

Believers can yield to the influence of the world and be defeated.

Temptations of sex, food, drink, and other lusts such as gambling, the love of money, or an inordinate desire for material possessions can be identified immediately as sins of the flesh. Sometimes the devil accentuates and emphasizes these things if he knows one of them is your weakness. However, most of the time what people are battling is simply their own flesh.

In Galatians 5:19 Paul gave an outline of the works of the flesh: adultery, fornication, uncleanness, lasciviousness, idolatry, witchcraft, hatred, variance, jealousies, wrath, strife, divisions, heresies, envyings, murders, drunkenness, revellings, and so forth.

When Jesus said to pluck out your eye or cut off your hand if it offended you (Mark 9:43–47), He was not speaking literally. He was talking about fleshly lusts and appetites. Paul spoke similarly of "mortifying" our flesh, or putting it to death (Rom. 8:13; Col. 3:5).

The pleasures of the flesh are not demons or evil spirits. Eating is a lust or a pleasure of the flesh that, when pushed to the extreme, is gluttony. But it is not necessarily a demon at work. It can be a lack of temperance or self-control (Gal. 5:23). Actually, the greatest war the believer will ever wage is not with the devil but with the flesh.

The world system includes many things that are beautiful and attractive. It also includes knowledge, humanitarian concerns, social programs, art, music, and politics. None of these are evil in themselves, but none of them are totally founded on God and His principles.

We often overlook the fact that religion is part of the world's system. Children of God do not observe a "religion." They enter into and develop a relationship with God the Father.

Religion is Adam and Eve covering their nakedness with leaves from the tree.

Religion is always man's self-efforts to cover his nakedness, rooted in pride.

Religion appeases the mind into thinking it is in right-standing with God.

Christianity involves the shedding of innocent blood to atone for man's sins. God clothed Adam and Eve in animal skins after the animals' innocent blood was shed. That is true Christianity.

The world, the flesh, and the devil all make their first approach to a person through the mind. If thoughts come indirectly through the world's entertainment system, the ultimate source is the satanic world order. If the thoughts are triggered by the flesh, they are also traced indirectly to Satan through the fall of Adam and Eve.

We can overcome these thought attacks by meditating on the truth of God's Word. In the next chapter, I want to give you essential information about another way of resisting Satan—spiritual warfare.

17

Spiritual Warfare and Angels

We are not too unlike the flea on the head of the elephant who, just after the elephant crossed an aging bridge, leaned over to the ear and whispered, "Wow! Didn't we shake that bridge!"[1]

—Judson Cornwall

I have been amazed at the recent proliferation of teachings in the church on directly attacking Satan's evil angels. It seems people have become aware that we are at war. Movements and organizations are bringing new understandings in this area to the church.

Many of these men and women have great ministries and unusual abilities at communication. They also have valid insights into the Bible and a passion to win the world for Jesus, which I admire with all of my heart.

However, I believe a basic misunderstanding about the battle between Satan's troops and the church can lead to errors and possible extremism. I could not write a book about angels without talking about how we can stand against evil angels and demons and cooperate with the angels of God. Conversely, I find it is necessary to write about how not to deal with them.

Although there is much truth in what spiritual warfare groups are saying, I believe that in some cases they are operating out of faulty interpretation of Scripture. The reason I am so sure of this is that I made the same mistake in my first book, *The Power of Praise and Worship*. I used the three primary scriptures that they use, and I since have seen that my interpretation was inaccurate. Those three scriptures are Ephesians 6:12, 2 Corinthians 10:3–5, and Daniel 10:12. The mistake is this: the Greek word for "strongholds" in 2 Corinthians 10:4 is *okuroma*. It appears only once in the New Testament, and I

151

did what so many others have done: I built a major doctrine on that one word.

How many spiritual warfare choruses have been written lately about pulling down strongholds?

How many "militant" choruses have been written and sung by Christians who actually are losing the real battle with Satan in their minds and flesh?

How many are projecting the sin in their own hearts onto demonic forces, venting anger and hatred, yet not dealing with those things in themselves?

How many cities can say they have lower crime rates because principalities and powers were "pulled down"?

I had connected those verses in 2 Corinthians 10 with Paul's outline of spiritual hierarchy in Ephesians 6:12 and used the Old Testament example of Daniel to "prove" that we should use our weapons against principalities and powers. Actually, those verses do not connect in this way, although most of the books I have read on spiritual warfare make the same artificial connection that I once did. The facts are these:

1. "Strongholds" in 2 Corinthians 10 are explained very explicitly as "imaginations," "high things" (or thoughts) that exalt themselves above the knowledge of God. Paul wrote that we should bring every thought into obedience to Christ. Some translations are even plainer, saying "arguments," "theories," "reasonings," "speculations," or "pretensions." The mind is the number-one battleground between Christians and Satan.

   These verses in no way depict a cosmic struggle against territorial spirits that rule over our cities. In fact, *none* of the verses about warfare in the New Testament really involve Christians coming against heavenly powers.

   For example, in 2 Timothy 2:3–4, the warfare in which Paul exhorts Timothy to be "a good soldier" involves the affairs of this life, not evil angels and authorities. In James 4:1–2, James calls "wars and fightings" the lusts that war in your members. "War" for the Christian obviously refers to the war of the spirit against the flesh, as does 1 Peter 2:11. It has nothing to do with fighting evil angels or spirits.

2. Ephesians 6:12, at first glance, may seem to endorse Christians fighting against evil angels in ruling positions. "For we wrestle not against flesh and blood, but against principalities, against powers, against the rulers of the darkness of this world, against spiritual wickedness in high places."

    However, taken in the context of verses 10 to 18, Paul is not writing about pulling fallen angels out of the heavens but about resisting the enemy's attacks in everyday life. He is talking about the shield of faith, the helmet of salvation, the breastplate of righteousness, the sandals of peace, the sword of the Spirit, truth as a covering for the "loins," knowing the Word and prayer (Eph. 6:13–18).

3. In Daniel 10, an angel visited Daniel in answer to his prayer and fasting. In addition to the answer Daniel sought, the angel told him that the prince of Persia had "withstood" the angel until he got help from the archangel Michael (v. 13). This verse is the foundation of most of the present teaching on "territorial spirits" and is used to explain Ephesians 6:12.

    I would like to point out that this story from Daniel took place under the old covenant. After Jesus died, rose, and ascended, there is no indication in the New Testament that territorial spirits are able to stop or hinder our prayers from getting through to God.

We are sons of God and have immediate access to the throne of grace at any time. We are told to come boldly to the throne of grace in Hebrews 10:19 because of Jesus' blood. In John 15:7, the Word says, "If ye abide in me, and my words abide in you, ye shall ask what ye will, and it shall be done unto you." This obviously allows no opportunity for satanic intervention. When we understand our authority in God's kingdom, there will be no fear of territorial spirits interfering with our prayers.

Let me make it clear that I do believe there are territorial spirits, and I have encountered them in the more than eighty countries where I have traveled and ministered.

It seems clear from the Bible that Satan's evil angels are arranged in ranks of various authorities. However, I believe that Christians have not been told to pull them down. The only strongholds believers are to deal with are in their own minds, flesh, and lives. The only evil spirits we are to deal with are demons that sometimes must be cast out of people through personal ministry.

Genuine spiritual warfare mostly has to do with the mind and the flesh, which, of course, involves the influences from the world and the devil.

Genuine spiritual warfare involves fighting "the good fight of faith." That means keeping our mind renewed, our flesh in check, and resisting the temptations of the world. That is the bulk of the fighting that Christians are called to do.

To borrow a phrase from Judson Cornwall, we need to see clearly whose war this really is.

Whose War Is It Anyway?

If Jesus defeated Satan, and if He "spoiled principalities and powers," then why should believers have to do that?

> And having spoiled principalities and powers, he made a show of them openly, triumphing over them in it.   —Colossians 2:15

Since we are seated with Christ "together in heavenly places" (Eph. 2:6), that means we already are positioned above principalities and powers. Some people are leasing airplanes to get to a high altitude and pull down "high places." Others are renting the top floors of tall buildings for this purpose.

What difference does natural altitude make? Would it have been more effective if Jesus' cross had been on Mount Everest instead of Mount Calvary?

It seems that if strongholds needed to be pulled down over cities, Scripture would give examples of the apostles doing so at such notorious locations as Ephesus, Corinth, or Rome. Hagin Sr. wrote that instead: "Paul was busy drawing attention to Jesus. He was preaching the Word so people could come out from under Satan's control."[2]

Spiritual warfare traditionally has meant simply praying about something until the answer came. Even in the Book of Daniel, angels of God—not Daniel—fought the evil territorial spirit on Daniel's behalf. The authors of *The Foundations of Pentecostal Theology* commented:

> Nowhere are Christians told to fight the devil. Our Lord did that once for all on the cross. Our part is to claim, by faith, and stand in His victory. "Resist the devil"—do not fight him—and he is the one who will "flee from you" (James 4:7). [First] Peter 5:9 explains how this is to be done: "Whom resist, steadfast in the faith." Faith in the account of Christ's victory over the devil, and faith in God's promises, is the secret to victory....Faith in God's Word is the secret of the believer's daily triumph.[3]

So what does it mean to wrestle against things that are not flesh and blood? Vine's expository dictionary says the meaning of the Greek word *pale*, translated "wrestling," is akin to *pallo*, which means "to sway" or "to vibrate."[4] Vine wrote that this is used figuratively concerning spiritual conflict. Yet many of the proponents of territorial warfare interpret this literally and believe that we actually wrestle with territorial spirits in the heavenlies.

Paul was trying to draw a word picture for believers that opposition comes from the enemy, not from other people. The whole point he is making in Ephesians 6 is not about spiritual warfare in the heavenlies but who the enemy is. He was trying to keep Christians from fighting among themselves or even against unbelievers over things the devil stirred up.

What a wrestling match it is to dismiss past failures!

What a wrestling match it is to remember that snide comments and derogatory remarks from friends or relatives do not make them our enemies! Our enemy is the one who provoked those thoughts in their minds or who reminds us of past faults and failings that have been placed under the blood of Jesus.

What a wrestling match it is to avoid self-righteousness and believe that good deeds gain us status in heaven and not to take part of the glory for what God does through us!

Spiritual Territoriality

I have no argument with those who say there are territorial spirits. My only difference is in whether or not we are to pull down defeated foes that are already defeated.

The situation is no different with evil angels than with Satan. Few believers would slip into thinking they have to bind and pull down Satan himself. They know all they have to do is resist him in all areas of their lives. The same holds true for his angels. (Concerning demons, please see Appendix B.) If Satan is a defeated foe, then so are his angels.

Satan knows his ruling spirits cannot be pulled down or bound before his "lease" runs out. Remember, his lease is not for the world, nor does it involve the kingdom of God. Satan's dominion is a time-lease on the systems that rule all areas of this planet.

We can resist him by voting in political elections as God witnesses to us through the Holy Spirit. We can cut the ground out from under Satan's ruling spirit by removing from office those people who have been in agreement with his ideas.

We can resist him in our culture by buying videos or going to movies that reflect God's ways, by buying godly books and magazines, and by watching television programs that promote the concepts of God.

We can resist him in education by becoming active on local school boards.

We can resist him by fasting and praying about any of these areas.

In other words, we can resist Satan by living a biblical, "normal" (as taught in the Word) Christian life.

The most important thing about that passage in Daniel is not that there are territorial spirits. It is not even that good angels fight them.

The most important thing is that God answers sincere heartfelt prayer, even if it means dispatching angels to bring the answer.

Personally, I am concerned that the devil is enjoying all this attention paid to something that he knows is wasting Christians' time and energy. In books and articles and at spiritual warfare conferences, so much time is spent focusing on Satan's power and influence that our eyes are off what Jesus already has done.

Judson Cornwall said the bigger problem with some spiritual warfare is that "the emphasis is upon the power vested in us far more than the power in the blood of Jesus Christ. It walks a very fine line between Christianity and humanism, which teaches the deity of mankind.... True warfare occurs when we exalt Christ in righteousness and faith."[5]

Cornwall concludes:

> I am confident that what is going on under the title of spiritual warfare is neither spiritual nor warfare. It is fleshly activity, energized by soul power. [It] is far more mass hysteria than it is warfare. It accomplishes nothing in the heavens, and often what it accomplishes on earth is divisive, mystifying, and destructive to the participants.[6]

A Spiritual Balance

We should not back off from praying for our cities, states, and nations simply because some are operating in error or extremism.

We should pray for our countries and for those in authority ((2 Chron. 7:14; 1 Tim. 2:2).

We should pray for people's hearts to be open to the gospel.

To live victorious lives, we must not underrate or overrate our enemy, Satan. We cannot understand how to relate either to good or to evil angels if we do not understand authority in the spirit realm.

Kenneth Hagin Sr. has described the real reason why Christians cannot pull down territorial spirits over cities:

> We do not have Scripture for breaking the power of the devil over an entire city once and for all time, because a city is composed of people. People have free choice, and they can choose whom they will serve—Satan or God—and in every city many people choose to serve Satan and to continually yield to him. But we can push back the influence of darkness in prayer so that the Word has an opportunity to prevail in people's hearts and lives through the preaching of the gospel.[7]

What Hagin has said is so important, I suggest you go back and reread it. A lack of understanding concerning levels of authority is the root of the pitfalls into which some are falling in the field of spiritual warfare.

That's why understanding the lines of authority in the angelic realm is relevant information for living the Christian life.

18

Who Is in Charge?

It seems impractical, if not impossible, to fight against the kingdom of darkness, while trying to worship the God of light. They dwell in incompatible kingdoms and do not even share the same phone line. So if you're talking to the devil and wish to speak to God, hang up and redial. The reverse is equally true. God and the devil will not accept conference calls. You can only speak to one at a time.[1]

—Judson Cornwall

Why do many people believe that all supernatural beings are benign?

Why are Christians unable to recognize "doctrines of devils" in books about the afterlife?

Why do Christians address God and the devil in the same "prayer" as if they are equal in authority?

Why are some of our Christian leaders moving in an area that amounts to presumption? (The word *presumption* means "assuming prerogatives that are not yours.")

Why are there conflicting teachings on who is really in charge: Jesus, the devil, or the church?

The answers to all of the above questions can be found in one particular event in history, which few truly understand. In my study of good and evil angels, I came to the realization that one event is central to understanding the true role of angels in the world. That event was the death, resurrection, and ascension of Jesus Christ.

That God could love mankind so much that He would send His Son to die for them is still a mystery that even the angels seek to understand (1 Pet. 1:12). Fully understanding what happened at Calvary is the only way for us to understand the present levels of spiritual authority.

What happened when Jesus "gave up the ghost" and expired on the cross?

What happened during the three days He was in the grave?

What did it mean to Satan when Jesus was crucified—and then rose from the dead? What did it mean to him as "prince of the power of the air" and as "god of this world"?

First, let's look at what was happening to people under the old covenant when they died.

The Terms of the Old Covenant

A story Jesus told of a rich man and a beggar (Lazarus) gives us some insight into the real conditions of life after death (Luke 16:19–31). Both men died, and the angels carried Lazarus to "Abraham's bosom," or paradise. (From this we infer that angels escort the righteous dead when they leave this earth.)

On the other hand, the rich man found himself in "torments." He looked up and saw, on the other side of an abyss, the beggar—whom he had scorned—being welcomed by Father Abraham.

Why were Abraham and Lazarus able to see one another in this story?

Why wasn't paradise (or Abraham's bosom) in the third heaven with God?

Paradise is in heaven now, but that was not its location until after Jesus rose from the dead. Under the old covenant, after death all mankind went to a lower spiritual realm where there were two regions: the place for the righteous dead and the place for the wicked dead. In Hebrew this place was call *sheol,* and in Greek it was called Hades (which is the word poorly translated as "hell" in Luke 16:23.)[2]

As we describe what happened when Jesus' body was in the tomb, we will see what happened to the righteous dead who were kept in Hades.

From the Cross to the Throne

After hanging on the cross for several hours, Jesus cried out in a loud voice and "gave up the ghost," meaning that He died (Luke 23:46). He committed His spirit to the Father. In other words, He entrusted Himself completely into the hands of God.

David tells us prophetically what was happening:

> For thou wilt not leave my soul in hell [*sheol*]; neither wilt thou suffer thine Holy One to see corruption.   —Psalm 16:10

On the Day of Pentecost, Peter told his listeners that this verse referred to Jesus, not David (Acts 2:29–31). So Psalm 16:10 tells us two things about Jesus.

1. He must have gone into Hades, the place of the dead.

2. His body did not suffer corruption or begin to decay. (In those times, a body would normally begin to decay after three days, as happened with Lazarus.)

In Ephesians 4:9–10, Paul specifically said that Jesus descended into the lower parts of the earth as well as ascended far above all heavens. Peter was even more specific. He wrote that Jesus preached to the "spirits in prison" who disobeyed God before the flood (1 Pet. 3:18–20).

Yet another piece of the puzzle is found in Luke 23:39–43, where the two thieves were hanged with Jesus. One thief defended Jesus and asked to be remembered by Him in His kingdom. Jesus told him, "Today shalt thou be with me in paradise."

Using these Scriptures and others, I believe we can outline what happened to Jesus from the cross to the throne.

Jesus Descends to Hades

Jesus' spirit descended into Hades, where He apparently went first to the place of the righteous dead, called paradise or Abraham's bosom. When the penitent thief died, Jesus was there to receive his spirit because Jesus died first. It also is most probable that Jesus declared the good news of redemption to the righteous dead.

From paradise, He proceeded across the abyss into the portion of Hades reserved for the wicked dead. The word translated "preached" in 1 Peter 3:19 is not the kind of preaching we do today. It actually means "making a general proclamation," something similar to an announcement by a herald. Why this was necessary we are not told, and it is better not to speculate. It is enough simply to know that He did it.

Some people say that Jesus fought with Satan in Hades. I do not believe this is true because Scripture never describes Satan as being in the lower regions. There is no verse in the Bible that says the devil has ever been to hell or Hades.

On the other hand, there is evidence that the devil and his fallen angels live in the second heaven. There is a time in the future when Satan will be sent to *gehenna,* the lake of fire, which is the final destination of all wicked angels and humans (Rev. 20:15). (*Gehenna* is sometimes confused with Hades because both are described as having flames. [See Matthew 25:41; Luke 16:24.])

In other words, the part of Hades where the rich man was kept was similar to a holding cell for prisoners awaiting judgment. The lake of fire is the final prison of the universe. The sentence is eternal, forever and ever, with no possibility of parole.

Why were the righteous dead being held in the same realm instead of being in fellowship with God?

The reason is that, until the penalty for sin was paid, no human being could be in the presence of God. The animal sacrifices of the old covenant were like a deposit on a purchase (a promissory note). The purchase was planned and foreknown by God, but until the balance was paid, the purchase was not complete.

Without the blood of Jesus being deposited on the heavenly altar (Heb. 9:12–28), no human descendant of Adam could stand in the presence of God. The righteousness of a total pardon was promised to those whose hearts followed God. However, until Jesus actually was crucified, died, and resurrected, His righteousness was promised but not imputed.

Jesus Ascends to Heaven

Today, when a Christian dies, he or she is carried by angels directly to the presence of Jesus.

In Ephesians 4:8, Paul wrote that Jesus ascended and "led captivity captive." Paradise ascended with Jesus and is no longer in the realm of Hades, the "place of the dead." We see this in the death of the first martyr, Stephen. As Stephen was being stoned to death, he saw Jesus standing at the right hand of the Father in heaven and said, "Lord Jesus, receive my spirit" (Acts 7:59). Immediately afterward he died, and I believe his spirit went directly to Jesus.

There are many other verses that also support this, such as 2 Corinthians 5:8 in which Paul wrote of being "absent" from the body and "present" with the Lord.

In Revelation 1:18, Jesus said He had the keys of Death and Hell (Hades). I agree with British Bible scholar Derek Prince that Death and Hades are dark angels.[3] They are described as riding horses (Rev. 6:8), which could be a figurative or symbolic representation. However, both are described as being cast into the lake of fire along with the devil (Rev. 20:14). Symbols are not consigned to hell; only spiritual beings are.

Death, I believe, is the dark angel who has power over people's bodies, power to induce physical death. Hades is the dark angel who presides over the place of the dead where the wicked are being held pending judgment (Rev. 20:11–15).

In the Bible, to have keys means to have authority. So Jesus took the authority away from the angels who were in charge of death and hell. That must have been a dramatic scene

Paul wrote in Ephesians 4:8 that Jesus ascended after He descended. During the ascension, He led captives in His train and gave gifts to men.

I believe Jesus' appearance at His tomb was during His ascension to the Father. That's because only at the tomb did He tell someone not to touch Him. When the Old Testament high priest carried the blood into the holy of holies on the day of atonement, no one could touch him. If they did, they would be smitten dead. Jesus was our high priest taking His blood to the holy of holies in heaven.

When Mary saw Jesus in the garden, He said, "Touch me not; for I am not yet ascended to my Father" (John 20:17). Several other translations put this in the present tense: "I am ascending to My Father." (Howard Ervin, professor of Greek at Oral Roberts University, assures me this is the accurate translation.)

Later that same day, however, Jesus appeared to the disciples and told them to touch Him. During the next forty days, people not only saw Him in the flesh but also touched Him. He also ate and drank with them.

After Jesus appeared to Mary at the tomb, I believe He continued His ascension into the first heaven (the atmosphere) and on into the second heaven, the realm where both good and evil angels operate. This was where I believe the events of Colossians 2:15 took place:

> And having spoiled principalities and powers, he made a show of them openly, triumphing over them in it.

Judson Cornwall gives tremendous insight into the Greek word for "spoiled"—*apekduomai.* It is a term that referred to a military ceremony where a victorious Roman general would stand before a defeated enemy in the presence of their respective armies. While the defeated general stood at attention, the conquering general stripped his uniform of all insignia, medals, badges, and other symbols of authority. He also stripped him of all of his military names and titles and claimed them as his own.[4]

I am suggesting the possibility that in the same way, on His way to glory, Jesus stripped Satan of every vestige of power that God had given him before he rebelled and was expelled from heaven. Any authority that Satan once had now belonged to Jesus.

For a limited time, Satan had been the daystar, an angel of light, the anointed cherub, and the prince of this world. But for all eternity Jesus would be the bright and morning star, the light of the world, the anointed one, and the prince of life.[5]

Cornwall wrote:

> Every angel in the eternal abode knows that Satan has been completely stripped....Both hell and heaven know that Satan is merely a figurehead, a puppet, an exile. It is only mankind that seems unaware that the roaring lion (1 Pet. 5:8) has had his teeth pulled out and is on a leash to the lion of the tribe of Judah (Rev. 5:5).[6]

It must have been an incredibly dramatic moment as Jesus came to the gates of heaven with the righteous dead, having completed His victory over Satan and evil angels. David gives us a picture in Psalm 24 when he says:

> Lift up your heads, O ye gates; and be ye lift up, ye everlasting doors; and the King of glory shall come in. Who is this King of glory? The Lord strong and mighty, the Lord mighty in battle.
> —Psalm 24:8–9

Now we understand why Jesus had every right to say that "all power is given unto me in heaven and in earth" (Matt. 28:18). Because Jesus has authority, the church has authority. Jesus defeated Satan through His finished work and delegated His authority immediately and completely to the church (Mark 16:15–18; Acts 1:8).

The Authority of the Believer

What does all this have to do with the believer today?

Does the believer have authority over demons and fallen angels?

Do demons and fallen angels retain any authority over people?

The answer to these questions is found when believers realize the authority delegated to them through the finished work of Christ. Neil Anderson of Biola University wrote:

> When you don't understand the doctrinal truths pertaining to your position in Christ, you have no ground for success in the practical arena. How can you hope to stand firm against the schemes of the devil (Eph. 6:11), if you have not internalized that you are already victoriously raised up with Him and seated with Him in the heavenly places in Christ Jesus?[7]

If we are seated with Christ, then our position is far above all principalities and powers of darkness. Kenneth Hagin Sr., wrote: "Our position as the church is a position of authority, honor, and triumph—not failure, depression, and defeat."[8]

The truth of the authority of the believer has everything to do with authority in the angelic world. Our knowledge of authority affects both the good and bad angels. Both respond to authority. They understand authority, which many human beings do not. The biggest problem with the church is that we have never fully realized the finished work of Christ and how it relates directly to us.

When we understand that we already have authority over principalities and powers, we do not try to "pull them down" as if we still had to gain the ascendancy.

When we understand that we already have authority, we do not go to battle against the territorial spirits over our area. When we fight to take authority over Satan, we are attributing to him authority he does not have.

Why are the hosts of darkness ruling in so many countries, then? They rule because the systems of those countries are Satan's territories and believers are not walking in enough light to transform those territories through the Great Commission (Mark 16:15–18).

Why are the powers of darkness ruling in so many believers' lives? They rule because believers are not exercising the authority of Jesus, even if they know they have it.

We need to understand, however, that our authority in Christ gives us no authority over another person's will and right to choose. Even Jesus does not exercise His authority to make everyone get saved.

Authority Among Fallen Angels and Demons

What is authority anyway?

What does it mean to be "in authority"?

It means "to rule" something, "to be in charge." Some people confuse *authority* and *power.* Authority is the right to rule; power is the strength or force involved in enforcing authority.

In the heavenly realm, both good and evil angels operate without exception along lines of authority.

In earlier chapters, we have seen the apparent ranks among Satan's angels (Eph. 1:21; 6:12; Col. 1:16; 1 Pet. 3:22). I believe it helps to know what kind of a territorial spirit is over certain areas. You can then find the right scriptures to preach or pray against its thought systems. Where I differ with recent spiritual warfare teachings is with the strategies being taught and the doctrine behind the strategies.

"Spiritual mapping" is a fairly new teaching. It suggests studying the history and social patterns of areas to find what evil spirit is in charge of their spiritual systems. Why are some areas more oppressive, more idolatrous, more spiritually barren than others? George Otis Jr. asks these good questions:

> Why, for instance, has Mesopotamia put out such a long string of tyrannical rulers?
>
> Why is the nation of Haiti the premiere social and economic eyesore in the Western Hemisphere?
>
> Why do the Andean nations of South America [especially Colombia] always seem to rank near the top of the world's annual per capita homicide statistics?
>
> Why is there so much overt demonic activity in and around the Himalayan Mountains?
>
> Why has Japan been such a hard nut to crack with the gospel?[9]

Spiritual territoriality has a great deal to do with the way things are in any part of the world. In my twenty-five years of ministering in the Soviet world, I have been able to identify various spiritual powers over geographical areas.

In 1980, I was attending a Charismatic leadership conference near St. Louis. Fifty or sixty men had gathered to discuss what God was doing in the world. In the middle of the conference, a Roman Catholic lay leader walked in with the news that Pope John Paul had been shot.

The speaker immediately suggested we get on our knees and pray. As I began to intercede, a spiritual darkness came over me. I knew that a territorial spirit was behind the attack on the pope's life, and I recognized that spirit because I had dealt with it in the Soviet Union. I suspected the intelligence agency, the KGB, had something to do with the attack. (I was familiar with them because they had interrogated me five times.)

I said as much to the group. However, the next day the news reports said the man who shot the pope was a right-wing Muslim fundamentalist from Turkey. I am sure that it appeared as if my conclusions were wrong. I left it at that because I couldn't prove a subjective recognition of a spirit. About a year and a half later, though, the truth was revealed by the Mossad, Israel's intelligence service, that the pope's assassin actually had been trained by the KGB in Bulgaria.

There is no question in my mind that there are territorial spirits because the evidence of their activity is so apparent. However, one might ask this question: If the church has authority over evil powers, why are they still operating?

- Satan and his evil angels will operate until Adam's lease runs out.

- The believer has a lack of knowledge (Hosea 4:6).

- Sin in someone's life opens the door for oppression.

- A missing "shield of faith" lets fiery darts slip through (Eph. 6:16).

- An evil angel or demon cons someone into accepting it as an angel of light and receiving its thoughts and doctrines. This is happening right now across the United States and other countries through books, films, and videos about "angels."

However, the bottom line of all these questions is that God is in charge. Jesus has delegated all power and authority in heaven and earth to the church. Believers have authority over all the power of the enemy as they carry out Jesus' commission to evangelize the world (Mark 16:15-18).

The questions we now need to answer are these: What is the connection between angels and the Holy Spirit? If we, as believers, have authority over all the power of the enemy, then why do we still have the ministry of angels today when, as Christians, we have the Holy Spirit within to guide and direct us?

We are going to look into these questions in the next chapter.

19

The Holy Spirit, Angels, and Us

*Understanding the times properly requires that we reach
beyond our event-oriented mentalities to cultivate an appreciation for the concept of spiritual seasons. If we have
indeed entered a new season of divine initiative, we need to
understand what this really means.*[1]

—George Otis Jr.

Some years ago, I was ministering in Argentina with Omar
Cabrera, who founded the Centrifuge Church in Argentina,
which has a membership of more than 120,000 people. He
asked me a surprising question.

"Why don't people in your country ever see angels?" he asked
and then answered for himself: "People in the West are so educated,
so trained to be rational, that you believe only what you can experiment with in test tubes. People in Argentina are very simple. They
live next to nature. They talk to the invisible world, and the invisible
world talks back to them. Almost every Sunday in our church, someone comes in with a story of having talked to an angel."

My response was typical for a skeptical Westerner, "We have a
lot of people in America who see angels on occasion, but I question
the validity of their experiences."

Omar said, "We check out these stories here and find that most
are authentic."

He then asked me a second question, "Have you ever noticed
the connection between the Holy Spirit and angels in the Book of
Acts?"

In all of my years of ministry no one had ever asked me that or
even indicated that such a connection existed. On the airplane back
to Miami, I began to read through Acts, and again I was surprised.

In Acts 8, Philip was in the middle of a great evangelistic crusade in Samaria when an angel appeared to him with directions to leave and go south on the road from Jerusalem to Gaza. Philip obeyed.

He started out on the road and met an important official from Ethiopia who was in charge of the state treasury for the queen. This man apparently was a God-fearer who had been to Jerusalem to worship and was now riding in his chariot, reading from a scroll of Isaiah. How did Philip know what to do next? Did the angel appear again and tell him what to do?

No, the Bible says the Holy Spirit then spoke to Philip and told him to approach the chariot and stay near it (Acts 8:29). An angel set up the encounter, and after Philip obeyed, the Holy Spirit took over with final instructions. It is obvious, therefore, that the Holy Spirit and angels work together.

The same thing happened when Peter was sent to Cornelius, a Roman centurion in the elite Italian regiment who also was a God-fearer. An angel appeared to Cornelius and told him specifically to send for Peter, who at that time was in the home of Simon the tanner in Joppa.

God gave Peter a vision of clean and unclean animals as a symbol of the fact that, to God, Gentiles were cleansed by the sacrifice of Jesus on the cross.

> While Peter thought on the vision, the Holy Spirit said unto him, Behold, three men seek thee. Arise therefore, and get thee down, and go with them, doubting nothing: *for I have sent them.*
> —Acts 10:19–20, emphasis added

The Bible says the angel sent them, but it also says the Holy Spirit sent them. Angels, therefore, are under direct orders of the Holy Spirit.

The pattern seems to be that the Holy Spirit may send an angel to get you headed in the right direction, but He will also give follow-up instructions Himself.

When Philip obeyed the Holy Spirit and drew near to the chariot, he saw the man reading Scripture. The obvious way to start a conversation with this stranger was to ask him, a non-Jew, if he understood what he was reading. Neither the angel nor the Holy

Spirit put words in Philip's mouth or led him through the assignment by the hand.

The same thing was true of Peter and Cornelius. The angel headed them in the right direction, the Holy Spirit gave the basic assignments, but the details of carrying out the assignments were left to the two men.

Angelic Assignments

After my father's retirement, he lived for a time on Point Roberts in Washington State. Although this peninsula is a part of the United States, it can only be reached from Canada. Several years ago, I went to visit him with some relatives. At the end of our visit, we were traveling back in a van through some very steep mountains in British Columbia.

As my father was sitting in his home drinking coffee, an angel suddenly appeared to him and said, "Terry and his friends are in very grave danger." He saw a mini-vision of our van going off a cliff and hurtling through the air.

My father has a strong knowledge of the Word of God, not just of the verses and facts but also of the principles involved. He knew from the Holy Spirit what needed to be done, and he did it. He knew it was up to him to do something, or the angel would not have appeared to him.

He spoke out of his heart, "In the name of Jesus, take care of that situation!"

The angel left immediately and after a while appeared again, saying, "The situation is taken care of, and they are all right." Then he vanished again. We completed our journey safely.

This may not sound like the same circumstances as Philip's or Peter's because it involved the safety of family members, not someone's salvation. However, the principle is the same: First, the angel brings a message; then, knowledge comes from the Holy Spirit about what to do (which my father already knew); and finally, action on the part of those involved.

My father knew about the role of angels from personal experience as well as from studying the Bible. When I was still a teenager, Dad was spared a tragic death by an angel. He farmed as well as pastored, and one summer he rented our farm of more than six hundred acres to another farmer. One day, my father was helping this man, who had gotten a large tractor stuck in a pothole. He wanted Dad to pull him out with a second and much smaller tractor.

It was very hilly terrain, and the first tractor was mired down to the axles and pointed up a steep incline. My father was concerned and had an impression that he should not attempt this. (That impression was what is called a "check" or a "witness" from the Holy Spirit.) He told the farmer how he felt, but the man insisted it was safe, that he had done it before.

Against his better judgment, Dad climbed onto the smaller tractor, which had hydraulic pipes surrounding the tractor seat. Climbing into the driver's seat was almost like climbing into the cockpit of a small airplane. When Dad let out the clutch, the tractor bucked and went straight up in the air in a somersault.

As it began to flip, Dad heard a voice call out, "Jump!" He knew it was an angel, and he tried to jump, but he couldn't get untangled from the pipes quickly enough. Then he felt himself lifted up and set gently down on the ground some twenty feet away.

The farmer did not see him pulled out of the tractor seat by the angel. He only saw the tractor flip over and smash into the ground. He shouted in fear. He believed my father was under the tractor, so he threw himself down on the ground and began to dig furiously, trying to get him out. When Dad called out to him, he turned around white as a sheet, obviously shocked. The man then knelt down by the tractor wheel and began to shake.

My father did not hear the Holy Spirit tell the angel to intervene, but he knew that was what had happened. He knew this from Hebrews 1:14: "Are they not all ministering spirits, sent forth to minister for them who shall be heirs of salvation?"

What does that mean?

How far do angels go to fulfill this assignment?

They go as far as the Spirit sends them and as far as the believer will receive them.

I want to demonstrate through the following examples that ministry on behalf of those who are heirs of salvation is an interaction of the angels of God, the Holy Spirit of God, and the children of God operating in willing submission.

A man in our time who described having a number of visits from angels was the late Roland Buck, pastor of Central Assembly of God in Boise, Idaho. I have mentioned that he was a friend of mine. Charles and Frances Hunter, Texas evangelists, wrote a book about his encounters with angels that stirred up quite a bit of controversy. Fifteen to twenty years ago, people were not as ready to talk of angels.

Regardless of the controversy, the important thing to me was that I knew Roland personally, and he was a good man. He was as humble and unassuming a man as I have ever met. I had a great respect for him. He and the angels who appeared to him played a part in my life's assignment.

Let me explain. As a thirteen-year-old boy, I attended a camp meeting at Nanoose Bay in Vancouver Island, British Columbia. One night a speaker from the American Assemblies of God gave a stirring call for commitment and a challenge for missions, and the Holy Spirit began to move on me. I have recounted in another book what a rebellious teenager I was and what a struggle I went through before yielding to the call of God.

After the meeting, I did not want to go back to the cabin where my folks were staying, so I remained in the meeting hall. I had been deeply stirred and sensed God moving in my heart, but I did not know what it meant. Everyone else left for the night, and the lights were turned out. Midnight passed, 1:00 a.m. passed, and then around 2:00 a.m., the evangelist returned.

His name was Dwight McLaughlin, and he had left his Bible on the pulpit. I was sitting on a bench in the shadows where he could not see me, but I could see him in the moonlight. I sat motionless, but he sensed someone was there and called out. When I answered, he felt his way to where I sat in a back corner.

He said, "You know, the Lord must have sent me to you," and explained that he had awakened and felt impressed to go get his Bible. Then he asked if he could pray for me. When he laid his hand on me, warmth radiated through me. I started to tremble.

He said, "Young man, I see a vision. God has called you, and He is going to send you around the world to preach the gospel. I see crowds of thousands and hundreds of thousands."

He described a broad field with multitudes of faces, and he saw me standing before them with an open Bible in my hand. Although these people did not speak English, my words somehow went straight to their hearts.

Now, I did not want to be a preacher. I had been a "preacher's kid" all my life, and we had lived on "love offerings"—all love and no offerings! However, I believe what McLaughlin saw was the crowd that God gave us in Poland many years later. Three hundred thousand people gathered in an outdoor field—a half-mile of people on each side of the podium.

The next morning at camp meeting, McLaughlin called me up in front of the crowded tabernacle and told everyone to take a good look at me because I was called to a worldwide mission. I was more embarrassed than anything else at that point.

Years later, in 1977, I was traveling with my music group Living Sound and came to minister at Roland Buck's church in Boise, Idaho. Roland and I were outside the church one night sitting in his car when he told me a story.

He began by saying very quietly, "Terry, I talked with Gabriel last week."

At the time, I knew no more about angels than the average Christian, perhaps less than some, and I said, "Gabriel who?"

When he told me it was the angel Gabriel, I said, "Oh, Roland, come on! Gabriel hasn't been heard from since the days of the early church." I was like the Greek professor who told Charlie Shedd when he wrote an essay on angels that "much of the Bible is history, and we should respect it as such."[2]

Then next year I was back at Roland's church, and he told me some more about angels. The most descriptive way of explaining my reaction is that he simply "blew my mind" with his stories. The year after, 1979, I flew directly to his church for a missions conference after a preaching engagement in Australia.

As my co-evangelist, Gordon Calmeyer, and I were sitting at breakfast with Roland one morning, Gordon shocked me with a question for Roland about angels.

"Well, pastor," he said, "if these angels are talking to you all the time, and your church is a strong supporter of our ministry, why don't you ask the angels about us?"

I was embarrassed and said, "Oh, Gordon, you don't ask angels things like that."

Actually, I did not know what you asked angels because I had never seen one to ask him anything. But Roland sat there with a slight smile and did not say anything. We went our separate ways, and I forgot about the conversation.

Three months later I was asked to appear on a national Christian television program to introduce Roland. A recent book about him was attracting attention to what he said was happening in Boise with the angels. Before the program went on the air, we were in a room backstage together, just the two of us.

He said, "Terry, do you remember when you were a thirteen-year-old and attended a camp meeting in Canada?"

I had never told another soul what happened that night.

Roland said, "Do you remember about 2:00 a.m., the camp evangelist"—and he actually named Dwight McLaughlin—"walked into the building? Do you remember that you were sitting there praying, and he walked over and laid hands on you?"

I said, "Roland, how do you know about that night?"

He looked at me and just smiled. I exclaimed, "Are you kidding me? The angels told you this?"

He nodded and said the angels had awakened McLaughlin because that was the night God had chosen for my ordination into ministry.

"The angels told me a lot about you," he said. "They told me of times in your childhood when you went through great difficulties. You had to learn as a child to stand up against odds and overcome them. God was getting you ready for your ministry. He was building iron into your character because one day you would have to deal with the KGB.

"When you go into the Soviet Union, there is a ministering band of angels that goes in first and prepares the way. Then there is another band that comes from behind to protect you while you are there. The angels have been with you all this time. They have been working with you." Those ministering band of angels have traveled with me wherever I go, and, as I shared with you earlier, even in the most dangerous places in the world, like the Middle East.

From that time on, I lost my skepticism about angels ministering today for the saints.

Fullness-of-Time Moments

There is an interesting word in the Greek language, *kairos,* which is translated "the fullness of time" in the Bible. The Greeks coined this word to describe the arrival of these crisis times, these crossroads in life when changes occur. The Bible speaks of only two such major events: the fullness of time when Jesus was born (Gal. 4:4) and the fullness of time when He will return again (Eph. 1:10). However, there are *kairos* moments occurring all through history and even in our own lives.

The fullness of time means the time when all things are in place so that changes can be made. When the earth reaches exactly the right point in its rotation around the sun, seasons change. In the fullness of time, spring arrives out of winter and summer out of spring. This term conveys a unique sense of God's timing.

Today, *kairos* moments are all about us in the world. Extraordinary events are flowing out of the intercession of God's people, directed by God's timing.

George Otis Jr. wrote in *The Last of the Giants* that if we are into a new season of God (and I believe we are), "new rules apply, old bets are off, and we cannot return to business as usual, ever."[3]

Otis says that *kairos* events, especially if they involve the demise of kings and ideologies, tend to create spiritual vacuums. If God's people do not understand their role and seize the moment, chaos results. The enemy is then able to turn things to his advantage.

Today particularly, we need to be as the sons of Issachar in the early days of Israel: "men that had understanding of the times, to know what Israel ought to do" (1 Chron. 12:32).

Look at the vacuum left by the outdated worldview of Marxism in Eastern Europe. Millions are bereft of their spiritual moorings. They realized their philosophy is bankrupt. The result is more freedom but also chaos and confusion, which many feel is leading to another and even worse regime.

What would the sons of Issachar say the former Soviets should do?

What would their "understanding" tell them America should do today?

We can miss the part that angels and the Holy Spirit are calling us to play during the *kairos* in this new millennium. Consequently, something might not be turned for the purposes of God.

Suppose Philip had not obeyed the angel? Would Ethiopia have had the gospel?

Suppose Peter had not gone with the men sent by Cornelius, or suppose Cornelius had not sent them? I am sure the Gentiles still would have been evangelized because that was always God's sovereign plan. However, the lives of Peter and Cornelius might have been quite different.

Would you know what to do at a *kairos* moment in your life? Do you know what role angels may play in the fulfillment of God's plan for you? They stand by, ready to be activated into action.

20

"Activating" Angels

Bless the LORD, ye his angels, that excel in strength, that do his commandments, hearkening unto the voice of his word.

—Psalm 103:20

I hesitate to say "activating" angels since that term has been misused in recent years to imply that angels are our servants, not just fellow servants of God. However, used in the sense that we can make it possible for them to help us, activating is an accurate term. They stand by watching, "unactivated," if we are not "on the right road" at the right time and place.

Essentially, angels are agents of the government of God, the sovereign ruler of the universe (Isa. 46:8–11; Rom. 11:36; Eph. 1:11). Activities of angels in the Bible were directly related to God's sovereign plan.

Nothing done by any man controlled the angels. Their primary motivation is obeying and serving God. However, men can do some things that activate angels, or put them in motion to act on their behalf.

In studying angels, I have discovered five biblical principles that seem to activate them to fulfill their role of serving God by serving His people. In other words, our actions seem to influence their actions. Those five principles are: authority, sacrifice, prayer, giving in obedience (or alms), and praise and worship.

Authority

The first principle is obedience and submission to authority. When angels see us operating properly under authority, they are released to minister for us as the Holy Spirit wills.

The entire universe runs on the authority principle—including Satan's kingdom. The one place where authority is generally resisted is here on Earth.

As often as I have studied the subject of angels, I have been impressed time and again with the principle of authority as it relates to angels.

God's angels operate under God's authority.

Satan's angels operate under Satan's authority.

There is order in Satan's evil kingdom because it is an imitation of God's orderly, righteous kingdom. The most important point of all, however, as we consider just what the angelic hierarchy may signify, is that Jesus is high above them all. He has no equal and no superior.

He delegated His authority over evil spirits to the disciples even before He was crucified and resurrected. His example shows us how we are to walk in that delegated authority.

> Behold, I give unto you power to tread on serpents and scorpions, and over all the powers of the enemy: and nothing shall by any means hurt you.
>
> Notwithstanding, in this rejoice not, that the spirits are subject unto you; but rather rejoice, because your names are written in heaven.
> —Luke 10:19–20

Evil spirits can tell whether a person is operating in the authority of God's Word.

A biblical example involves seven sons of a Jewish priest named Sceva. They attempted to cast out an evil spirit in the name of Jesus "whom Paul preacheth." But they were not born again, so they did not have the right to use the authority of Jesus, and the evil spirit overcame all seven of them (Acts 19:13–16). In fact, the possessed man tore the clothes off the seven men and chased them down the street.

The spirit's reply to these men was, "Jesus I know, and Paul I know; but who are ye?" (Acts 19:15). You can almost hear the taunting belligerence in the tone of that spirit. He would not obey anyone who did not have authority over him. This is a law in the spirit realm—the law of authority.

Neil Anderson says, "Spiritual authority is not a tug-of-war on a horizontal plane; it is a vertical chain of command." He wrote:

> Jesus Christ has all authority; He is on top.
>
> We are underneath Jesus, because He gave His authority and power to His servants to be exercised in His name.
>
> And Satan and his demons? They're at the bottom, subject to the authority Christ has invested in us. They have no more right to rule your life than a buck private has to order a general to clean the latrine.[1]

If the church could get hold of this, the world would become a different place, even in the midst of the *cosmos diabolicus.*

Authority *carries* responsibility, and authority *follows* responsibility; it does not precede it.

The Great Commission demonstrates this. Jesus said, "*All authority* in heaven and on earth has been given to me. Therefore go and make disciples of all nations," (Matt. 28:18–19, NIV, emphasis added). This is an incredible responsibility for the church. To get the job done, He has delegated His authority completely to the church. In other words, Jesus said, "Since I gave you the responsibility, you also have the authority of My name to do it."

If we don't take responsibility in this certain area, then our authority is canceled out. You may rule or govern by force, through some kind of power, but there is no authority behind it. Like the seven sons of Sceva, there is no point speaking to demons, much less principalities and powers, if you have not assumed responsibility for the lusts of your flesh.

Another element of authority is submission. Submission to authority is an act of obedience, but it is also a form of faithfulness.

If we want authority in the kingdom of God, we must learn first to be good followers and to submit to authority with the right attitude. God told the Israelites that if they were "willing and obedient" they would "eat the good of the land" (Isa. 1:19). Obedience under duress or with a reluctant heart is not true obedience.

In other words, if you want to operate in authority, you have to come under authority. That's because the levels of authority in the world are established by God. If you want to find out if you're under authority, see how you measure up to these seven guidelines. (These seven levels of authority are listed in order of supremacy.)

1. We must be obedient to the sovereign will of God. This is the highest level of authority. It is absolute and infallible.

2. We must be obedient to the veracity (truth) of God's Word. God's Word holds the position in the universe of veracious authority, with *veracious* meaning it is "always true."

3. We must not go against our own conscience. Some people's consciences will not permit them to do what other people can do. An angel of God would not ask you to go against your conscience—but an angel of light might.

4. We must obey the laws of the land and of our churches, as long as those directives do not conflict with those of the first three levels of authority. That's because all authority in the church and the world is delegated by Christ (Rom. 13:1). However, I am not advocating blind obedience to any law or man, but accepting civic and church authority as ordained and delegated by God.

   Attempts to coerce obedience by emotional or spiritual force—fear, shame, guilt, and other negative manipulative techniques—are abuses of authority. Tyrannical political systems, such as Nazism and communism, are abusive authorities, not true representations of God-ordained authority.

5. We must honor stipulative authority, which is authority that is specified by agreement. An example of this kind of authority is parties signing a contract that is legally binding.

6. We must honor tradition if it has not become abusive or is not in conflict with other levels of authority. For example, tradition is wrong when it is given higher authority than the Word of God (Matt. 15:3–6).

7. We must honor the authority of others, which stems from their talents, abilities, or skills. This is called functional

authority, and, again, it's origin is in God. We go to a doctor when we're sick—not a mechanic.[2]

Angels and the words we speak

The authority of our words depends on whether or not we obey or submit to the levels of authority over us.

Let's compare the difference between Mary's words of faith and Zacharias's words of doubt when they had visits from the angel Gabriel. It must have been difficult for both of them to believe Gabriel; Zacharias was too old to have a child, and Mary was a virgin.

Zacharias asked a question that was full of doubt—he almost seemed to be asking for a sign that what Gabriel said would really happen (Luke 1:18). "Whereby shall I know this? for I am an old man, and my wife well stricken in years," he said. Gabriel acted quickly to stop Zacharias's words of unbelief (Luke 1:20). Zacharias was struck dumb and could not speak until John was born. He got his sign, but it probably wasn't the kind he wanted. Angels are sensitive to what we say. It appears our words of faith or doubt can "activate" or "deactivate" them.

Mary *submitted* to the authority of God's Word and said, "Be it unto me according to thy word." I believe she became pregnant at that very moment. Her faith activated the Word of God, which immediately became flesh inside of her. Her submission to authority became faith that resulted in the conception of Jesus, the Son of God, in her womb. Her response is one of the most powerful faith statements in the Bible.

Jesus taught that we are redeemed, justified, or made righteous by our words, and we are also condemned by our words (Matt. 12:37). When we are sensitive to God, it is easy to discern the oppressive atmosphere created by words of doubt and unbelief.

The church teaches angels

Through Jesus, the church has been raised higher than the angels. We are of the family of God and seated at the right hand of the throne of God with Jesus. What a position of authority this gives to the church! Jesus delegated His authority to the church, and because angels understand authority, they are watching to see what we do with that authority.

When Christians get the revelation of their position in Christ, when they stand against the enemy in the power of the name of Jesus, recognizing the authority God has given to the church, angels understand that authority. If our desire is to see God's will done on earth, and we are under authority, angels will flow with us.

Sacrifice

Sacrificing in any area out of love for God is the second principle that I believe activates angels. It shows a wholeheartedness toward God that brings a response. Sacrifice is actually closely related to praise and worship.

I wrote about sacrifice in one of my earlier books:

> God required that Cain and Abel bring a sacrifice to Him. Abel offered the animal sacrifice that was pleasing to the Lord (a substitution of a living being for himself). Cain offered the Lord the first part of his harvest, the fruit of the ground, but this was unacceptable (involving no sacrifice). As a result, Cain killed Abel out of jealousy.
>
> Abraham and David clearly understood the principle of sacrifice. Abraham was willing to sacrifice his son Isaac to the Lord on Mount Moriah. An angel appeared as Abraham raised his knife, prepared to take Isaac's life. David had to offer a sacrifice to God on the threshing floor of Ornan the Jebusite in order to stop the death angel whose sword was stretched over Jerusalem to destroy it.[3]

Why does God require sacrifice?

From the time Adam and Eve disobeyed, man has been the creature separated from the Creator by sin. The only way to approach God's holiness was through the substitutionary death of a living creature. The penalty for disobedience, required of all the human race after Adam fell, was death (Gen. 2:17). Until Jesus died vicariously once and for all, there had to be a death. Blood is a proof of such death, because the life is in the blood (Deut. 12:23). Animal sacrifice was a substitution—a merciful token of the one-time sacrifice of Jesus yet to come.

Why did David refuse to take the threshing floor of Ornan (Araunah) as a gift, but insist on paying full price for it before he made sacrifice to God (2 Sam. 24:18–25; 1 Chron. 21:17–30; 2 Chron. 3:1)?

David knew it was not a real offering unless it had cost him something. Human nature (our souls) would far prefer to praise God when things are going well, but to grumble and complain when they are not!

We tend to say, "God, what have You done for me lately?"

That attitude will not activate angels on our behalf.

Sacrificial worship provides a legal right for the angels to ascend and descend to and from God's throne bringing help to the saints. Gideon and Manoah and his wife offered sacrifices while they were being visited by angels, and the angels returned to heaven while the sacrifices burned (Judg. 6:21; 13:20). Most churches have praise and worship services, but most do not really understand what they are doing.

When Gabriel appeared to Zacharias to announce the birth of John the Baptist, it was while the priest was offering a sacrifice of incense to the Lord. Incense is a symbol of pure worship. In other words, Zacharias's sacrifice unto the Lord brought the angel to him with an answer to his lifelong prayer for a son.

I have found that if I can lead people into a sacrifice of praise, something about that brings angelic involvement. This is especially true of those who are sick and suffering.

Prayer—the Word of God on Our Lips

The third principle that activates angels is prayer, especially praying God's Word back to Him. There is no question that prayer activates angels on our behalf. Moses' prayers of repentance on behalf of the Israelites saved them from destruction several times (Num. 14:11–21; 21:5–9; and others). Abraham's intercession on behalf of Lot and his family activated angels to rescue them (Gen. 18:17–33). Those are two of many biblical examples.

The primary way to renew our minds so that any thoughts dropped in by evil spirits cannot find a lodging place is to meditate on the Bible. I have found that something special happens in the angelic kingdom when Christians speak God's Word in the midst of contrary circumstances. It somehow releases the angelic world to work alongside us.

Our prayers are much more effective when we pray God's Word back to Him. That allows us to get in agreement with Him instead of wasting time and energy imploring Him to get in agreement with us. Many times we tend to pray the problem and talk about the problem so much that we finally operate in "negative faith"—faith that something bad is going to happen or is happening.

Problems do not activate angels. God's Word activates angels.

Promises from God's Word bring provisions, including the assistance of angels if that is needed. Someone has said there are seven thousand promises in the Bible. God does not want to hear the problem. He wants to hear the promise that fixes the problem. He wants to hear us praise Him in advance for that promise. He honors prayer that costs us something.

Remember, prayer by the church brought an angel to Peter in prison. Prayer brought an angel to shut the mouths of lions for Daniel. Faith words (prayer) by the three Hebrew children brought the fourth man into the fiery furnace.

Giving in Obedience

The fourth principle that activates angels involves giving to God's work, God's people, or to the poor and needy. Something about money and its use by the church touches the world of angels. Sacrificial giving activates angels as much as sacrificial praise. Evil spirits are trying today to hinder giving by God's people.

Cornelius, the first Gentile to be filled with the Holy Spirit, was a giver. The angel told him his prayers and his alms (money) had come up as a memorial before God (Acts 10:3).

When Satan became "god of this world" (2 Cor. 4:4), the finances of the world also passed under Satan's authority. The world economic system is Satan's system, his way of handling trade and money, not God's.

However, through the work Jesus did on the cross, the authority over the world's resources once again became God's. Because God has given us the responsibility to reach the world, He also has given us the authority to get the job done. Through the delegation of that authority, the church should be taking dominion over the silver and gold through biblical principles. Our stewardship in finance demonstrates probably more than anything else whether we have come under God's authority. The angels are aware of how we handle our money.

Kenneth Hagin Sr. used to say that when the Lord showed him the ministry of angels, it included help with finances. He was given these three steps to activate angelic help:

1. Claim what you need.

2. Tell the devil to take his hands off your money or resources.

3. Tell the ministering angels to go forth and bring you what is needed.

Hagin said the angels of the Lord are waiting for the church to give orders according to the Word of God and under the direction of the Holy Spirit.

Willie George, pastor of Church on the Move in Tulsa, Oklahoma, also believes very firmly that angels are involved with finances on behalf of the children of God.

The principle of giving in obedience was demonstrated to me when I was a very young pastor. This incident changed the course of my entire life. In 1967, I pastored a little church in Hatton, Saskatchewan, on the prairies of western Canada. My father was pastor of a larger church in Medicine Hat, Alberta, fifty miles away. My congregation numbered about twenty-five; it was an event when thirty people showed up for a meeting!

Obviously, a congregation this size could not pay me a full salary, so I supplemented my income by working with a local farmer, Ed Stahl. Ed was a successful farmer with a herd of five hundred purebred Herefords running on thirteen square miles of fairly barren, dry prairie land. Finding water for their stock was one of the biggest problems for area ranchers and farmers.

However, Ed was a very unusual man and one of the most godly, honest men I have ever known. He did not walk when he worked; he trotted, and all day long he prayed and talked to the Lord. One night, in a vision, God showed him where pockets of water form on the prairies. After that, Ed found water everywhere he dug for it.

He also had large wheat and hay operations, and my work included branding cattle in the spring and riding a tractor sowing wheat seed. During the summer, I spent long periods baling hay, hauling the heavy hay bales, and stacking them in the yard. Then, in the fall, I rode the combine and helped with the wheat harvest.

In the late summer of 1967, I heard that Oral Roberts was coming to Edmonton, Alberta, for a healing crusade. Edmonton is about three hundred fifty miles north of Medicine Hat, and I got permission from Ed to take off work to attend one of the meetings. I had never seen Oral Roberts in person and did not know very much about his ministry.

I made the trip during the day. That night Roberts preached and prayed for the sick, which I watched intently, then I left for the parking lot.

In the lobby, I passed a large table with books and tapes and another table with literature promoting a school just started in Tulsa, Oklahoma, named Oral Roberts University. I paused at the book table for a moment, then picked up one of the brochures about the university.

As I picked it up, I had an overwhelming inner awareness that I was to attend ORU. I felt the call of God so strongly that I literally groaned. The last thing I wanted to do was go to school two thousand miles away! The biggest problem would be tuition and other expenses. My weekly salary was only about fifty dollars. There was no way I would be able to save the money. Besides that, like many other young preachers, I felt I was ready to "turn the world upside down" with the Bible school education I already had!

During the long trip home tears rolled down my cheeks as this strong call from God echoed inside me. For the next three months I wrestled with this, not telling anyone else about it, not even my father or mother. I did not mention it to Ed as we worked side by side during those three months. However, after three months of struggling every night with this call and my uncertainty about finances, I finally gave up.

One night, I said to the Lord, "All right! I'll go to Tulsa!"

The next day Ed and I were working together digging holes for fence posts. This is hard, back-breaking work, and I paused for a moment with a posthole augur in my hand and with sweat rolling down my forehead. Ed was standing at the back of a half-ton pickup truck pulling fence posts out of the truck bed to drop into the holes I dug.

I said, "Ed, I made a major decision last night. I believe the Lord has called me to attend Oral Roberts University, and I have made up my mind. I don't know how yet, but I'm going to go."

Tears came into his eyes so suddenly that I thought he had dropped a post on his toe.

He said, "Get in the truck. I want to show you something."

So I jumped in, and we traveled a couple of miles across the prairie up to the top of a hill.

"Do you see that spot over there?" he said. "Three months ago I was working in the field with one of the bulls when suddenly an angel of the Lord stood before me.

"The light was so bright I didn't dare look at him, and I fell on my knees. The angel spoke to me and said, 'Terry Law is going to make a decision. He is going to go to Oral Roberts University in Tulsa. When he makes that decision, God the Father wants you to cover the financial obligations of his university education. You are to pay the bills and make sure everything is taken care of.'"

It was my turn for tears to well up in my eyes. The decision I had struggled with, which looked so impossible, had been taken care of by the Lord even while He was calling me to go. Ed was faithful to the command of the Lord and covered my entire university education.

Since my graduation, I have seen literally hundreds of thousands of people make decisions for Jesus Christ in my missionary travels around the world. I believe that Ed Stahl has a share in every one of those people because he was obedient to the words of the angel sent by God.

Praise and Worship

The fifth principle that seems to activate angels is praise and worship of God.

As I mentioned in chapter fourteen, before he fell, I believe Satan led the angelic hosts in praise and worship to the Father. He was heaven's choir director. Music was not created as a tool—even for evangelism—although God does use it that way. Music was origi-nally ordained for one purpose—to worship the Father.

When Lucifer took his eyes off God and focused them on his own beauty and brilliance, something happened inside him. He became filled with pride. He began to desire worship for himself instead of giving and leading worship to God.

Satan's primary drive today is still to get worship for himself in any way that he can. His temptation of Jesus was designed to get the Lord to worship him! As Chafer wrote, one can hardly think of a more audacious, arrogant, conceited act. He failed with Jesus, who told him it was written that only God shall be worshiped and served.[4]

Satan's challenge concerning Job was one of the greatest insults he has ever given God.[5] He implied that God really cannot be loved for Himself, but only for what He does for people or for what He gives them. Satan was saying God has to bribe people to serve Him. No wonder the Lord allowed Job to be tested! God knew what Satan was saying could be proven false. He knew Job's heart.

Jesus asked the same thing of the multitudes who followed Him after the miracle of the loaves and fishes. In effect, He said, "Are you following Me because of who I am, or because of what I can do for you?" (See John 6:26–27.)

True worship comes out of love and reverence, not fear, coer-cion, or a desire to be better off. This is what Satan has never under-stood. Judson Cornwall wrote:

> Satan is still far more interested in worship than in sin. He is more likely to be in church than in the worst den of iniquity in any area. This fallen angel would rather pervert a person's worship than cor-rupt his morals, for he knows that if he can pervert our worship, we will corrupt our morals.[6]

Satan is a very religious being who desires and probably needs praise and worship. His goal is far less to destroy mankind than it is to receive worship from those created to worship God. He knows the power that praise and worship generate in the spiritual realm. He knows that praise and worship generate healing, such as the woman whose hearing was restored and the little boy who was healed of asthma. (See chapter nine.)

If Satan cannot subvert it to attention on himself, he tries to kill praise and worship altogether by turning it into ritualistic religion.

Today, Satan is working on people, whispering in the ears of anyone who appears to have talent, promising them popularity and prosperity. Many top music groups today actually give Satan the credit for the lyrics they "receive" while high on drugs. Some groups perform songs seeking sympathy and worship for Satan. Christians who chant Satan's name or sing choruses about him as a part of spiritual warfare do not realize it, but he counts that as worship, not warfare.

Music played an incredibly important role in the Bible. There are more than eight hundred references to music, while hell is only mentioned seventy times. Our church services would be more productive in spiritual terms if we could learn that music is not a preliminary to the message, nor an icebreaker to get people warmed up. The song service is the protocol that God designed for the body of Christ to come into His presence.

Protocol is the procedure to be followed in approaching royalty and dignitaries on earth, a "code of ceremonial forms."

When we were invited to the Vatican, a monsignor took me aside and instructed me on the proper protocol. He said, "Terry, you are a Protestant leader. When a Protestant meets the pope, he does not respond to him as a Roman Catholic would. I want to tell you the proper phrases so that you will feel comfortable. You will not feel as if you are compromising your beliefs, or fear that you might show disrespect to a head of state."

I was taught protocol because addressing a cardinal, as we knew him first in Poland, and addressing the pope require different approaches. When I met Pope John Paul II, I felt as comfortable talking with him as I had when he was a cardinal. I knew the proper way to approach him.

The highest office in the universe is God the Father. If earthly officials require a certain protocol to approach them with respect, how much more should we feel that way about the Creator? Visitors usually bring gifts to heads of state. My group and I also took gifts to the pope: a cowboy hat from Oklahoma and other things.

The psalmist David indicated that the first step in the protocol of approaching God is thanksgiving. In Psalm 100:4, David wrote that we should enter into His gates with thanksgiving. The next step is to enter His courts with praise. Using the pattern of the tabernacle, David was saying, "Come into the outer court of God with thanksgiving and into the holy place with praise."

Thanksgiving in the Bible is retelling what God had already done for people. How often God's children come to Him with shopping lists of what we need or want Him to do. How seldom do we come with a "thanksgiving list" from the past. However, giving thanks for past blessings is one of the greatest faith builders that I know.

In the story of Jehoshaphat, king of Judah, we see an example of protocol in approaching God (2 Chron. 20:1–29). Jehoshaphat's heart was filled with fear when he found that three kings had invaded his territory with their armies.

The king first went to the Lord with thanksgiving. He reminded him of His greatness and of what He had done for the Israelites previously (2 Chron. 20:5–12). Then he essentially asked God to do it again.

A plan given to Judah by God through a young prophet was to send the Levites, the priests, out ahead of the army singing and praising the Lord for His mercy that endures forever. A group of singers heading out toward the enemy ahead of the soldiers would have been afraid, but they obeyed in the face of fear. They brought gifts to God of sacrificial praise, and God "set ambushments" (2 Chron. 20:22). The result was that the three armies—Moab, Ammon, and Mount Seir—turned on one another and destroyed one another.

As I read this one day, the word *ambushments* caught my attention. I began to trace it through the Bible. I saw that God consistently uses angels to set up ambushes. Some of these were for individuals such as Balaam. Others were *for* Israel and Judah. Still other ambushments of God were *against* Israel and Judah when the nations departed from following God's ways.

Perhaps the angels sang along with Jehoshaphat's priests. As you've read earlier in the book, there have been many reports of people seeing angels during praise and worship services. Other people have heard angels singing along with the congregation. So, angels may not only watch us worshiping, but also join in.

21

The Truth About Angels

You cannot put [God] off with speculations about your next door neighbours or memories of what you have read in books. What will all that chatter and hearsay count (will you even be able to remember it?) when the anaesthetic fog which we call "nature" or "the real world" fades away and the Presence in which you have always stood becomes palpable, immediate, and unavoidable?[1]

—C. S. Lewis

For fifty years we have been in one of those periods, a cycle in history, when belief in the supernatural has been repressed so much that it seems weird, foolish, and irrational. Now the pendulum is swinging the other way. But without the balance of teaching from the church, too much of the supernatural is being accepted without question.

When God moves to restore a truth, it seems that human nature always goes to the extreme with it. One of three things happens:

1. People go overboard and get caught up in emotional extremes.

2. The enemy exaggerates fears that things are out of control or becoming emotional and fleshly so that well-meaning Christians are the ones who quench the move of the Spirit. William DeArteaga's *Quenching the Spirit* shows this pattern through revival after revival.

3. The Holy Spirit brings a balance and integrates the restored truth with previous truths to make a solid foundation for the next restoration.

When God moves in restoration, the secular world also somehow receives the truth released into people's spirits. Because nonbelievers don't have a personal relationship with Jesus, they translate the thoughts or influence of the Holy Spirit into secular terms.

The spiritual movement to take us back to the basics of the faith has translated in the secular world as a "back to the earth" movement, back to one's roots in nature.

The spiritual move of breaking out of religious traditions became the Jesus Movement, but at the same time, hippies rebelled against all establishment, including God.

The neo-Pentecostal (or Charismatic) movement emphasized the supernatural gifts of the Holy Spirit. This was translated by the world into interest in the occult. Satan never misses open doors. His trade is wildfire—or no fire at all.

The purpose of the move of God that we call charismatic was to restore the knowledge that He loves mankind. However, many Christians as well as nonbelievers somehow became "babies" who wanted toys and presents as a demonstration of love. God's love was viewed in many cases as permissiveness, with no emphasis on a holy walk. This resulted in a generation of spoiled baby boomers and baby Christians, similar to those Paul dealt with at Corinth. We call this the "Me Generation."

The move of God to pull down the walls of racial separation in His church is being translated by the world into political correctness, tolerance carried to extremes.

The Current Move Is About Angels

For His own reasons, God is showing us that we need to know about angels today. Believers are coming into a time, I believe, when that knowledge will be as important as it was to the early church. When God moved to restore this truth to His people, Satan began to thrust his "ringers" forward, catching the world's attention. He is forever the counterfeiter.

Many Christian leaders realize that something is happening today. It is very hard to miss. No matter which school of eschatology you subscribe to, it seems there are troubles ahead that all of us will have to live through. In fact, these already have started: stronger earthquakes, heavier floods, famines, and persecution against Christians and the Christian way of life.

For years the angels protected my associates and me behind the Iron Curtain. Now they protect us as we travel to the Middle East, and I have no doubt they will continue to protect us. This is a biblical truth for every child of God. I am not special. Many missionaries, evangelists, and pastors—in fact, all believers—can testify to the same protection. Psalm 91 spells this out for us, as do Jesus' words in Mark 16:15–18.

Other church leaders see the "fullness of time" approaching. The threads of events and circumstances that will make up the second major *kairos* of the New Testament are being woven together. As George Otis Jr. pointed out, in times like this, multitudes of lesser *kairos* moments are occurring. We need angelic assistance now more than ever.

Those who stuck a toe in the waters of New Age in the mid-sixties have now launched out into the deep things of Satan (Rev. 2:24). They are convinced they are more "spiritually mature" than "those intolerant Christians." Michael Green wrote:

> Magic is the attempt to bring the spirit world under one's knowledge and control. It is the precise opposite of religion, which seeks surrender to the Divine, not control over it, and operates by faith, not knowledge...Further, it is an endeavor to "conjure up spirits of the universe that are alien to God Almighty."[2]

Robert Lightner has pointed out that when people turn away from God's authority, they turn to themselves for authority. He wrote:

> Having experienced humanism's total failure and frustration, man is now turning to the world of evil spirits for answers to his most perplexing problems.[3]

The problem today is that many people think these evil spirits are God's good angels.

What Is the Truth?

No human being knows all of the truth about anything. However, it is possible to identify real truth in the midst of error, counterfeit, subtractions, and additions that are all presented as "truth." The standard by which all these stories, doctrines, reports, and speculations must be measured is the Word of God.

Hodge wrote that there is a difference between believing what is possible and believing only what is certain. It is illustrated by the different approaches of Martin Luther and John Calvin to the devil and his works.[4] Luther was disposed to credit all evil to the spirits of darkness. Calvin credited nothing to their agency that could not be proved actually to be their work. In this case, I have to agree with Calvin.

The same thing applies to angels. Let us be like Calvin in this case and be neither too skeptical nor too gullible.

It is intellectually and spiritually dishonest to blame the devil or evil angels for sins of the flesh.

It is intellectually and spiritually dishonest to believe everything an angel says without testing it.

It is intellectually and spiritually dishonest to attribute things that cannot be explained to angels or demons.

Prove All Things

Believers must not, and nonbelievers should not, accept anything supernatural without testing its source. Paul said to "prove all things" and to "hold fast that which is good" (1 Thess. 5:21).

John wrote:

> Beloved, believe not every spirit, but try the spirits whether they are of God: because many false prophets are gone out into the world.
>
> —1 John 4:1

How do you test an angel?

You do this by seeing if his visit matches those in the Bible, if his words line up with the Bible, and if the purpose that his visit achieves is biblical.

- Does he tell you he is the spirit of a dead friend or ancestor? In other words, does he draw your attention to himself or to beings other than Jesus and the Father? That is not a real angel of God. God's angels never testify of themselves.

- Does he bring you revelation that cannot be found in the Bible, say that all religions are of God, and tell you that the hereafter is a good place for everyone? That is not a real angel of God.

- Does he entertain, socialize, and hang around after his "assignment" is over? That is not a real angel of God.

- Does he use spectacular lights, weird sounds, or odd odors to get your attention? That is not a real angel of God. When a real angel appears, he gives you a message or helps you out of danger—and then vanishes.

- Does he flatter you and build up your pride, perhaps telling you how spiritual you are? That is not an angel of God. An angelic visitation is not proof of spiritual maturity.

- Does he leave you feeling anxious, fearful, or confused? That is not an angel of God.

- Does he try to force you to do something against your inner witness? That is not an angel of God.

- Do these encounters bear spiritual fruit? Do they cause you to change for the better in some way? Or are the results harmful to you or those around you? That is not an angel of God.

If an angel tells you that you can talk to him anytime or call him in some way, or if he tells you that angels can live within you—he is a counterfeit. Real angels never become part of you, nor can you ever become an angel.

How can you test an angel if you do not know the Bible? The answer is, you can't!

Knowing the Bible Is Essential

Doug LeBlanc wrote in *Moody Monthly* magazine that Christians are less informed in a Christian worldview today than they were even a few decades ago. He wrote:

A startling number of Americans who consider themselves Christians are unable to say who preached the Sermon on the Mount...With their secular neighbors, evangelicals lap up the evolution-as-fact premises of *Jurassic Park*, the sexual exploitation of MTV, and the dumbed-down factoids of *USA Today*.[5]

Gallup polls on whether there had been religious training in people's backgrounds showed that:

In 1968, 9 percent said no.

In 1978, 17 percent said no.

In 1988, 25 percent said no, and 49 percent of parents told Gallup in 1988 that their children are receiving no religious training.

What has occurred in the last two decades can be called "the secularization of consciousness," says Os Guiness of The Trinity Forum.[6] Several years ago the cover of *Christianity Today* declared we are in the first post-Christian generation.[7]

The famous historian Will Durant predicted in the 1950s that the last major confrontation of Western history would not be between democracy and communism but between the Western Christian mind-set and Eastern religions. Russell Chandler wrote that this confrontation is embodied in the New Age movement.

The New Age has touched you. You've heard its ideas, listened to its music, viewed its artwork, watched its superstars, read its literature, and bought its products. You may even have participated in its therapies, shared in its rituals, and embraced its philosophies— all without knowing them as New Age.[8]

Peter Jones points out that "in spite of its apparently tolerant, pluralistic, and diffuse nature," the New Age has a real agenda, "orchestrated from a diabolical center," that is moving toward "ecological disaster of the spirit."[9]

Another best-selling new book is by a man who writes of an after-death experience that initiated a series of out-of-body experiences and communications from heavenly beings. A council of "thirteen beings of light" told him to build a series of centers where people can "heal their spirits and build a strong faith in God." That sounds good, does it not? However, in the context of the unbiblical picture of the afterlife that they have presented, the "god" on which their faith is built is not the Creator, God of the universe, but a different god.[10]

This man has lectured in Russia, presenting his concept of "spiritual capitalism," which is "that all people should be free to worship the way they choose" on "many paths to righteousness."

Another popular book sounds very biblical and spiritual, even giving good guidelines for testing angels. Yet a certain percentage of the book is taken up with information learned from angels that is similar to Swedenborg's, a teaching on meditating with a passive mind, and a "pilot program" angels have instituted.[11]

This pilot program involves "seeding" of angels among human beings, "a new way" of angels working with their "wards." This is alleged to have started about two hundred fifty years ago. Without a sound grounding in Bible knowledge and in God's ways, many Christians may totally accept this book and others like it.

For the first time in its history, idolatrous thinking and practices underlie American society more than Judeo-Christian principles. Environmentalism is a fairly recent movement that is beginning to look like "idolatrous thinking." It seems to be developing into the core of a New Age religion.

There is no question we should be better stewards of the earth than we have been. In fact, we must assume responsibility for our environment. Along with the original mandate from God to man— take dominion, multiply, and subdue—came a fourth directive. That was to "replenish" (Gen. 1:28).

Stewardship in the Bible means to take care of everything for God, the real Owner (Ps. 24:1). Man was not given ownership of the planet but simply rule (or dominion) over it.

However, conservation and concern for the environment, which is valid in many areas, has become a religion in itself. Paulist Father Robert A. Sirico wrote in the *Wall Street Journal* that environmentalism has spawned a revival of pagan earth worship, which has attracted the feminist movement. The idea is that the earth itself is living and divine, which Romans 1 calls worshiping creation instead of the Creator.

While this "new" religion was not started by an angel, many of the angels featured in the proliferation of popular books on angels are helping to build it. One has to submit that angels are involved heavily in this aspect of the New Age, as well as in personal guidance.

It seems very clear that we are living in one of those *kairos* moments of history.

When the Earth Meets the Sky

A *kairos* moment happens when the earth and the sky seem to meet. Some would call it a "paradigm shift"—moving from one worldview to another.

It is a point in time when the veil between the natural and the supernatural becomes opaque, and everything familiar seems turned upside down.

It is a time when God is saying, "Once again, I will shake everything that can be shaken." (See Hebrews 12:26–27.)

It is a time when God sovereignly intervenes in our programs and plans in order to forward His own purpose and plan.

It is a time when Christians can clearly see God's promises arching over us like a rainbow—if we walk through the storms and the rain in faith and claim His peace. Have you ever seen a double rainbow? God's promises are like a sky full of rainbows.

This is the time when we can know, if we stand and resist the enemy, that the biggest "pot of gold" we could possibly win is out there in front of us. That reward is life forever and ever with God the Father, with God the Son, and with God the Holy Spirit.

When the earth literally meets the heavens, that will be a "pot of gold" for the children of God. However, it will be an awful moment for wicked angels and human beings who have not believed in Jesus:

- The lie of Satan's government will be judged in the complete and final exhibition of its anti-God character.

- The *cosmos diabolicus*, whose princes "crucified the Lord of glory" (1 Cor. 2:8), will vanish from power and from sight.

Some who have accepted the counterfeit angels of light will see more real angels than they want to as angels harvest the earth and Jesus trods out the grapes of wrath (Rev. 14:14–20).

Becoming Overcomers

In the introduction and the first chapter, I asked a lot of questions about what is going on in the world now regarding angels. Hopefully, those questions have been answered for you. I have presented what I believe is the truth concerning the present furor about angels.

I am not saying now is the end of the world.

I am not saying the rapture is going to be in this decade.

I am saying God is getting ready to do something again, and I want to be a part of it. I want to let go of those things in my life and ministry that can be shaken. I hope every reader feels the same way.

Every being that calls itself an angel is not necessarily a godly angel. In fact, probably 75 percent of what is being written, said, and seen today about angels is probably a satanic counterfeit.

What should we do about the evil in the world?

In the apostle John's revelation, the saints overcame Satan by three things.

> And they overcame him by the blood of the Lamb, and by the word
> of their testimony; and they loved not their lives unto the death.
> —Revelation 12:11

In the same chapter, Michael and the angels clean up the heavens. Notice that the believers do not overcome the devil by cleaning up the heavens. Their part is on earth; the angels' part is in the heavens.

Why have the angels not cleaned up the heavens yet?

It is because they are waiting for believers to get in line with the principles of almighty God. They are waiting for believers to overcome the enemy in their own lives by the blood of the Lamb and the word of their testimonies.

Angels and Christians are to be working in cooperation with the blood of Jesus and the direction of the Holy Spirit.

Angels will not come down here and do our job—preaching the gospel—while we are wasting our time and energies trying to do their assignment. They are waiting for us to come under authority. Meanwhile we are operating in our own authority.

That's not how the church will be victorious.

The day is upon us when earth and heaven literally are meeting, and God will have a victorious church on earth. This is the time when believers must get hold of the truth of God's Word and begin to preach, pray, and witness. "Not loving your life to the death" does not always mean martyrdom. It can also mean commitment, consecration, and total dedication to God of everything you are and have.

When God takes the church to glory, He is not going to send Jesus for a beaten, defeated, downtrodden group of people. He is going to send for a victorious church that understands authority, a church that walks in authority and under authority.

We are going home victorious!

We are not leaving this world beaten by a foe who lies, cheats, and steals.

The Victorious Church

Many Christian leaders are sensing that this *kairos* heralds the greatest move of God we have ever seen, certainly the greatest in this century and probably in all of history.

Many church leaders are announcing this major move of God. Pat Robertson wrote in a recent newsletter:

> I also believe we are going to see a dramatic increase of signs, wonders, miracles, healings, revelations, visitations of angels, and dreams. I believe God is pouring out His Spirit on the church, and it is going to become more intense in the next few years.
>
> We are living right on the edge of the turnover of our universe. The most cataclysmic events and the greatest revivals our world has ever known may happen in our lifetimes. Our responsibility as Christians is to prayerfully remain focused on God's eternal purposes.[12]

The preaching, prayer, praise, and giving that accompanied the evangelistic crusades of Dwight Moody, Charles Finney, and others opened the windows of heaven over areas. This is about to happen in a greater way as God's people humble themselves and pray.

Finney ushered in one of the greatest revivals America has ever seen. He always said the "secret" to this was prayer. History shows that about 80 percent of his converts remained faithful to God. Finney used to get up at 4:00 a.m. and pray until 8:00 a.m. every morning. When enough Christians begin to do this, evil angels will get out of the way.

Rick Joyner wrote:

> The Welsh revival was initiated and carried by a devotion to prayer and intercession that also spread throughout the worldwide Christian community. Much of the fire that continues in some of

the great prayer movements of today could likely trace their origin to a lingering spark from the Welsh Revival.[13]

In the Welsh revival, the early revivals of the twentieth century, and in meetings of the British evangelist Smith Wigglesworth, ungodly places closed down because no one would go there anymore. Criminal activity was minimal.

As the church begins to move in its authority and takes the gospel to the world, angels will deal with the territorial powers over the areas where righteousness reigns. Many seemingly unsolvable problems in society will be eliminated, almost overnight.

It is time, church, to open our eyes. Angelic activity—good and bad—is telling us that *kairos* is upon us.

Appendix A

The Sons of God and the Daughters of Men

And it came to pass, when men began to multiply on the face of the earth, and daughters were born unto them, that the sons of God saw the daughters of men that they were fair; and they took them wives of all which they chose.... There were giants in the earth in those days; and also after that, when the sons of God came in unto the daughters of men, and they bare children to them, the same became mighty men which were of old, men of renown.

—Genesis 6:1–2, 4

Were the "sons of God" mentioned in the verses above actually fallen angels, or were they sons of Seth who began to intermarry with women from the line of Cain?

Those who say this account in Genesis must be referring to the sons of Seth (not angels) cite as evidence Jesus' comment that angels neither marry nor are given in marriage (Matt. 22:30; Mark 12:25; Luke 20:34–36).

On the other hand, *The Foundations of Pentecostal Theology* says the Seth/Cain connection may be "an over-simplification of the problem, for it raises almost as many difficulties as it meets."

The difficulties these theologians mention are:

1. On what basis could the descendants of Seth be called "sons of God"? Both Seth and Cain were born to parents of a fallen nature. Seth was said to have been born in the "likeness" and "image" of Adam, or with an Adamic nature (Gen. 5:3).

2. Everywhere else in the Old Testament, the term "sons of God" (*B'nai* or *Bene Elohim*) refers to angels, never to men (Job 1:6; 2:1; 38:7).

3. How could the union of these two family lines with the same original ancestor result in the birth of unusual off-spring such as giants?

4. Jesus also said people would not marry or be given in marriage in *heaven*, yet they certainly do marry and reproduce on earth.

5. If these "sons of God" are not angels, then why does the Book of Jude say the sins of those angels who "kept not their first estate" and who are held in everlasting chains until judgment were "fornication" and "going after strange flesh" (Jude 6–7)?[1]

Chafer also pointed out that considering the "sons of God" to be the sons of Seth is based on the following assumptions not found in Scripture:

1. That Seth's descendants lived apart from the descendants of Cain until shortly before the flood. "It is very unlikely," Chafer wrote, "that the descendants of Seth and Cain would not intermarry very soon."

2. That Seth's descendants remained a "pure and holy" race. We can see from Genesis 4:16–24 that many of Cain's line probably were ungodly, but nowhere do we see that Seth's descendants remained separated and pure. All had fallen natures, or Noah would not have been the only righteous man left (Gen. 6:5–8).

3. When Moses wrote "the daughters of men," he must have meant that the "sons of God" were not of mankind, because "man" or "men" always signified the entire human race, male and female.[2]

Because the Old Testament is a Hebrew book, what did the Jews of Jesus' day and before think of these verses?

Chafer wrote that the "sons of God" was accepted as referring to angels by the ancient Jewish synagogues and by Hellenistic Jews at and before the time of Christ. The Christian church also accepted that the sons of God referred to fallen angels until the fourth century. Then the interpretation again was believed during the time of the Reformation.[3]

Jewish and early Christian beliefs were based on a supposedly more detailed description of what occurred in Genesis 6, found in a book called *1 Enoch.* In *1 Enoch,* the characters who joined together with women were called "holy ones" and "watchers" before they succumbed to temptation. All sexual perversions originated, or were taught to men, by these fallen angels, according to *1 Enoch.*

(*First Enoch* is not to be confused with *2 Enoch,* which came out of Gnosticism after A.D. 250. Not only was *1 Enoch* accepted by Jews, but it was also accepted by Christians until about the fourth century. It is quoted in the New Testament by Jesus, Peter, Paul, and in Jude.[4] But by referring to it, we are in no way suggesting it is divinely inspired as one of the sixty-six books of the canon.)

Jude 6–7 may be speaking of the punishment God gave to the angels (if that is who it was) who joined together with women. In the Jewish New Testament, those verses in Jude are translated this way:

> And the angels that did not keep within their original authority, but abandoned their proper sphere, he has kept in darkness, bound with everlasting chains for the Judgment of the Great Day. And S'dom, 'Amora and the surrounding cities, following a pattern like theirs (the fallen angels), committing sexual sins and perversions, lie exposed as a warning of the everlasting fire awaiting those who must undergo punishment.[5]

The parallel verses of 2 Peter 2:4–5 read this way:

> For if God spared not the angels that sinned, but cast them down to hell, and delivered them into chains of darkness, to be reserved unto judgment; and spared not the old world, but saved Noah the eighth person, a preacher of righteousness...

The word translated "hell" in the King James Version actually is *tartarus,* which means "the lowest abyss of Hades," according to Strong's concordance.[6] If this is not a special category of fallen angels, then it must mean all fallen angels. In which case, we must ask, What beings are ruling now as principalities, powers, and rulers with Satan?

The only explanation that fits all of the facts seems to be that some fallen angels transgressed not only by taking on human bodies —as we know fallen angels sometimes do—but by operating in all of the functions of those bodies, including sex. This transgression was so much worse than even rebellion against God that they were chained in darkness before the flood or at the time of the flood.

Also, this points out that not even these angels are yet in the lake of fire but are "in the lowest part of Hades," apparently a sort of jail for holding prisoners awaiting judgment.

This whole question is one that cannot be definitely proved either way.

Appendix B

Oppression, Obsession, and Possession

The term *demon possession* apparently originated with Josephus, the famous first-century Jewish historian, and then became part of church language.[1]

The Old Testament has five different Hebrew words that are translated "demon," although Hebrew has no exact equivalent for the Greek word *daimonion*. The Hebrew words are *shedhim, seirim, elilim, gad,* and *qeter,* or "destruction." The "destruction that wasteth at noonday" was considered to be an evil spirit.[2]

The New Testament uses four main terms to describe a person under the influence of a demon:

1. *Daimonizomai*—one who is demonized

2. *Echon*—one having a demon

3. *En*—one with an unclean spirit

4. *Ochloumenous*—one vexed with an unclean spirit[3]

Daimonizomai was the term used most frequently in the New Testament. The meaning seems to be that the demon cannot be successfully resisted by the victim, and it indwells him. The word *demonized* is never used to speak of demonic influence that can be resisted. Demonized persons usually are indwelt bodily by at least one demon, as indicated by the scriptural references to casting out, entering in, or going out (Matt. 8:16, 32; 9:33; 12:22–24; Mark 1:13, 34).

The second term, meaning "one having a demon," is also used frequently. The implication of this usage is that a victim is under demonic influence.

The word for "one with an unclean spirit" is only used twice (Mark 1:23; 5:2). It pictures the person as being under the domination or power of a demon.

The last reference, "one vexed with an unclean spirit," is used only once (Acts 5:16).

New Testament writers gave examples, not explanations, of dealing with demons or of people with demons. However, Jesus did teach on demonization one time (Matt. 12:43–45). In this text He explained how a person can be set free of demons yet not remain free. But He was not talking primarily about demons but was using this as an analogy of the spiritual condition of leaders of the scribes and Pharisees.

Nevertheless, here are several lessons to be found in Jesus' teaching:

1. Demonization involves the indwelling of a demon or demons within the body of a human being.

2. Demons desire such indwelling.

3. Such indwelling does not come as easily as some people assume. It involves finding a "willing" host.

4. Demons may leave victims temporarily and then return.

5. Those once demonized are particularly susceptible to renewed invasion if they are not in proper spiritual condition.

Most Christian leaders who believe that Christians can be the target of demons describe three levels of attack:

- Oppression, or influence, which includes evil thoughts that encourage carnal sins or affect the mind and emotions.

- Obsession, which involves a continuous attack in certain areas—from lust to religion. Anything that has become an obsession, a compulsion, or a perversion of the natural could fit this definition. In this case, demons might have taken up lodging in a Christian's soul or body.

- Possession, which means having an indwelling demonic spirit or spirits that essentially run the person's life. They actually dwell in the human spirit.

The majority of church scholars, teachers, and pastors do not believe Christians can be possessed. That's because a person who is truly born again is a new creature, with the Holy Spirit indwelling his spirit. There is no place for an evil spirit in the spirit of a new creature. However, the soul and body of man are not instantly reborn. Salvation of the soul is an ongoing process (James 1:21; Phil. 2:12), and salvation of the body will occur at the resurrection (1 Cor. 15:44).

Kenneth Hagin Sr. explained it this way:

> If you lived in an old house that had termites in it, that doesn't mean you have termites in you. Well, your body is just the house you live in. Your body isn't the real you. The real you is the spirit man on the inside. And if you're born again, the spirit man can't have a devil in him. But your body—the house of your spirit—can have an evil spirit afflicting it...
>
> Total possession implies giving over spirit, soul, and body to an evil spirit because to possess something means "to own it"....A Christian can be demonized (oppressed, influenced, or obsessed) by evil spirits. But, no, a Christian cannot be possessed spirit, soul, and body by evil spirits.[4]

Appendix C

The Angel of Jehovah

The term "the angel of the Lord" in the Old Testament is considered by many to denote a theophany or Christophany, which means a manifestation of the Godhead in the Person of Jesus in visible and bodily form before His incarnation.

Others believe that only some of those visitations might have been Jesus, with the rest being angels. Others teach literally what is said—"the angel of Jehovah," an angel sent by God on very special assignments.

There are several arguments for this angel being Jesus. These include:

1. The language, *malak Yaweh*, is a singular and peculiar title showing that this personage was more than an angel.

2. In the Old Testament, He is consistently presented as Jehovah: the angel appeared, but God, or the Lord, spoke.

3. Promises made or direction given by this being are such as only God would give.

This angel, identified as Jehovah, nevertheless is presented as distinct from Jehovah and calls upon Jehovah. Therefore, this angel seems to be the preincarnate Son of God, Jesus Christ. Also, his ministries parallel those of Jesus.[1]

Those who believe this is simply an angel on special assignment representing Jehovah say that:

1. This identification would make Jesus an angel, which resembles the doctrines of the Muslims, Mormons, and others.

2. Although angel does mean "messenger," it takes away from the deity of Jesus to consider Him simply a "messenger" of God.

3. Jesus has a special angel whom He called "My angel" sent "to testify to you these things" in Revelation (Rev. 22:16). So why would God not also have a special angel He sends on special missions who speaks for Him?

4. In Matthew, the angel who appeared to Zacharias and Mary is called "the angel of the Lord" (*Kurios*), then identified as Gabriel. *Kurios* is the Greek equivalent of Jehovah, according to *Vine's Expository Dictionary*.[2] As the "angel of the Lord," Gabriel had authority to act and speak for the Lord, as we already have seen.

Roy Hicks Sr. has written that if the angel of the Lord was Jesus, then we have to accept that He is the One who administered death to the Assyrian soldiers attacking Hezekiah (2 Kings 19:35) and carried out other such incidents. And he asks whether or not that is how we see the character of Jesus.[3] In Revelation, it is angels who carry out judgment, not Jesus.

Hicks also points out that Scripture occasionally attributes the words of an angel to God even when it is not the angel of Jehovah. This should not be troubling, because whether the angel of Jehovah is God or His angel, it still represents God directly intervening in the affairs of men.

Again, this issue cannot be settled beyond question by Scripture, so I leave you to draw your own conclusions.

Notes

Introduction

1. Kenneth Woodward, "Angels," *Newsweek*, December 27, 1993, 53.
2. Nancy Gibbs, "Angels Among Us," *Time*, December 27, 1993, 65.
3. Ibid., 56.
4. Woodward, "Angels," 57.
5. Gibbs, "Angels Among Us," 65.

Chapter 1: Personal Encounters of an Angelic Kind

1. William Shakespeare, *Hamlet*, act 1, scene 5, line 166, as quoted in John Bartlett, *Familiar Quotations*, 13th ed. (Boston: Little, Brown and Company, 1955), 173.
2. S. Ralph Harlow, "The Day We Saw the Angels," in *Footprints in the Snow* (Nashville, TN: Dimensions for Living, 1992), 102–103.
3. Sophy Burnham, *Angel Letters* (New York: Ballantine Books, 1991), 87–89.
4. Bob and Penny Lord, *Heavenly Army of Angels* (N.p.: Journeys of Faith, 1991), 167–168.
5. Wesley Bradshaw, *National Tribune*, December 1880.
6. Martin Mitchell, "Popularity of Angels Continues to Soar," *Tulsa (Okla.) World*, January 12, 1994, Midtown Tulsa Zone sect., 1.
7. Editorial, *The National Christian Reporter*, January 7, 1994.
8. Sophy Burnham, *A Book of Angels* (New York: Ballantine Books, 1990).
9. Timothy Jones, "Rumors of Angels," *Christianity Today*, April 5, 1993, 20. Jones also has written a book, *Celebration of Angels* (Nashville, TN: Thomas Nelson, 1994).
10. Peter Rojcewicz, folklorist and cultural critic at the Julliard School in New York City, as quoted in the editorial, *The National Christian Reporter*, January, 7, 1994.
11. Gibbs, "Angels Among Us," 56.
12. Jones, "Rumors of Angels," 19.
13. Ibid.
14. Thomas J. Herron, academic dean of the theology department at St. Charles Borromeo Seminary, as quoted in a story by Tanya Barrientos, *Tulsa (OK) World*, January 2, 1994, "Living" section, 2.
15. Gibbs, "Angels Among Us," 56, 65.
16. The two books offered were written by Karen Goldman: *The Angel Book: A Handbook for Aspiring Angels* and *Angel Voices* (New York: Simon and Schuster, 1993 and 1994 respectively).

Chapter 2: Nothing New Under the Sun

1. George Santayana, *Life of Reason*, vol. 1 (Charles Scribner's Sons, 1905; reprint, New York: Dover Publications, 1980), chapter 12, "Flux and Constancy in Human Nature."

2. John E. Ronner, *Know Your Angels* (Murfreesboro, TN: Mamre Press, 1993), 150.

3. Geddes MacGregor, *Angels, Ministers of Grace* (New York: Paragon House, 1988), 113.

4. J. I. Packer, Merrill C. Tenney, and William White Jr., *The Bible Almanac* (Nashville, TN: Thomas Nelson, 1980), 450–451.

5. William Whiston, ed., *Works of Josephus* (Peabody, MA: Hendrickson Publishers, 1980), book 1, chapter 3, page 28. This book was originally published in the 1700s.

6. Alexander Hislop, *The Two Babylons* (Neptune, NJ: Loizeaus Brothers, 1916). Donald Grey Barnhouse, the late Presbyterian pastor and radio Bible teacher, called Hislop's book "one of the great books in the Christian literature of apologetics" (from the front cover of *The Two Babylons*).

7. Kenneth Boa, *Cults, World Religions and the Occult* (Wheaton, IL: Victor Books, 1977), 131.

8. F. L. Cross and E. A. Livingstone, *The Oxford Dictionary of the Christian Church*, 2nd ed. (New York: Oxford University Press, 1990), 573. Gnosticism makes a distinction between a supreme and unknowable "divine being" and the creator god, who is said to be a lesser god. Jesus is never considered all-God and all-man but an emissary of the Supreme Being assigned to bring *gnosis*, or knowledge. Jesus is thought to have come as a spirit being (much as angels appear to men), or is said to have temporarily inhabited (possessed) a human being named Jesus. Until the mid 1940s, most of what was known about Gnosticism came from the anti-Gnostic writings of the early church fathers from the second to the fourth centuries.

9. James Strong, *Strong's Exhaustive Concordance of the Bible* (Nashville, TN: Thomas Nelson, 1990), Greek dictionary, #1108.

10. Russell Chandler, *Understanding the New Age* (Dallas: Word Publishing, 1988), 17, 43.

11. Ibid., 125.

12. Ibid., 33.

13. Ibid., 233.

14. Peter Jones, *The Gnostic Empire Strikes Back* (Phillipsburg, NJ: P and R Publishing, 1992), 44.

15. Israel Gutwirth, *Kabbalah and Jewish Mysticism* (New York: Philosophical Library, 1987), 17–22; Solomon Grayzl, *A History of the Jews*

(New York: New American Library, 1968), 328, 335–336; "Demons and Spirits in Jewish Tradition" in *The Jewish People's Almanac*, David G. Gross, ed. (New York: Doubleday and Co., 1981), 93.

16. Price, *Angels Within Us*, 10.

17. *Encyclopaedia Judaica*, vol. 2 (Jerusalem: Keter Publishing House Ltd., 1972), 962.

18. Chandler, *Understanding the New Age*, 50. This was a comment from Martin Katchen, an orthodox Jew and analyst of historical trends and patterns.

19. Mortimer Adler, *The Angels and Us* (New York: Collier Books, 1993), 41.

Chapter 3: Angels and the Church

1. Hope Price, *Angels* (London: Macmillan, 1993), 86. This quote and those following are used by permission.

2. Burnham, *Book of Angels*, 164.

3. Malcolm Godwin, *Angels, an Endangered Species* (New York: Simon and Schuster, 1990), 23.

4. Everett Ferguson, ed., *Encyclopedia of Early Christianity* (New York: Garland Publishing, 1990), 268.

5. Adler, *Angels and Us*, 35.

6. Adler, *Angels and Us*, 19.

7. *New Catholic Encyclopedia*, vol. 1 (Washington DC: The Catholic University of America, 1967), s.v. "angels."

8. Gibbs, "Angels Among Us," 56.

9. MacGregor, *Ministers of Grace*, 82–83.

10. *Angels* (London: Fount, Harper Collins Publishers, 1993), 52.

11. Edward Welch, "Early Roots of the Codependency Movement," *S.C.P. Journal* 18, no. 3 (1994): 21, 23. The *S.C.P. (Spiritual Counterfeit Project) Journal* is published in Berkeley, CA.

12. Paola Giovetti, *Angels* (York Beach, Maine: Samuel Weiser., 1993), 98.

13. Ronner, *Know Your Angels*, 157.

14. Alfred J. Crosby, *America's Forgotten Pandemic: The Influenza of 1918* (New York: Cambridge University Press, 1989), 203–207. The influenza epidemic is said to have "almost single-handedly thrust the year of 1918 back into the previous century." Multiplied millions of people died in a year or less. Crosby said nothing else—not infection, war, or famine—has ever killed that many in such a short period of time. The combined deaths of the U.S. armed forces in World Wars I and II, and the Korean and Vietnam wars was much less than the loss of life in the U.S. due to the flu in 1918—423,000 (deaths by those wars) to more than 600,000 (by flu). An estimated 40 million people died worldwide, and the count may be higher

through side effects or deaths later from related causes. The trauma of that thirty-year period (1914 to 1944) changed the course of events forever. Society retreated into the "Roaring Twenties," bootleg gin, jazz, and the new moving, talking pictures—the "eat, drink, and be merry" syndrome.

15. A. C. Gaebelein, *What the Bible Says About Angels* (Grand Rapids, MI: Baker Book House, 1993), 75.

16. Maria Woodworth-Etter, *A Diary of Signs and Wonders* (Tulsa, OK: Harrison House, 1971).

17. Roy H. Hicks, *Guardian Angels* (Tulsa, OK: Harrison House, 1991), 41–42. This quote and those following are used by permission.

18. C. Douglas Weaver, *The Healer-Prophet, William Marion Branham* (Macon, GA: Mercer University Press, 1987), 34–36, 73–75, 87, 119, 123, 151–162. Reprinted with permission by Mercer University Press, 1400 Coleman Avenue, Macon, GA 31207.

19. J. Rodman Williams, *Renewal Theology* (Grand Rapids, MI: Academie Books, Zondervan Publishing House, 1988), 170–171.

20. Charles and Frances Hunter, *Angels on Assignment* (Kingwood, TX: Hunter Books, 1979).

Chapter 4: Angelic Warriors in the Twentieth Century

1. C. S. Lewis, *Mere Christianity*, rev. ed. (New York: Macmillan Publishing Company, first paperback edition, 1960), 146. Used by permission.

2. Price, *Angels*, 92–102.

3. Ibid.

4. Katherine Pollard Carter, *The Mighty Hand of God* (Kirkwood, MO: Impact Christian Books, 1991), 169.

5. Price, *Angels*, 102.

6. Carter, *The Mighty Hand of God*, 16.

7. Ibid., 19. Editor's note: The original source did not give exact details as to how many Nazi planes were in the air, nor how many planes there were in each British squadron. However, history describes British aircraft as greatly outnumbered by the Nazis during the entire Battle of Britain. It is possible that an exact count of Nazi planes during this particular skirmish was not ever determined.

8. Billy Graham, *Angels, God's Secret Agents* (Dallas: Word Publishing, 1986), 167–168. This quote and those following are used by permission.

9. Hicks, *Guardian Angels*, 25.

10. Carter, *The Mighty Hand of God*, 26.

11. Ibid., 25–27.

12. John MacArthur Jr., *God, Satan, and Angels* (Panorama City, CA: Word of Grace Publications, 1983), 123–124.

13. Douglas Speare, *The Dimensions of Prayer* (New York: Woman's Division of Christian Service of the Methodist Church, 1962).

Chapter 5: Angels of Light

1. Paul Thigpen, "Spiritual Warfare in the Early Church," *Discipleship Journal*, May/June 1994, 29. Used by permission.

2. Ibid., 29.

3. Burnham, *Angel Letters*, 123–127.

4. Most of the information about Islam and Mormonism was synthesized from *Cults, World Religions, and the Occult; The Oxford Dictionary of the Christian Church*, and George Mather and Larry Nichols, *Dictionary of Cults, Sects, Religions, and the Occult* (Grand Rapids, MI: Zondervan, 1993).

5. George Otis Jr., *The Last of the Giants* (Grand Rapids, MI: Chosen Books, Fleming H. Revell, a division of Baker Book House, 1991), 61, 75.

6. Ibid., 79–80.

7. Giovetti, *Angels*, 97–115.

8. Information concerning the Kabbalah is taken from *Cults, World Religions, and the Occult; Dictionary of Cults, Sects, Religions, and the Occult;* Burnham's *Book of Angels*, 178–183; and from Roy A. Anderson, *The Illuminati 666* (N.p.: The Institute of Religious Knowledge, 1983), 87–91.

9. Georg Wilhelm Friedrich Hegel, who ruled German philosophy in the early nineteenth century, thought the Geist (German for spirit, mind, soul, and idea), or "God," had its beginning at creation and realized its full potential, not in heaven, but on earth. Whatever nation is in ascendency is the Geist expressing itself. [Anthony Campolo, *Partly Right* (Dallas: Word Books, Jarrell Imprint, 1985), 48–63.]

10. *Dictionary of Cults, Sects, Religions, and the Occult, s.v.* "Mormons."

11. Otis, *Last of the Giants*, 104.

12. Ibid., 105.

Chapter 6: Angelic Encounters in Modern Times

1. George Otis Jr., "An Overview of Spiritual Mapping," in *Breaking Strongholds in Your City*, C. Peter Wagner, ed. (Ventura, CA: Regal Books, 1993), 35. Used by permission.

2. Taken from the *Agape* Newsletter, Little Rock, AK, May/June, 1988, 3. This newsletter is published by Agape Church, pastored by Happy Caldwell.

3. Larry Libby, *Somewhere Angels* (Sisters, OR: Questar Publishers, 1994), 32.

Chapter 7: Goodness and Mercy—God's Special Agents in the Middle East

1. *Washington Post*, courtesy of the Associated Press, Wednesday, October 12, 2005, "Full Text of Iraqi Constitution" Draft document to be presented to voters Saturday, http://www.washingtonpost.com/wp-dyn/content/article/2005/10/12/2005, 10, (accessed April 18, 2006), italics added.

Chapter 8: Guardian Angels

1. Gibbs, "Angels Among Us," 56.

2. Adler, *Angels and Us*, 73.

3. Marilyn Hickey, *Angels All Around* (Denver, CO: Marilyn Hickey Ministries, 1991), 87. This quote and those following are used by permission.

4. Carter, *The Mighty Hand of God*, 207–211.

5. Hickey, *Angels All Around*, 45–47.

Chapter 9: Angels and Healing

1. Hicks, *Guardian Angels*, 91–92.

2. Ibid., 95.

Chapter 10: Angels in the Bible

1. C. Fred Dickason, *Angels: Elect and Evil* (Chicago: Moody Press, 1975), 17. This quote and those following are used by permission.

2. Norvel Hayes, *Putting Your Angels to Work* (Tulsa, OK: Harrison House, 1989), 8, 23.

3. Fred H. Wight, *Manners and Customs of Bible Lands* (Chicago: Moody Press, 1953), 112–113.

4. Hickey, *Angels All Around*, 131–132.

Chapter 11: Angels and Jesus

1. H. V. Morton, *In the Steps of the Master* (New York: Dodd, Mead, and Company, 1934), 128–129.

2. Hal Lindsey, *Satan Is Alive and Well on Planet Earth* (Grand Rapids, MI: Zondervan, 1972), 55. This quote and those following are used by permission.

3. MacArthur, *God, Satan, and Angels*, 123; and Gaebelein, *What the Bible Says*, 9–10.

4. Graham, *Angels, God's Secret Agents*, 121.

5. Lindsey, *Satan Is Alive and Well*, 54.

6. Hickey, *Angels All Around*, 17.

7. Strong, *Strong's Exhaustive Concordance*, Greek dictionary, #1247.

8. Guy Duffield and Nathaniel Van Cleave, *The Foundations of Pentecostal Theology* (Los Angeles: L.I.F.E. Bible College, 1983), 485–486. This quote and those following are used by permission.

9. There are some discrepancies between the four Gospels about how many angels were at Jesus' tomb and exactly where they were. The answer may be that all of the accounts are accurate, just reported from the perspective of different people.

10. Hicks, foreword to *Guardian Angels*, 5.

Chapter 12: What Are Angels?

1. John Milton, *Paradise Lost*, 1667, Book IV, Line 677; Book VII, Line 569, Project Gutenberg Consortia Center Renascence Editions Collection, viewed at http://www.worldebooklibrary.com on May 24, 2006.

2. Dickason, *Angels: Elect and Evil*, 58.

3. Lehman Strauss, *Demons Yes But Thank God For Good Angels* (Neptune, NJ: Loizeaux Brothers, 1976), 88.

4. Henry Clarence Thiessen, *Lectures in Systematic Theology* (Grand Rapids, MI: William B. Eerdmans Publishing Company, 1986), 134.

5. Robert Lightner, *Evangelical Theology* (Grand Rapids, MI: Baker Book House, 1986), 138, 135.

6. Theissen, *Lectures in Systematic Theology*, 134, 139.

7. John Ronner, *Do You Have a Guardian Angel?* (Murfreesboro, TN: Mamre Press, 1985), 153.

8. Hunter, *Angels on Assignment*, 45.

9. Pascal Parente, *Beyond Space* (Rockford, IL: TAN Books and Publishers, 1973), 24.

10. Price, *Angels*, 120.

11. Graham, *Angels, God's Secret Agents*, 34–35.

12. Dickason, *Angels: Elect and Evil*, 43.

13. Lewis Chafer, *Systematic Theology* (Grand Rapids, MI: Kregel Publications, 1993), 23. This quote and those following are used by permission.

Chapter 13: What Do Angels Do?

1. Hunter, *Angels on Assignment*, 47.

2. Duffield and Van Cleave, *Foundations of Pentecostal Theology*, 467.

3. Gaebelein, *What the Bible Says*, 34–35.

4. Ibid., 59.

5. Andrew Bandstra, "A Job Description for Angels," *Christianity Today*, April 5, 1993, 21.

6. Graham, *Angels, God's Secret Agents*, 52.

7. The list of biblical terms for angels was adapted from Dickason, *Angels: Elect and Evil*, 58–61.

8. Ibid., 61–62.

9. Ibid., 62.

10. Chafer, *Systematic Theology*, 21; The framework for the section on ministry of angels is taken from chapter 8 of *Angels: Elect and Evil* by Dickason.

11. James Montgomery Boice, *Foundations of the Christian Faith*, rev. ed. (Downers Grove, IL: InterVarsity Press, 1986), 169.

12. Lester Sumrall, *Angels, the Messengers of God* (South Bend, IN: LeSea Publishing, 1993), 75.

13. Dickason, *Angels: Elect and Evil*, 78.

14. Hickey, *Angels All Around*, 57.

15. Graham, *Angels, God's Secret Agents*, 31–32.

16. Hunter, *Angels on Assignment*, 177–180.

17. Ibid., 75–89.

Chapter 14: The Rise and Fall of Lucifer

1. Duffield and Van Cleave, *Foundations of Pentecostal Theology*, 500.

2. Gibbs, "Angels Among Us," 61. The telephone poll was conducted by Yankelovich Partners, Inc. on December 2, 1993.

3. Lightner, *Evangelical Theology*, 141.

4. Boice, *Foundations of the Christian Faith*, 172.

5. Duffield and Van Cleave, *Foundations of Pentecostal Theology*, 497.

6. Chafer, *Systematic Theology*, 35.

7. Theissen, *Lectures in Systematic Theology*, 135.

8. Augustine, *The City of God*, trans. Henry Bettenson (New York: Penguin Books, 1972), part 2, book 12, chapter 4, page 474.

9. Chafer, *Systematic Theology*, 84–85, italics added.

10. Dickason, *Angels: Elect and Evil*, 117.

11. Kenneth Hagin Sr., *The Triumphant Church* (Tulsa, OK: Faith Library Publications, 1993), 7–9. This quote and those following are used by permission.

12. Chafer, *Systematic Theology*, 79.

13. Derek Prince, *The Spirit-Filled Believer's Handbook* (Lake Mary, FL: Charisma House, 1993), 455.

14. W. E. Vine, Merill Unger, and William White Jr., *Vine's Expository Dictionary of the Old and New Testaments* (Nashville, TN: Thomas Nelson, 1985), s.v. "world."

15. Chafer, *Systematic Theology*, 83.

16. Lindsey, *Satan Is Alive and Well*, 83, 99.

17. C. Peter Wagner, "The Visible and the Invisible," in *Breaking Strongholds in Your City*, 52.

18. Ibid., 59.

19. Chafer, *Systematic Theology*, 100, 103.

20. LaMar Boschman, *The Rebirth of Music* (Shippensburg, PA: Destiny Image Publishers, 1980), 11, 16.

21. Mark Bubeck, *The Adversary* (Chicago: Moody Press, 1975), 71.

Chapter 15: The Reality of Demons

1. C. S. Lewis, *The Screwtape Letters* (Old Tappan, NJ: Fleming H. Revell, 1978) as quoted by Neil Anderson, *The Bondage Breaker* (Eugene, OR.: Harvest House Publishers, 1990), 100.

2. David Stern, *Jewish New Testament Commentary* (Jerusalem: Jewish New Testament Publications, 1992), 556. This is the second Messianic Jewish commentary ever published and the first since 1912.

3. Lewis, *Screwtape Letters*, as quoted by Anderson, *Bondage Breaker*, 100.

4. Duffield and Van Cleave, *Foundations of Pentecostal Theology*, 479–482.

5. Ibid., 484.

6. William DeArteaga, *Quenching the Spirit* (Lake Mary, FL: Charisma House, 1992), 17.

7. Augustine, *City of God*, book 7, chapter 6.

8. Rick Renner, *Seducing Spirits and Doctrines of Demons* (Tulsa, OK: Pillar Books, 1988), 33.

9. Ibid., 43.

10. Eric Klein, *The Crystal Stair*, 3rd ed. (Livermore, England: Oughten House Publications, 1994), "Ascension Books for the Rising Planetary Consciousness," 34–35.

11. Ibid., 39.

12. Ibid., 74.

13. Renner, *Seducing Spirits*, 143.

14. Jones, *Gnostic Empire*, 103, footnote 10. Jones said his information came from Religious News Service, January 4, 1992, "Many Christians Found to Hold New Age Beliefs," and from *Culture Wars: The Struggle to Define America* by James Davison Hunter (New York: Basic Books, 1991).

15. Marcia Ford, "Mormon Book Lures Christians," *Charisma*, July 1994, 64; Letters, *Charisma*, July 1994, 10; *Christian Retailing*, June, 18 1994, 26. The book is *Embraced by the Light* by Betty Eadie (Utah: Gold Leaf Press, n.d.).

16. Jones, *Gnostic Empire*, 85. Quoted from "The Emerging Reality of a New World Order" by Tal Brooke, *S.P.C. Journal* 16, no. 2 (1991), 21.

Chapter 16: Evil Angels and Thought

1. Charles Hodge, *Systematic Theology* (New York: Charles Scribners Sons, 1895), 642. An original copy of this book was found in the Oral Roberts University library collection (Tulsa, OK). A paraphrased and

abridged version was published by Baker Book House/Revell (Grand Rapids, MI) in 1993.

2. Ibid.

3. Judson Cornwall and Michael Reid, *Whose War Is It Anyway?* (Essex, England: Sharon Publications, 1993), 132.

4. Neil Anderson, *Victory Over the Darkness* (Ventura, CA: Regal Books, 1990), 168, 170.

Chapter 17: Spiritual Warfare and Angels

1. Cornwall, *Whose War Is It Anyway?*, 15.

2. Hagin, *The Triumphant Church*, 208–209.

3. Duffield and Van Cleave, *Foundations of Pentecostal Theology*, 508–509.

4. *Vine's Expository Dictionary*, s.v. "wrestle, wrestling."

5. Cornwall, *Whose War Is It Anyway?*, 14, 17.

6. Ibid., 16.

7. Hagin, *The Triumphant Church*, 244.

Chapter 18: Who Is in Charge?

1. Cornwall, *Whose War Is It Anyway?*, 144.

2. *Vine's Expository Dictionary*, s.v. "hades" and "sheol."

3. Prince, *Spirit-Filled Believer's Handbook*, 455–456.

4. Cornwall, *Whose War Is It Anyway?*, 38.

5. Compare Isaiah 14:12 and Revelation 22:16; 2 Corinthians 11:14 and John 8:12; Ezekiel 28:14 and Acts 10:38; John 14:30 and Acts 5:31; 3:15.

6. Cornwall, *Whose War Is It Anyway?*, 42.

7. Anderson, *Victory Over the Darkness*, 54.

8. Hagin, *Triumphant Church*, 150.

9. Otis, "An Overview of Spiritual Mapping," in *Breaking Strongholds*, Wagner ed., 36–37.

Chapter 19: The Holy Spirit, Angels, and Us

1. Otis, *Last of the Giants*, 35.

2. Charlie Shedd, *Brush of an Angel's Wing* (Ann Arbor, MI: Servant Publications, 1994), 49.

3. Otis, *Last of the Giants*, 35.

Chapter 20: "Activating" Angels

1. Anderson, *Bondage Breaker*, 61.

2. Buddy Harrison, *Understanding Authority for Effective Leadership* (Tulsa, OK: Harrison House, 1982), 21–46. Ralph Mahoney, "The Use and Abuse of Authority," *Acts* magazine, vol. 11, no. 4, 2–11.

3. Terry Law, *The Power of Praise and Worship* (Tulsa, OK: Victory House, 1981), 161–162.

4. Chafer, *Systematic Theology*, 73.

5. Ibid.

6. Cornwall, *Whose War Is It Anyway?*, 29.

Chapter 21: The Truth About Angels

1. Lewis, *Mere Christianity*, 183. Used by permission.

2. Michael Green, *Exposing the Prince of Darkness* (Ann Arbor, MI: Servant Publications, 1981), 13, 118.

3. Lightner, *Evangelical Theology*, 134.

4. Hodge, *Systematic Theology*, 637–638.

5. Doug LeBlanc, "Living in a Christian Culture," *Moody Monthly*, June 1994, 11.

6. Ibid., 12.

7. *Christianity Today*, September 1994.

8. Chandler, *Understanding the New Age*, 232, 19.

9. Jones, *Gnostic Empire*, 97.

10. Dannion Brinkley, *Saved by the Light* (New York: Villard Books, Random House, 1994), 159–160.

11. Eileen Elias Freeman, *Touched by Angels* (New York: Warner Books, 1993).

12. Pat Robertson, CBN World Watch, July/August 1994, 7–8.

13. Rick Joyner, *The World Aflame* (Charlotte, NC: MorningStar Publications, 1993), 25.

Appendix A: The Sons of God and the Daughters of Men

1. Duffield and Van Cleave, *Foundations of Pentecostal Theology*, 481.

2. Chafer, *Systematic Theology*, 115.

3. Ibid., 116.

4. *1 Enoch* (Thousand Oaks, CA: Artesan Sales, 1980), 3.

5. David Stern, trans., *Jewish New Testament* (Jerusalem: Jewish New Testament Publications, 1989).

6. Strong, *Strong's Exhaustive Concordance*, Greek dictionary, #5020.

Appendix B: Oppression, Obsession and Possession

1. Merrill Unger, *Biblical Demonology: A Study of the Spiritual Forces Behind the Present World Unrest* (Wheaton, IL: VanKampen Press, 1952), 101.

2. Dickason, *Angels: Elect and Evil*, 152.

3. Alex Konya, *Demons: A Biblically Based Perspective* (Schaumburg, IL: Regular Baptist Press, 1990), 20–25. Konya has one of the clearest expla-

nations I have found of demonology in the New Testament. However, he believes the casting out of demons was an apostolic gift that vanished from the church before A.D. 100.

4. Hagin, *The Triumphant Church*, 73, 87.

Appendix C: The Angel of Jehovah

1. The arguments for the angel of Jehovah as a theophany are taken from Dickason's *Angels: Elect and Evil*, chapter 6.

2. *Vine's Expository Dictionary*, s.v. "lord, lordship."

3. Hicks, *Guardian Angels*, 28.

Bibliography

Author's Note: This bibliography includes resources from secular as well as Christian sources. I have identified some of them as New Age. Inclusion in this bibliography does not imply endorsement of the work or the author.

Adler, Mortimer. *The Angels and Us.* New York: Collier Books, 1993.

Anderson, Neil. *The Bondage Breaker.* Eugene, OR: Harvest House Publishers, 1990.

———. *Victory Over Darkness.* Ventura, CA: Regal Books, 1990.

Anderson, Roy. *The Illuminati 666.* The Institute of Religious Knowledge, 1983.

———. *Angels.* London: Fount, HarperCollins Publishers, 1993.

Augustine. *The City of God,* trans. Henry Bettenson. New York: Penguin Books, 1972.

Boa, Kenneth. *Cults, World Religions and the Occult.* Wheaton: Victor Books, 1990.

Boice, James Montgomery. *Foundations of the Christian Faith,* rev. ed. Downers Grove, IL: InterVarsity Press, 1986.

Boschman, LaMar. *The Rebirth of Music.* Shippensburg, NJ: Destiny Image Publishers, 1980.

Bubeck, Mark. *The Adversary.* Chicago: Moody Press, 1975.

Burnham, Sophy. *A Book of Angels.* New York: Ballantine Books, 1990. (New Age)

———. *Angel Letters.* New York: Ballantine Books, 1991. (New Age)

Brigidi, Stephen and Robert Bly. *Angels of Pompeii.* New York: Ballantine Books, 1991.

Campolo, Anthony. *Partly Right.* Dallas: Word Books, Jarrell Imprint, 1985.

Carter, Katherine Pollard. *The Mighty Hand of God.* Kirkwood, WA: Impact Books, Inc., 1991. Originally published as *Hand on the Helm.*

Chafer, Lewis. *Systematic Theology.* Grand Rapids, MI: Kregel Publications, 1993.

Chandler, Russell. *Understanding the New Age.* Grand Rapids, MI: Zondervan Publishing House, 1991.

Cornwall, Judson and Michael Reid. *Whose War Is It Anyway?* Essex, England: Sharon Publications, 1993.

Crosby, Alfred. *America's Forgotten Pandemic: The Influenza of 1918.* New York: Cambridge University Press, 1989.

Cross, F. L. and E. A. Livingstone. *The Oxford Dictionary of the Christian Church,* 2nd ed. New York: Oxford University Press, 1990.

Davidson, Maxwell Jr. *Angels at Qumran.* Sheffield, England: Sheffield Academic Press, 1992.

DeArteaga, William. *Quenching the Spirit.* Lake Mary, FL: Charismatic House, 1992.

Dickason, C. Fred. *Angels: Elect and Evil.* Chicago: Moody Press, 1975.

Duffield, Guy and Nathaniel Van Cleave. *The Foundations of Pentecostal Theology.* Los Angeles: LIFE Bible College, 1983.

Eadie, Betty. *Embraced by the Light.* Utah: Gold Leaf Press, 1994. (New Age)

Encyclopaedia Judaica. Jerusalem: Keter Publishing House Ltd., 1972.

1 Enoch. Thousand Oaks, CA: Artesan Sales, 1980.

Ferguson, Everett, ed. *Encyclopedia of Early Christianity.* New York: Garland Publishing, 1990.

Gaebelein, A. C. *What the Bible Says About Angels.* Grand Rapids, MI: Baker Book House, 1993.

Gibbs, Nancy. "Angels Among Us." *Time,* December 27, 1993, 56–65.

Giovetti, Paola. *Angels.* York Beach, Maine: Samuel Weiser, 1993.

Godwin, Malcom. *Angels, an Endangered Species.* New York: Simon and Schuster, 1990.

Goldman, Karen. *The Angel Book: A Handbook for Aspiring Angels.* New York: Simon and Schuster, 1993. (New Age)

————. *Angel Voices.* New York: Simon and Schuster, 1994. (New Age)

Graham, Billy. *Angels, God's Secret Agents.* Dallas, TX: Word Publishing, 1986.

Green, Michael. *Exposing the Prince of Darkness.* Ann Arbor, MI: Servant Books, 1981.

Gross, David, ed. *The Jewish People's Almanac.* New York: Doubleday and Co., 1981.

Gutwirth, Israel. *Kabbalah and Jewish Mysticism.* New York: Philosophical Library, Inc., 1987.

Harrison, Buddy. *Understanding Authority for Effective Leadership.* Tulsa, OK: Harrison House, 1982.

Hayes, Norvel. *Putting Your Angels to Work.* Tulsa, OK: Harrison House, 1989.

Hendrikson, William. *The Bible on the Life Hereafter.* Grand Rapids, MI: Baker Book House, 1959.

Hagin, Kenneth E., Sr. *The Triumphant Church.* Tulsa, OK: Faith Library Publications, 1993.

Hicks, Roy H., Sr. *Guardian Angels.* Tulsa, OK: Harrison House, 1991.

————. *Avoiding Ditches.* Tulsa, OK: Harrison House, 1994.

Hickey, Marilyn. *Angels All Around.* Denver, CO: Marilyn Hickey Ministries, 1991.

Hislop, Alexander. *The Two Babylons.* Neptune, NJ: Loizeaus Brothers, 1916.

Hodge, Charles. *Systematic Theology.* New York: Charles Scribners Sons, 1895.

Hunter, Charles and Frances. *Angels on Assignment.* Kingwood, TX: Hunter Books, 1979.

Jeremias, Joachim. *Jerusalem in the Time of Jesus.* Philadelphia: Fortress Press, 1969.

Jones, Peter. *The Gnostic Empire Strikes Back.* Phillipsburg, NJ: P and R Publishing, 1992.

Jones, Timothy. "Rumors of Angels." *Christianity Today,* April 5, 1993.

Klein, Eric. *The Crystal Stair,* 3rd ed. Livermore, England: Oughten House Publications, Ascension Books for the Rising Planetary Consciousness, 1994. (New Age)

Law, Terry. *The Power of Praise and Worship.* Tulsa, OK: Victory House, 1981.

Lewis, C. S. *Mere Christianity*, rev. ed. New York: Macmillan Publishing Company, First Paperback Edition, 1960.

Lewis, C. S. *Screwtape Letters*. Old Tappan, NJ: Fleming H. Revell, 1978.

Libby, Larry. *Somewhere Angels*. Sisters, OR: Questar Publishers, 1994.

Lightner, Robert. *Evangelical Theology*. Grand Rapids, MI: Baker Book House, 1986.

Lindsey, Hal. *Satan Is Alive and Well on Planet Earth*. Grand Rapids, MI: Zondervan Publishing House, 1972.

Lockyear, Herbert Sr., ed., *Nelson's Illustrated Bible Dictionary*. Nashville, TN: Thomas Nelson Publishers, 1986.

Lord, Bob and Penny. *Heavenly Army of Angels*. N.p.: Journeys of Faith, 1991.

MacArthur, John Jr. *God, Satan, and Angels*. Panorama City, CA: Word of Grace Publications, 1983.

MacGregor, Geddes. *Angels, Ministers of Grace*. New York: Paragon House, 1988.

Martin, Walter. *The Kingdom of the Cults*. Minneapolis, MN: Bethany House, 1965.

Mather, George and Larry Nichols. *Dictionary of Cults, Sects, Religions and the Occult*. Grand Rapids, MI: Zondervan, 1993.

Melton, J. Gordon. *Encyclopedic Handbook of Religious Cults in America*. New York and London: Garland Publishing, 1986.

Morton, H. V. *In the Steps of the Master*. New York: Dodd, Mead, and Company, 1934.

New Catholic Encyclopedia. Washington DC: The Catholic University of America, 1967.

New Bible Dictionary, 2nd ed. Wheaton, IL: Tyndale House Publishers, 1982.

Otis, George Jr. *The Last of the Giants*. Grand Rapids, MI: Chosen Books, Fleming H. Revell, division of Baker Book House, 1991.

Packer, J. I., Merrill C. Tenney, and William White Jr. *The Bible Almanac*. Nashville, TN: Thomas Nelson Publishers, 1980.

Parente, Pascal. *Beyond Space*. Rockford, IL: TAN Books and Publishers, 1973.

Price, Hope. *Angels*. London: Macmillan, 1993.

Price, John Randolph. *The Angels Within Us*. New York: Fawcett Columbine, 1993. (New Age)

Prince, Derek. *The Spirit-Filled Believer's Handbook*. Lake Mary, FL: Charisma House, 1993.

Renner, Rick. *Seducing Spirits and Doctrines of Demons*. Tulsa, OK: Pillar Books, 1988.

Richmond, Gary. *All God's Creatures*. Dallas, TX: Word Publishing, 1991.

Ronner, John. *Know Your Angels*. Murfreesboro, TN: Mamre Press, 1993.

———. *Do You Have a Guardian Angel?* Murfreesboro, TN: Mamre Press, 1985.

Saucy, Robert. "The Eschatology of the Bible," in *The Expositor's Bible Commentary*, ed. by Frank Gaebelein. Grand Rapids, MI: Zondervan, 1979.

Stern, David. *Jewish New Testament*. Jerusalem: Jewish New Testament Publications. 1989.

———. *Jewish New Testament Commentary*. Jerusalem: Jewish New Testament Publications, 1992.

Sumrall, Lester. *Angels, the Messengers of God*. South Bend, IN: LeSea Publishing Company Inc., 1993.

Theissen, Henry Clarence. *Lectures in Systematic Theology*. Grand Rapids, MI: William B. Eerdmans, 1986.

Unger, Merrill. *Biblical Demonology: A Study of the Spiritual Forces Behind the Present World Unrest*. Wheaton, IL: VanKampen Press, 1952.

Wagner, C. Peter, ed.. *Breaking Strongholds in Your City*. Ventura, CA: Regal Books, 1993.

Weaver, C. Douglas. *The Healer-Prophet, William Marion Branham*. Macon, GA: Mercer University Press, 1987.

Whiston, William, ed. *The Works of Josephus*. Peabody, MA: Hendrickson Publishers, 1980. This book was originally published in the 1700s.

Williams, J. Rodman. *Renewal Theology*. Grand Rapids, MI: Academie Books, Zondervan, 1988.

Woodward, Kenneth. "Angels." *Newsweek*, 27 Dec. 1993, pp. 52–57.

Woodworth-Etter, Maria. *A Diary of Signs and Wonders*. Tulsa, OK: Harrison House, 1971.

Wight, Fred H. *Manners and Customs of Bible Lands*. Chicago: Moody Press, 1953.

Other Books by Terry Law

The Power of Praise and Worship

How can I praise God when I feel so bitter and angry? Praising God in a time of overwhelming personal tragedy was almost more than Terry Law could do. The encouragement and revelation the Lord gave him will show you how to reach out for your surpassing breakthrough! $9.00

Also available as a talking book! $25.00 (8 tapes)

How to Enter the Presence of God

There's a passion in every human being to be where God is. God made us that way, and that desire is never satisfied until we are in His presence. This popular teaching by Terry Law has helped thousands enter into God's presence. $8.00

Praise Releases Faith

Unleash God's power in your life! This book will not only build your faith, it will give you a foundation that will enable you to stand in the face of all assaults. Stop being hindered by your critical thinking and learn to receive God's promises by faith. $9.00

To order books or to find out more information about Terry Law Ministries and World Compassion, write or call:

Terry Law Evangelism, Inc.
P. O. Box 92 • Tulsa, OK 74101-0092
(918) 492-2858

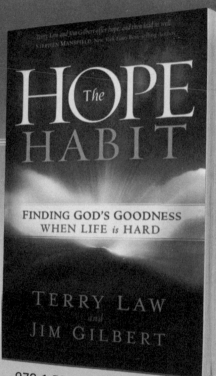

FREE NEWSLETTERS
TO HELP EMPOWER YOUR LIFE

Why subscribe today?

❑ **DELIVERED DIRECTLY TO YOU.** All you have to do is open your inbox and read.

❑ **EXCLUSIVE CONTENT.** We cover the news overlooked by the mainstream press.

❑ **STAY CURRENT.** Find the latest court rulings, revivals, and cultural trends.

❑ **UPDATE OTHERS.** Easy to forward to friends and family with the click of your mouse.

CHOOSE THE E-NEWSLETTER THAT INTERESTS YOU MOST:

- Christian news
- Daily devotionals
- Spiritual empowerment
- And much, much more

SIGN UP AT: **http://freenewsletters.charismamag.com**

8178